8 ⁹⁵

MAGISTERIUM

TEACHING AUTHORITY
IN THE
CATHOLIC CHURCH

FRANCIS A. SULLIVAN S.J.

Paulist Press   *New York/Ramsey*

Library of Congress Catalog Card Number 83-61858

ISBN: 0-8091-2577-3

First published by Paulist Press, 545 Island Road, Ramsey, N.J. 07446

Printed and bound in the United States of America

Contents

Abbreviations

AAS   *Acta Apostolicae Sedis*
AG   *Ad Gentes*
CDF   Sacred Congregation for the Doctrine of the Faith
CTSA   Catholic Theological Society of America
D-S   Denzinger-Schönmetzer, *Enchiridion Symbolorum, Definitionum, Declarationum*
DV   *Dei Verbum*
DH   *Dignitatis Humanae*
GS   *Gaudium et Spes*
ITC   International Theological Commission
LG   *Lumen Gentium*
L Th K, Vat. II
        Lexikon für Theologie und Kirche, Das Zweite Vatikanische Konzil
RSPT   *Revue des sciences philosophiques et théologiques*
TS   *Theological Studies*
UR   *Unitatis Redintegratio*

Introduction

A little over twenty years ago, when lectures at the Gregorian University were still being given in Latin, I wrote a Latin text-book for the use of my students, in which I included several theses *de magisterio*. At that time I would never have thought of writing a book on this subject in English for the general reading public. Still less would I have expected that people would know at once what the book was about, if I used the Latin word *magisterium* as its title. Since then, however, much has happened to focus attention on the magisterium, to the extent that it has become practically a household word.

The first of these events, of course, was that extraordinary exercise of collegial magisterium: the Second Vatican Council (1962-65). In 1968 came the encyclical *Humanae Vitae* (a controversial exercise of ordinary papal magisterium). In 1970 Hans Küng published his book entitled *Infallible? An Inquiry*, which sparked a lively discussion about the possibility of an infallible exercise of the magisterium, and eventually resulted in the judgment of Rome that he could no longer be approved as a Catholic theologian. More recently a good deal of attention was given to the 'colloquium' to which Edward Schillebeeckx was summoned in 1979 by the Vatican Congregation for the Doctrine of the Faith.

These events have stimulated a very considerable amount of theological publication in the past two decades. Scholarly books have appeared, treating questions like the theology of the ecumenical councils and their relation to the papacy, the background and interpretation of the First Vatican Council, the problem of infallibility, the justification of dissent from ordinary papal teaching, etc. Ecumenical dialogues have also resulted in the publication of common statements and preparatory studies dealing with teaching authority in

1

the Church. Far more numerous, of course, than the books have been the articles in theological journals, a number of which have devoted whole fascicles to questions about the magisterium.

But with all the abundance of literature on the subject, I do not know of any one book that offers a systematic presentation of modern Catholic thinking about the nature and function of teaching authority in the Church. This is what I have set out to provide in this book. While taking into account the various issues raised by the events of the past twenty years, this book intends to provide the broad picture in which each of these details finds its proper place. It takes as its point of departure the belief which a great many Christians besides Catholics share, namely, that the Church of Christ is maintained in the truth of the Gospel by the Holy Spirit. It then goes on to study the various ministries by which the Gospel has been handed on and interpreted for each generation of believers. Special attention is given to the question of the biblical and historical basis for the teaching authority of bishops. This leads to a consideration of the particular role of the Bishop of Rome in settling disputes about the faith, and the eventual recognition in the western church of his authority to define dogmas of faith. Then comes the question of the infallibility which is attributed to such dogmatic definitions, whether issued by an ecumenical council or by a pope.

Two questions are then treated which have come into prominence in connection with the encyclical *Humanae Vitae*: namely, whether a moral doctrine like that on methods of contraception has been, or ever could be, infallibly taught, and, if the teaching of the encyclical is not infallible, just what binding force it has on the assent and moral practice of Catholics. The final chapter is devoted to the thorny question of the relationship between the magisterium and Catholic theologians. It gives the full text and a commentary on the theses which were the fruit of the discussion of this question in 1975 by the International Theological Commission.

While I expect that this book should prove useful to students of theology — in fact I have been encouraged to write it by the comments of students on my lectures on the subject — I do not think of it as a text-book, and it is surely different in style and content, as well as language, from the text-book

I wrote twenty years ago. I have written this book with non-specialists in mind. It is my hope that it may help many Catholics (and others as well) to achieve a better understanding of the ministries by which the Gospel is proclaimed and interpreted in the Catholic Church.

I wish to thank Christopher O'Donnell, O. Carm., Edward Yarnold, S.J., and Gerald O'Collins, S.J., for reading this work in manuscript and giving me many helpful suggestions for its improvement.

Francis A. Sullivan, S.J.
Gregorian University, Rome

1.

The Infallibility of the People of God

The indefectibility of the Church

One of the fruits of the recent discussion on infallibility, both of that stimulated by Hans Küng's critique of the official teaching on the subject,[1] and of the ongoing ecumenical dialogue, most notably the Lutheran-Catholic dialogue in the United States,[2] has been to focus attention on the basic and widely shared Christian belief in the indefectibility of the Church. For a great many Christians besides Roman Catholics, it is a matter of faith that the Church of Christ has a divine assurance of its remaining not only in existence, but also of its being maintained in fidelity to Christ and his Gospel, until the end of time.[3] Indeed there is clear evidence that the New Testament Church shared such a belief. For even if we prescind from the question whether the historical Jesus said to Peter: 'Upon this rock I shall build my church and the gates of hell shall not prevail against it' (Mt 16:18), it is at least obvious that the evangelist could not have attributed this saying to Jesus unless the Christian community was persuaded that nothing could ever destroy his Church. Likewise, whether or not the risen Christ's last words to his disciples were actually the last words of Matthew's Gospel: 'I am with you always, to the close of the age', there is no doubt that these words witness to the faith of the early Christian community that their risen Lord would never abandon them, and that his Church would enjoy his presence and assistance to the end of time.

If we ask what could have been the basic motive for this confidence that Christ's Church would never succumb either to external hostility or to internal corruption, the answer is

4

also to be seen in the texts we have cited: it is because this will always be Christ's own Church: the one he himself built on rock and continues to build, and because he will always remain faithful to his promise to remain with his Church. Or to put it another way: belief in the indestructibility of Christ's Church is a corollary of the far more basic Christian belief that 'Jesus is Lord'. For, to believe that Jesus is Lord is to believe that he is risen and glorified at the right hand of the Father, that he has won a decisive, 'eschatological' victory over the powers that are hostile to God in this world, and that no enemy will ever be able to snatch from him the fruits of this glorious victory. The New Testament conviction that the Church is Christ's 'body' and his 'bride' suggests the utter incompatibility between the triumph of Christ, on the one hand, and any future defeat of the Church which 'he nourishes and cherishes, as a man nourishes and cherishes his own flesh' (cf. Eph 5:29). If 'Christ loved the Church and gave himself up for her' (Eph 5:25) how could he ever allow her to be corrupted and lost to him? Needless to say, Christian faith in the indefectibility of the Church is not based on any claim to merely human fidelity: it is totally a matter of confidence in divine promises and divine grace. The Second Vatican Council expresses it in the following way: 'Moving forward through trial and tribulation, the Church is strengthened by the power of God's grace promised to her by the Lord, so that in the weakness of the flesh she may not waver from perfect fidelity, but remain a bride worthy of her Lord; that moved by the Holy Spirit she may never cease to renew herself until through the cross she arrives at the light which knows no setting.'[4] The Church's confidence that she will 'remain a bride worthy of the Lord' is not a matter of human pride: it is a matter of humble faith in the power of God's grace and the abiding assistance of the Holy Spirit. It is only by the power of grace and the work of the Holy Spirit that she will be able to overcome the weakness of the flesh and never cease to renew herself. But she knows that her Lord has promised her this grace and this abiding presence of the Holy Spirit, and that his promises will never fail of their fulfilment.

The indefectibility of the Church in true faith
Christian conviction about the indefectibility of the Church

includes the conviction of its indefectibility in the true faith. The reason is not difficult to see. If indefectibility means permanence in existence, and if the very being of the Church is expressed by the term *congregatio fidelium*: community or congregation of believers, then the Church could hardly be said to persevere in authentic existence if it fell away from the truth of the Gospel. Indeed, the First Letter to Timothy describes the Church as the 'pillar and bulwark of the truth' (1 Tim 3:15): surely a reflection of the conviction of the New Testament community that the Church was assured of permanence in the truth.

Christians who believe that the Church is indefectible in the truth attribute this to the abiding presence and assistance of the Holy Spirit, especially in the light of the repeated promise of Jesus in his farewell discourse to send the 'Spirit of truth' to his disciples. 'I will pray the Father, and he will give you another Counsellor, to be with you for ever, even the Spirit of truth . . .' (Jn 14:16f.). 'But when the Counsellor comes, whom I shall send to you from the Father, even the Spirit of truth, who proceeds from the Father, he will bear witness to me' (Jn 15:26). 'When the Spirit of truth comes, he will guide you into all the truth; for he will not speak on his own authority, but whatever he hears he will speak, and he will declare to you the things that are to come' (Jn 16:13).

At this point we can prescind from the question raised by Hans Küng and others, whether or in what sense these promises have a particular application to those who have a special ministry of teaching in the Church. For now it is enough to note the quite general agreement among Christians that the Holy Spirit is promised to abide with the Church, as the Spirit of truth, who will guide the Church into all the truth. It is faith in this abiding presence and assistance of the Spirit of truth to the Church which founds the Christian conviction of the Church's indefectibility in the truth.

Indefectibility of the Church as community, not of the individual Christian

It hardly needs to be said that indefectibility in the true faith is understood as a property of the Church as a body, but not of its members as individuals. Experience, even within the time of the New Testament, was enough to show that individual Christians could indeed fall away from the faith, and even that groups of Christians could apostatise or form heretical sects. Such experience, however, did not shake the conviction that the Church as such could never make shipwreck of its faith.

Here we have to cope with the fact that we attribute to the Church, as a community, properties which are not attributable to its individual members as individuals. We say that the Church is indefectibly holy, that the Church is assured of persevering in grace, that the faith of the Church will always be faith 'formed by charity' — even though we know we cannot say these things of the individual Christian. Does this mean that we must think of 'the Church' in such statements as a kind of 'super-person', totally distinct from the real persons who are its members? Is the 'bride of Christ', to which we attribute indefectible holiness, a kind of ideal Church, altogether apart from the reality of its sinful members?

To answer this kind of question, I think it helpful to reflect on the reason which St Thomas Aquinas gives for saying that 'the faith of the Church is faith formed by charity' — that is, the faith of the *Church* is not the kind of faith that can persist even without charity or sanctifying grace, but is always faith animated by charity and grace. Now it is obvious that the faith of the individual member is not always such. But St Thomas insists that the faith of the *Church* is: and his reason is that such is the faith of all those who belong to the Church *et numero et merito.*[5] To use the terminology of Vatican II, St Thomas predicates of the *Church* what is actually true, at any moment, only of those members of the Church who are 'fully incorporated into it'. For, according to Vatican II, only those can be described as fully incorporated into the Church who, along with the other conditions, also 'have the Spirit of Christ'.[6] And we know from the official explanation given at the Council, that 'having the Spirit of Christ' means having the Spirit indwelling by grace.[7] Now these are the ones who, in the language of St Thomas, belong to the Church by merit and not only by number.

What this means, I believe, is that, following St Thomas, we attribute indefectible holiness, and indefectibility in the true faith, not to some ideal Church, but to the concrete People of God here on earth, whose properties are actually realised in its members, not in each and every one of them, to be sure, but in those who are fully incorporated in it. To say that the Church is indefectibly holy means that it will never lack members who are actually living in the grace of Christ; to say that the Church is indefectible in faith means that it will never lack members who maintain Christian faith in its purity. No individual member — not even the pope, as a private person — has any such guarantee of holiness or perseverance in the true faith. The guarantee is given to the Church, and there will always be those in whom it is concretely realised. This means, of course, that it is impossible that the whole Church, in all of its members, could ever lack sanctifying grace or charity, or could ever fall into the kind of error in faith that would put it into contradiction with the gospel of Jesus Christ.

Does this imply that the Church *consists* only of those members who are actually living in the state of grace, or who maintain the faith in its purity? Of course not. The pilgrim Church is a mixed community of saints and sinners, and will be such until the day of judgment. It is true that a person can cease to be a member of the Church by the wilful rejection of its faith or its communion (by a formal sin of apostasy, heresy or schism) — but other kinds of sin, even if they mean the loss of grace, do not mean the loss of membership in the Church. Nor do mere errors in belief have such an effect. So the pilgrim Church will always consist of those living in grace and those without it, of those with orthodox beliefs and those in error. While holding that all of these are members of the Church, what we are saying is that the properties which we attribute to the Church as community are always concretely realised in those of its members who are fully incorporated in it. I do not know how one could be sure that members such as these will always constitute the numerical majority in the Church. When St Thomas says that the faith of the Church will always be faith informed by charity, because such is the faith of those who belong to the Church *et numero et merito*, he does not seem concerned whether such will necessarily be a majority in the Church. He seems satisfied that we can attribute to the *Church* what is true of those who are fully living its life. Hans Küng says something similar: 'In the Church there will always be a sufficient number of people who so live

8

according to the gospel that the message can be perceived and that to speak of the ecclesial community remaining in the truth makes sense. . .'.[8]

The Church is indefectibly apostolic in its faith

In the 'Nicene Creed', which most Christians use as their liturgical profession of faith, we express our belief that the Church is 'one, holy, catholic and apostolic'. This means that not only the Church itself, but each of these four properties, is an object of our faith. The Church which is the object of our faith would no longer be what it is, if it ever ceased to be one, holy, catholic and apostolic. Therefore we believe that the Church is indefectibly one, holy, catholic and apostolic. Each of these properties has a divine assurance of permanence, just as the Church itself has, because it is the Church of Christ. Of course, *indefectibly* does not mean *perfectly*. Vatican II asserts on the one hand that the Church is indefectibly holy (LG 39), and on the other hand that 'on earth the Church is marked with a genuine though imperfect holiness' (LG 48). Each of these four properties is both a gift given and a goal to be striven for; none of them can be lost, but none of them will be perfectly possessed during the Church's pilgrimage on earth. Each of them is both an object of our faith and a test for our faith. For while we believe that the Church is indefectibly one (cf. *Decree of Ecumenism*, 4), it is only too obvious how far we are from perfect unity even within the Catholic Church itself, not to speak of the divided state of Christianity. The Church is indefectibly holy, but insofar as we ourselves are part of this pilgrim people of God, we are keenly aware of how imperfect that holiness is in us. The Church is indefectibly catholic, that is, universal, but how far it is from embracing all of mankind, even after two thousand years of missionary work. And the Church is indefectibly apostolic: but what a difference between the simplicity of the apostolic community of the New Testament, and the worldly splendour of the Renaissance papacy, to mention but one item of contrast.

What then do we mean when we say that the Church is indefectibly apostolic? First and foremost, we mean that the Church is indefectibly apostolic in faith. The Church accepts the witness of the apostles as normative for Christian belief for all time. Nothing can ever be accepted as an article of Christian faith which is in contradiction with this original witness, or does not in some real sense derive from it.

When we speak of the witness of the apostles in this context we do not restrict the meaning of this term to the original twelve disciples of Jesus. We certainly include St Paul among the apostles, and he himself tells us that the risen Christ, after appearing to James, appeared to 'all the apostles' — a term which hardly anyone nowadays takes as synonymous with 'the Twelve' to whom he had already appeared (cf. 1 Cor 15:5-7). Indeed, when we speak of the 'apostolic witness', we rightly include all the inspired writings of the New Testament, whether their authors were 'apostles' in the strict sense or not. Or to put the matter in its broadest terms, 'apostolic witness' is ultimately the witness of the apostolic Church, that is, the Christian Church of the period during which the New Testament was being written. This was the time of Christian revelation, and it is generally agreed that such revelation, which came to its definitive climax in Christ's resurrection and glorification as Lord at the right hand of the Father, was complete at the end of the apostolic period.

When we say that the apostolic period was the time during which the books of the New Testament were being written, we do not mean to restrict apostolic witness to these writings. As Vatican II puts it, 'the apostles, by their oral preaching, by example, and by ordinances, handed on what they had received from the lips of Christ, from living with him, and from what he did, or what they had learned through the prompting of the Holy Spirit. . . . Now what was handed on by the apostles includes everything which contributes to the holiness of life, and the increase in faith of the People of God. . . .' (DV 7-8). What the apostles handed on could not possibly be reduced to a series of propositions. For what they witnessed to was their experience of the Word of God made flesh. As the prologue of the First Letter of John puts it: 'That which was from the beginning, which we have heard, which we have seen with our eyes, which we have looked upon and touched with our hands, concerning the word of life . . . that which we have seen and heard we proclaim also to you, so that you may have fellowship with us; and our fellowship is with the Father and with his Son Jesus Christ' (1 Jn: 1-3). What the apostles handed on was not just the words of Jesus, as they remembered them, but the Word Himself, as they had experienced him: the whole Christ-event, which could never be reduced to words, so that any written account would never exhaust the reality of it: 'the world itself could not contain the books that would be written' (Jn 21:25).

As the apostles handed on their witness to Christ not only by preaching and writing but also by initiating a tradition of a Christian way of life, prayer and worship, so also the apostolic Church, and the Christian Church in each succeeding generation, 'in her teaching, life and worship, perpetuates and hands on to all generations all that she herself is, all that she believes' (DV 8). Needless to say, the inspired writings of the New Testament embody a privileged witness to apostolic tradition, but they could not possibly exhaust its riches. As the apostolic witness was originally handed on by preaching and by example, as well as in writing, so it continues to be handed on in the Church not only in the form of the written Scriptures, but in the Church's 'teaching, life and worship'. 'The wealth of this tradition is poured into the practice and life of the believing and praying Church' (DV 8). And thus, 'Sacred tradition and sacred Scripture form one sacred deposit of the word of God, which is committed to the Church. Holding fast to this deposit, the entire holy people united with their shepherds remain always steadfast in the teaching of the apostles, in the common life, in the breaking of the bread, and in prayers' (DV 10). Note that it is to the *Church* that the treasure of the word of God has been entrusted, and it is the *Church*, 'in her teaching, life and worship', that perpetuates and hands on to all generations 'all that she herself is, and that she believes'. Whatever may have to be said about the special role of the 'shepherds' in the handing on and interpreting of apostolic tradition, the primary fact, clearly stressed in these texts of *Dei Verbum*, is that it is the *Church* as such, the People of God, which has received the apostolic witness, and which unfailingly hands it on. In other words, the Church is indefectibly apostolic in its faith.

11

The faith of the Church is normative for the individual who wishes to belong to it

As the act of faith is free, so is the choice to belong to the community of Christian faith. No one can be forced to be a Christian against his or her will. But, on the other hand, once the free choice to be a member of the Church has been made, one is not free to choose one's own confession of faith, or to choose which articles of the Christian faith one will accept, which one will reject. The Christian Church has never understood itself as a collection of individualistic believers, each free to pick and choose among the various items offered for belief. It has always understood itself as a community of faith, united in the common profession which all accept when they are admitted into the community by baptism. This in fact is the significance of the recitation of the 'Apostles Creed' in the liturgy of baptism. The Church equivalently says to those seeking baptism: 'If you wish to enter the Church, this is the faith which we share and which you must share too. This is what we believe as Christians. If you wish to be a Christian, you must believe what the Church believes. Before you can be admitted to baptism, you must sincerely profess your faith as we do. You are joining a community that is united in the profession of the same apostolic faith.'

It is true, of course, that faith does not consist totally, or even primarily, in assent to the propositions enunciated in the creed. Faith is first of all an act of trust in God and of self-commitment to him. But because one trusts God and commits oneself to him, one also gives intellectual assent to what God has revealed to us. Again, what God has revealed to us does not consist in a series of propositions: the ultimate revelation of God, his self-revelation to mankind, is Jesus Christ, the Word of God made man. As we have already seen, no series of human words or propositions could ever adequately convey the total reality of this self-revelation of God in the Christ-event. Our knowledge of this revelation comes to us through the witness of the apostles and the apostolic Church. In order to communicate to others what they had 'heard, what they had seen with their eyes, what they had looked upon and touched with their hands concerning the word of life' (cf. 1 Jn 1:1), the apostles had to use human means of communication: words, gestures, actions. Not only

12

words, of course: for they communicated the sacramental presence of Jesus himself in the eucharist, and they communicated the Holy Spirit in baptism and the laying on of hands. They communicated the way of life which they had learned from watching Jesus live and die: they communicated this by their own way of living and dying for him.

Not only by words, then — but also by words, and necessarily by words, if the Christian community was going to be united in a common profession of faith. The sharing of a profession of faith necessarily involved putting the basic elements of faith into propositions to which all would give their assent. We see already in the New Testament a number of such brief, basic confessions in propositional form; the briefest of them being: 'Jesus is Lord!' (1 Cor 12:3). Others are 'Jesus is Lord, and God raised him from the dead' (Rom 10:9) and: 'Christ died for our sins in accordance with the scriptures, he was buried, he was raised on the third day in accordance with the scriptures, and he appeared to Cephas, then to the twelve' (1 Cor 15:3-5). In the First Letter of John we find a similar requirement of a common confession: for instance, 'By this you know the Spirit of God: every spirit which confesses that Jesus Christ has come in the flesh is of God, and every spirit which does not confess Jesus is not of God' (1 Jn 4:2-3).

The communication of the meaning of the Christ-event in human language, and the sharing of a common profession of Christian faith, necessarily involved expressing aspects of what God has revealed of himself to us, in human propositions. It is of course true that no human propositions could ever adequately express, much less exhaust, the fullness of the reality which had been revealed. It is also true that the act of faith does not terminate in the proposition as such, but in the reality of which the proposition always remains an imperfect sign.[9] All of this does not rule out the fact that propositions are necessary if the Church is going to have a common profession of faith, and indeed if there is going to be an intellectual content to which one gives intellectual assent in the act of faith. The practice of the Church, from the apostolic period on, of requiring of candidates for baptism the profession of faith according to a creed, is a clear indication of its realisation that basic elements of the faith could be expressed in propositions, and that the acceptance of cer-

13

tain propositions as enunciated in the creed was an appropriate way for the new Christian to profess his faith. The question we must now ask is: how important is it that the propositions in which the Church professes its faith be true propositions, and not erroneous ones? And if this is important, what assurance do we have that the propositions in which the Church professes its faith, are really true ones?

The indefectibility of the Church in true faith requires that the propositions in which its normative confession of faith is expressed be true and not false

There are a number of points in this assertion which need explanation and substantiation: I shall treat each of them in turn.

I have already treated the indefectibility of the Church in true faith. The term 'requires' relates to the question whether we could still describe the Church as indefectible in true faith, even if it could not express its faith in true propositions, or even if we had no assurance that the propositions in which it expresses its normative confession of faith would always be true ones.

First of all, we have to consider the question whether it is really possible to express divinely revealed mysteries in human propositions that are rightly called 'true'. We have to admit, of course, that no human proposition can ever adequately express a divine mystery; it will always fall short of the reality which it tries to express. Human language that tries to speak about God can only speak by analogy. It will always betray the weakness and limitations of the human mind confronted with the unfathomable mystery of God. Similarly, human propositions will always betray the limitation of a particular cultural background, conceptual framework, within which any human proposition has to be expressed. Human propositions will necessarily be historically conditioned; there will always be a particular, limited context in which they have to be understood.

Granted all this, and more that one could say along these lines, do we have to draw the conclusion that there can be no such thing as a *true* proposition where divine revelation is concerned? What indeed do we mean by a *true* proposition? First of all, we have to note the difference between a pro-

14

position and a sentence. A sentence is a particular verbal expression, in a particular language; the proposition is the *meaning* which the sentence intends to express. The same proposition is capable of various linguistic expressions: otherwise it would be impossible to translate it from one language into another. Similarly, mathematical propositions can be expressed either in words or in mathematical symbols. One consequence of this is that since, in the course of time, words might change their meanings, a sentence which originally conveyed one meaning, could eventually convey quite another meaning. In such a case, the original proposition remains true, but it now has to be expressed differently, because the sentence in which it was originally expressed no longer conveys the same meaning. So when we speak of 'true propositions', we do not identify the propositions, as such, with the sentences in which they have been expressed. A proposition is true if its *meaning* is true: strictly speaking, the proposition *is* the meaning.

Secondly, for a proposition to be true, it is not necessary that it be an adequate expression of the reality which it intends to convey: that it say all that could be said, or say it as perfectly as it could possibly be said. Human propositions, particularly those which attempt to grasp and express divine reality, can never do more than pick out some particular facet of the mystery, and say something, however imperfectly, about that particular aspect of the whole mystery.

If we grant that a proposition can have all these limitations, and still be true, I think there is no reason to deny the very possibility that the Church could express its normative faith in propositions that are really true. The next question is whether the indefectibility of the Church *requires* that the propositions in which it expresses its faith be true. Does it really make that much difference, as far as the indefectibility of the church is concerned, whether the propositions of its creed are true or false?

To answer this question, we can begin by agreeing that as far as salvation is concerned, 'orthopraxy' is more important than 'orthodoxy'. No errors in belief, however egregious, will keep a person from the love and mercy of God, as long as the person's heart is in the right place. The last judgment is not going to be an examination of catechism, where knowing the right answers will assure us of salvation. The recitation of the creed, no matter how true its propositions may be, will not guarantee eternal life.

Granted all this, does it follow that it makes no difference whether the propositions of the Church's creed are true or false? I say it does make a difference, and a crucial one at that, because we are talking about the propositions in which the Church community expresses the confession of faith which is *normative* for all its members. We are talking about what the ancient Church called the 'rule of faith' or the 'canon of truth': what candidates for baptism were obliged to believe and confess before they could be received into the Church, and what all members of the Church were obliged to continue to believe and confess, on pain of being excluded from the community. I am not talking here about less important or peripheral matters about which there could be legitimate differences of opinion among Christians. The question is: whether it would make reasonable sense to claim, on the one hand, that the Church of Christ is indefectible in truth, and to admit, on the other hand, that the propositions in which the Church obliges its members to confess their faith could really be false, rather than true. Again, this does not mean that the *sentences* in which these propositions have been expressed might not need to be re-formulated; in a changed cultural setting the sentences might well need to be changed in order to make their meaning intelligible. We are talking not about sentences as such but about the truth of the meaning which the sentences intend to express. I do not see how one can hold that the Church is really 'maintained in the truth' by the Holy Spirit, and at the same time hold that the Church could oblige its members to confess their faith in propositions which would actually be not merely human, partial, limited, capable of more adequate expression, culturally conditioned, etc., but downright false. In other words, the indefectibility of the Church in the truth requires that its normative confession of faith be expressed in propositions which, for all their inevitable limitations, are still true.

In what I have said thus far, I believe that I can count on the agreement of most Christians, for I have purposely limited the question of the indefectibility of the Church in truth to its consequences regarding the truth of the basic, normative

16

confession of Christian faith, such as we have from the second century in the 'Apostles Creed'. It is now time to take up a question on which there is a specifically Catholic point of view, with which many other Christians are not in agreement with us. Briefly, the question has to do with the 'development of doctrine' in the course of the Church's life, and with the 'infallibility' of the whole Church's belief that a particular doctrine is contained in revelation, even when this doctrine is not clearly found in Scripture or in documents of early tradition, and has not always been an explicit object of common Christian faith. On both of these points there are important passages in the documents of Vatican II, to which we shall now turn our attention.

The development of doctrine: Dei Verbum, n.8

'This tradition which comes from the apostles develops in the Church with the help of the Holy Spirit. For there is a growth in the understanding of the realities and the words which have been handed down. This happens through the contemplation and study made by believers, who treasure these things in their hearts, through the intimate understanding of spiritual things they experience, and through the preaching of those who have received through episcopal succession the sure gift of truth. For, as the centuries succeed one another, the Church constantly moves forward toward the fullness of divine truth until the words of God reach their complete fulfilment in her.'

For the present we shall prescind from the question of the 'sure gift of truth' which this text attributes to those in 'episcopal succession'. We are concerned for now with the role which all 'believers' are said to have in the development of doctrine. To make the matter more concrete, we can apply what is said here to such doctrines as the Immaculate Conception and the Assumption of the Blessed Virgin Mary. No one nowadays claims that these doctrines have always been explicit objects of Christian faith. They are not clearly taught in Scripture, nor is it easy to show that they necessarily follow from the scriptural evidence. It is highly unlikely, indeed extremely improbable, that there was any explicit oral tradition about either of these doctrines during the first centuries of the Christian era. However, as the text of Dei Verbum puts

17

it, there is growth in the understanding of the realities and words which have been handed down, through the contemplation of believers, who treasure these things in their hearts.

As we have seen above, the 'reality which has been handed down' is not a series of propositions, but God's self-revelation in his Word, Jesus Christ: the total Christ-event, as witnessed by the apostles. Now part of this total reality is the relationship of Jesus to his mother, and her role in the mystery of our redemption. It is already explicit in the New Testament that her role was not one of purely biological maternity (cf. Luke's account of the incarnation, and John's account of what happened on Calvary). As devout Christians continued to contemplate the mystery of Christ and of his mother, they came to see, for instance, that since the Son of Mary is truly divine, it is correct to speak of her as 'Mother of God'. Further contemplation led them to see more of the consequences which such a relationship must have entailed for the mother who shared so intimately in the mystery of her Son. It led to the realisation that, having been so closely associated with her Son in his incarnation and passion, she must also share in a unique way in the fruits of his death and resurrection. And so, over the course of the centuries, the conviction grew that Mary could never have been alienated from God by original sin, and that she must already share, body and soul, in the glory of resurrection which is his. Admittedly, these conclusions do not follow with metaphysical necessity from what Scripture tells us about Mary. They are seen to be contained in the total mystery of Christ, by a kind of intuition, rather than by a process of logical deduction. As contained in this total mystery, they are believed not only to be true, but to be revealed, since it is the whole Christ-event which is God's word to man.

What assurance can we have that such intuitions are really true? Here we turn to the other of the two texts: from *Lumen gentium*, n. 12:

> The body of the faithful as a whole, anointed as they are by the Holy One (cf. I Jn 2:20, 27), cannot err in matters of belief. Thanks to a supernatural sense of the faith which characterizes the People as a whole, it manifests this unerring quality when, 'from the bishops down to the last member of the laity', it shows universal agreement in mat-

ters of faith and morals. For, by this sense of faith which is aroused and sustained by the Spirit of truth, God's People accepts not the word of men but the very Word of God (cf. 1 Th 2:13). It clings without fail to the faith once delivered to the saints (cf. Jude 3), penetrates it more deeply by accurate insights, and applies it more thoroughly to life.

The infallibility of a universal agreement on a matter of faith

There can be no doubt about the fact that as Catholics understand the matter, the infallibility which this statement of Vatican II attributes to 'universal agreement in matters of faith and morals', was verified in the case of the doctrines of Mary's Immaculate Conception and bodily Assumption. Hence we can rightly have these doctrines in mind, when we analyse the claims made in this text. The first point which becomes clear when we apply what is said here to the case of these marian doctrines, is that the terms: 'the body of the faithful as a whole', 'the people as a whole', and 'universal agreement' mean concretely: 'the body of the Catholic faithful as a whole', 'the Catholic people as a whole', 'universal agreement among Catholic bishops and laity'.

It was only the Catholic bishops who received the papal questionnaires by which Popes Pius IX and Pius XII wished to assure themselves of the 'universal agreement from the bishops down to the last member of the laity', which would justify the solemn definition of these doctrines as dogmas of faith. It can hardly be doubted that in 1854 and 1950, when these dogmas were defined, the firm belief of the whole body of the Catholic faithful was taken as sufficient evidence that these doctrines must be contained in divine revelation. The 'body of the faithful as a whole' which 'cannot err in matters of belief' was simply understood to be the body of the Catholic faithful, and this is not surprising, since the official Catholic teaching at that time was that the Roman Catholic Church is the one true Church of Christ. In the very same year 1950 in which Pope Pius XII defined the dogma of the Assumption, he insisted in his encyclical *Humani generis* that the Mystical Body of Christ and the Roman Catholic Church are one and the same thing.[10]

The question that arises now, after Vatican II, is: if we no

19

longer exclusively identify the Church of Christ with the Roman Catholic Church, but recognise the presence and saving activity of Christ's Church in other Christian Churches and ecclesial communities, can we still attribute infallibility to the belief of the Catholic faithful, if their belief in a particular doctrine is not shared by the majority of other Christians? Should 'universal agreement of the whole body of the faithful' now require agreement among the faithful of all the major Christian communities? Would only a truly ecumenical agreement now satisfy the requirements for infallibility in belief?

In trying to answer these questions, the first point I would make is that a truly ecumenical agreement among all the Christian faithful would be the most satisfying basis for a judgment that the requirements for infallibility in belief are fulfilled. The second point is that it seems probable that in the future, when a question arises in the Catholic Church about defining a new dogma on the basis of the belief of the faithful, more attention will be paid to the belief of other Christians than was the case in 1854 or 1950.

Thirdly, in the light of the fact that Vatican II chose not to define any new dogmas, and in view of the greater ecumenical sensitivity in the post-Vatican II era, I think it less likely that in the future we shall see the dogmatic definition of Catholic beliefs which are not generally shared by other Christians.

However, despite what has just been said, I believe it would still be consistent with the teaching of Vatican II to attribute infallibility in belief to the Roman Catholic Church, even when its belief is not shared by other Christians. My reason for this is as follows. While Vatican II recognises that the Church of Christ extends beyond the limits of the Catholic Church, it nevertheless states that the Church of Christ 'subsists in the Catholic Church'.[11] If I am not mistaken, this means that all of the essential properties of the Church of Christ likewise subsist in the Catholic Church. We have an explicit statement of Vatican II to this effect with regard to the unity of the Church. The Decree on Ecumenism tells us: 'The unity which Christ bestowed on his Church from the beginning subsists in the Catholic Church as something she can never lose' (UR 4). I believe that the same must be said of the Church's holiness, apostolicity and catholicity. Where

20

the Church of Christ subsists, her indefectible properties must also be found. Without these qualities, it would no longer be the same Church of Christ.

If then, the unity of Christ's Church subsists indefectibly in the Catholic Church, and if this unity is necessarily unity in the true faith, then it would seem to follow that where the unity of Christ's Church subsists, there also must be found the infallibility of a universal agreement in faith. I conclude from this that it would not be inconsistent with the teaching of Vatican II to continue to attribute such infallibility to beliefs which are held universally within the Catholic Church. Of course in all this discussion we are talking about beliefs to which the faithful are deeply committed as to part of divinely revealed truth, and not about pious opinions, no matter how commonly held, which do not involve a definite commitment of faith. Later on we shall discuss the process and organs by which the necessary discernment between mere pious opinion and genuine faith-commitment can be made, and the presence of a universal agreement on a matter of revealed truth can be established.

For the present let us take another look at the text of *Lumen gentium* 12, which tells us that this infallibility of the whole People of God in its belief, is due to a 'supernatural sense of faith'.

The supernatural sense of faith (sensus fidei)

First let us see what this text of Vatican II says about this 'sense of faith'. It describes it as 'supernatural', and says that it is 'aroused and sustained by the Spirit of truth'. In other words, it is a gift of grace, given by the Holy Spirit. It is related to the fundamental grace-gift of faith. Secondly, it 'characterises the People of God as a whole'. In other words, it is not one of the charisms which the Spirit distributes to whom He chooses, which some receive and others do not; it is a gift of the Spirit which all receive.

Thirdly, the text describes the effects of this gift; four effects are named: (a) by this sense of faith God's People accepts not the word of men but the very word of God; (b) it clings without fail to the faith once delivered to the saints; (c) penetrates it more deeply by accurate insights; (d) applies it more thoroughly to life.

21

The first of these effects is to enable people to recognise the word of God for what it is, even though it comes to them through the words of men. The scriptural reference is to 1 Thess 2:13, where St Paul says: 'And we also thank God constantly for this, that when you received the word of God which you heard from us, you accepted it not as the word of men but as what it really is, the word of God, which is at work in you believers.' Paul was fully aware that it was only by a gift of God that the Thessalonians were able to recognise his message to them as truly a word from God. His was a human witness to the Gospel, but there was needed also the interior witness of the Holy Spirit, by which the hearers would be able to discern the very word of God in what Paul was telling them. The 'supernatural sense of faith', then, is a gift of grace to discern the word of God, to recognise it for what it is.

The second effect is that the faithful 'cling without fail to the faith once delivered to the saints'. Here we have the basis of that 'unerring quality' of the faith of the whole People of God, whereby 'the body of the faithful as a whole cannot err in matters of belief'. The 'sense of faith', then, must confer a kind of instinct to recognise and cling to the truth, and conversely to discern the presence of error and to reject it.

The third effect is that believers 'penetrate [the object of their faith] more deeply by accurate insights'. We have already spoken of the kind of insight by which the Catholic faithful came to see the consequences for Mary of her unique relationship with the Son of God. No mere exegesis or theological reasoning could have arrived at the certitude of faith in her Immaculate Conception or Assumption. This certitude is the fruit of insight guided by the supernatural sense of faith. We can invoke here St Thomas's idea of a kind of 'connaturality', by which a person deeply committed to a virtue will almost instinctively tend to make right judgments in matters that pertain to that virtue.[12]

The fourth effect is that the faithful are led to apply the word of God more thoroughly to life. Perhaps in our day we can recognise the fruits of this gift in the growing realisation that the word of God calls upon people of faith to resist and combat such evils as racial discrimination, unjust economic and social systems, and the like.

At this point it might be helpful to say a few words about

two other terms which are associated with the notion of *sensus fidei*, namely: *sensus fidelium* (sense of the faithful), and *consensus fidelium* (the agreement of the faithful).

As we have seen, the sense of faith (*sensus fidei*) is a supernatural gift, an aspect of the gift of faith itself, a kind of God-given instinct by which believers are able to recognise the word of God for what it is, to discern truth from error in matters of faith, and to have sound insights into what they believe. This then is a subjective quality of the one who believes.

The term *sensus fidelium* (sense or mind of the faithful) on the other hand generally has an objective meaning, referring not to the believer but to what is believed.[13] Thus, if one asks: 'What is the sense of the faithful on this matter?', one wants to know what people believe; what is the 'mind of the faithful' on an issue. The term *sensus Ecclesiae* (mind of the Church) is often used with much the same meaning. It is particularly frequent in the documents of the Council of Trent.[14]

The term *consensus fidelium* (agreement of the faithful) adds the element of universal agreement to the notion of *sensus fidelium*. It refers to the situation in which, on a particular issue of faith, the whole body of the faithful, 'from the bishops down to the last member of the laity', share the same belief. As we have seen, it is in such a *consensus* that the Second Vatican Council says that the whole People of God cannot be in error.

The last sentence of the paragraph of *Lumen gentium* which we have been considering introduces the subject to which we must now turn our attention. Having spoken of how God's People accepts the Word of God, clings to it, penetrates it more deeply and applies it to life, the paragraph concludes: 'All this it does under the lead of a sacred teaching authority (*magisterium*) to which it loyally defers.'

Following the lead of Vatican II, which said what pertained to the whole Church as People of God in Chapter Two of *Lumen gentium* before going on to speak about the hierarchy in Chapter Three, we have devoted this first chapter to a consideration of the indefectibility of the whole Church in its faith. We must now turn our attention to the particular role which the pastors of the Church have to play in maintaining the Church in the true faith.

2.

Magisterium

The meaning of the word magisterium

The English word that corresponds to the Latin *magister* is 'master', not only in the specific sense of 'schoolmaster', or teacher, but in the broad spectrum of senses in which a person can be a 'master': e.g. master of a ship, master of servants or slaves, master of an art or trade, etc. The Latin word *magister* always had a connotation of authority, coming as it did from the root *magis* (more), as contrasted with *minister*, from *minus* (less). Similarly the word *magisterium* in classical Latin meant the role and authority of one who was a *magister* in any of the various applications of this term. Perhaps the closest equivalent to this in English would be the word 'mastery'.

Of course one of the common applications of the word *magister* was to the schoolmaster or teacher, so that *magisterium* came to be used more and more frequently to mean the role and authority of the teacher. But it continued in late and medieval Latin to be used of other functions which involved some kind of authority. The English word magistrate reflects one such use of the term.

Magisterium in the writings of St Thomas Aquinas

In the vocabulary of the medieval schoolmen, *magisterium* came to mean the authority of one who teaches. The symbol of teaching authority was the 'chair', and they knew two kinds of such 'chairs': that of the bishop in his cathedral, and that of the professor in the university. So St Thomas spoke of two kinds of *magisterium*: 'magisterium cathedrae pastoralis' of the bishop, and 'magisterium cathedrae magistralis' of the theologian.[1]

For St Thomas both these instances of *magisterium* involved authority. The bishop's authority was based on his role as a prelate ('ex officio praelationis'), while the theologian's authority was based on his knowledge of theology.[2]

The modern use of the term magisterium

It is a fairly common thing for a word that originally had a wide variety of applications to come to be used principally or even exclusively with one particular meaning. This is the case with the ecclesiastical use of the Latin word *magisterium*, which has come in recent centuries to be used almost exclusively of the teaching office of bishops (what St Thomas called the *magisterium cathedrae pastoralis*). No one denies, of course, that theologians continue to have a teaching role in the Church, but the fact is that it is now generally the teaching role of bishops that is meant when the term *magisterium* is used.

The documents of the First Vatican Council offer several examples of the use of the term *magisterium* which illustrate its current meaning. For instance, *Dei Filius* speaks of doctrine that is taught by the Church, whether by solemn judgment or by its ordinary and universal teaching authority ('sive solemni iudicio sive ordinario et universali magisterio').[3] By this final phrase is meant the teaching authority which the bishops exercise when they are not gathered in an ecumenical council. Likewise, *Pastor Aeternus* declares that papal primacy includes the supreme power of *magisterium*,[4] and the chapter of this constitution in which papal infallibility is defined is entitled: 'On the infallible *magisterium* of the Roman Pontiff'.[5]

The term *magisterium* means the pastoral teaching office in the documents of Vatican II as well. *Lumen gentium* 18 speaks of the infallible *magisterium* of the Roman Pontiff; in n. 22 it says that the order of bishops is the successor to the college of the apostles in *magisterium*; in n. 25 it speaks of the 'authentic' and 'supreme' *magisterium* of the Roman Pontiff; later in the same number it declares that the bishops gathered in an ecumenical council exercise supreme *magisterium* along with the successor of Peter.[6]

So one aspect of the modern development of the Catholic use of the term *magisterium* is that it is hardly used at all except to refer to the teaching office of the hierarchy. Another, and even more recent development, is that the term *magisterium* has come to mean not only the teaching function of the hierarchy, but also the hierarchy itself as the bearer of this office. There are several examples of this usage in the documents of Vatican II; the clearest of these is found in the Constitution on Divine Revelation, *Dei Verbum*, n.10:

> The task of authentically interpreting the word of God, whether written or handed on, has been entrusted exclusively to the living *magisterium* of the Church, whose authority is exercised in the name of Jesus Christ. This *magisterium* is not above the word of God, but serves it, teaching only what has been handed on, listening to it devoutly, guarding it scrupulously, and explaining it faithfully by divine commission and with the help of the Holy Spirit; it draws from this one deposit of faith everything which it presents for belief as divinely revealed.

It seems obvious that it is not the teaching office as such, but the holders of that office who 'serve the word of God', who 'teach', 'listen', 'guard', 'explain', etc. The use of the term 'the magisterium' to mean the hierarchy as bearer of the teaching office, is a rather recent development, but it has become a common item of Catholic vocabulary.

The fact of the matter, then, is that the term *magisterium*, which St Thomas did not hesitate to apply to the teaching role of theologians as well as to that of bishops, has come to be used almost exclusively of what St Thomas called the *magisterium cathedrae pastoralis*: meaning either the pastoral teaching office, or, more recently still, the pastors who exercise this office.

'Authentic' magisterium

Another item of current vocabulary which requires some explanation is the use of the word 'authentic' in reference to the *magisterium*. Some examples of this usage in the documents of Vatican II are the following. *Lumen gentium* 25a describes the bishops as 'authentic teachers, that is, teachers endowed with the authority of Christ.' In 25b it speaks of the 'authentic magisterium of the Roman Pontiff.' In 25c it refers to the situation in which the bishops of the whole world are 'teaching authentically on a matter of faith or morals'. And the passage of *Dei Verbum* which we have quoted above says that 'the task of authentically interpreting the word of God has been entrusted exclusively to the living *magisterium* of the Church'.

In my opinion it is unfortunate that the translators of these documents have rendered the Latin *authenticum* and *authentice* in these passages by the English 'authentic' and 'authentically'. For the word 'authentic' in modern English means 'genuine'. It did once mean 'authoritative', 'entitled to obedience', but this meaning is now obsolete. And the fact is that what is now an obsolete meaning of the English 'authentic', is the correct meaning of the Latin 'authenticum'. In other words, the correct translation would not be 'authentic' but 'authoritative'.

Indeed the passages that we have cited not only show that the word 'authenticum' really means 'authoritative', but they also indicate the source of this authority, and tell us what kind of authority is involved. Thus, in *Lumen gentium* 25a, where bishops are described as *doctores authentici*, the source of their authority is also named: they are 'teachers endowed with the authority of Christ'. A bit later on in the same paragraph, it says that bishops 'are to be respected as witnesses to divine and catholic truth. In matters of faith and morals, the bishops speak in the name of Christ and the faithful are to accept their teaching and adhere to it with a religious assent of soul.' Likewise, the text of *Dei Verbum* which we have quoted above says that the authority of the magisterium is 'exercised in the name of Jesus Christ'.

If one asks on what basis the Council can declare that bishops are 'teachers endowed with the authority of Christ', or that they 'speak in the name of Christ', the answer is to be found in *Lumen gentium* 20: 'This sacred Synod teaches that by divine institution bishops have succeeded to the place of the apostles as shepherds of the Church, and that he who hears them, hears Christ, while he who rejects them, rejects Christ and Him who sent Christ.' One can also refer to *Lumen gentium* 21, which states: 'Episcopal consecration, together with the office of sanctifying, also confers the offices of teaching and of governing.' The mind of the Second Vatican Council is clearly that bishops receive their authority to teach in virtue of their inheriting from the apostles the mandate to teach in the name of Christ.

It is not my intention at this point to attempt to justify this teaching of the Council; I shall return to this question later on. For the moment I simply wish to make it clear what the mind of the Council is with regard to the kind of authority with which the bishops are endowed. It is particularly important to understand this, in order to avoid a misunderstanding of what the Council meant when it stated, in *Dei Verbum* 10, that 'the task of authentically interpreting the word of God, whether written or handed on, has been entrusted exclusively to the living magisterium, whose authority is exercised in the name of Jesus Christ'. As I have already pointed out, the word *authentice* should be translated by 'authoritatively', rather than by 'authentically'. But more than that, it is crucial to keep in mind that in this context, the word 'authoritatively' means specifically 'with authority to speak in the name of Jesus Christ, in virtue of episcopal consecration and succession from the apostles in their mandate to teach'. In other words, 'authoritatively' here means, 'with hierarchical authority', or as St Thomas put it, *ex officio praelationis*.

If this meaning of *authentice* is not kept in mind, one could think that the Council was making the absurd claim that only bishops could give a genuine interpretation of the Word of God, or that they were the only ones who would interpret Scripture or Tradition with any kind of authority at all. The Council surely did not intend to deny that theologians and exegetes speak with the authority which their expertise confers on them. What the Council attributes exclusively to the 'living magisterium' is authority to speak as pastors of the Church, endowed with the mandate to teach the Gospel in the name of Jesus Christ.

A twofold magisterium?

In the light of the way that St Thomas speaks of the *magisterium* of theologians as well as that of bishops, some Catholic writers have suggested that it would be appropriate now also to speak of a twofold *magisterium* in the Church.[7] They argue that to limit the term *magisterium* to the teaching function of the hierarchy seems to imply that only bishops can teach with authority in the Church.

Now a great deal needs to be said about the relationship between the teaching function of bishops and that of theologians and exegetes, and I intend to treat this question at some length in a subsequent chapter. For the moment I wish to discuss only the question of the use of the word *magisterium.* In my view, it would cause confusion and lead to misunderstanding, to use the term *magisterium* nowadays to describe the role of theologians and exegetes, and so to insist on there being a twofold *magisterium* in the Church. The fact is that in modern usage, the term *magisterium* has come to be associated exclusively with pastoral teaching authority. To say that theologians and exegetes constitute a second magisterium in the Church could create the impression that one is trying to set up a rival pastoral authority. Competent scholars can speak with authority in their own field, but they do not have the kind of authority that has come to be associated with the word *magisterium.* I agree with those who feel that the effort to reclaim the term *magisterium* for the role of theologians is ill-advised.[8]

The notion of pastoral teaching authority

It might be helpful at this point to explain further the Catholic notion of pastoral or hierarchical teaching authority, while leaving to a later chapter the question of the exegetical and historical basis of the Catholic position.

First of all, it is clear that where revealed religion is concerned, the ultimate authority is God the Revealer, and the absolute truth of his Word. The role of any human mediator, whether prophet, apostle, bishop or theologian, is to help others to know what God has said, and what his Word means here and now. Once the hearers recognise the message to be truly a Word of God, (and in this recognition the interior witness of the Spirit has its part to play), their act of faith is directed not to the human bearer of the message, but to the Word itself, and to God who has spoken it. The motive of the act of faith is not the reliability of the human messenger, but the truth of the Word itself as Word of God.

However, for the act of faith to be a reasonable decision, and not a rash leap in the dark, the hearers of the message need to be sufficiently certain that what is proposed to them as revealed truth is actually God's Word. The interior witness of the Spirit will help them to discern the presence of God's Word, but this is usually not sufficient by itself. The hearers have to be convinced of the reliability of the one who tells them that this is what God has said. It is the history of public revelation that only a few people have been chosen to be its direct recipients; all others have to rely on the testimony of witnesses to it.

The reliability or trustworthiness of the witness to God's Word, while not the motive of the act of faith, is important as providing reasonable certitude that God really has spoken this Word. It is at this point that the notion of 'authorised witnesses' enters the picture. All Christians agree that the apostles, and the 'apostolic men' who were the authors of the New Testament, were chosen by God as authorised witnesses to the Christ-event. By their witness to Christ they gathered disciples who accepted their testimony 'not as the word of men but as what it really is, the Word of God' (1 Thess 2:13). Those who received this Word 'devoted themselves to the apostles' teaching' (Acts 2:42). The teaching of the apostles was recognised as normative for the faith of the Christian community, for they were the authoritative witnesses to what God had revealed in his Son Jesus Christ.

We have seen above that the apostles entrusted their message to the Church, and that the faith of the Church is normative for the faith of the individual who wishes to belong to it. Since the Church is a community united in the profession of the same faith, it has to have a common creed and a common understanding of the basic truths of its faith. The pastors who are responsible for the well-being of the community have a special responsibility regarding its common profession of faith. When conflicts arise as to the terms of its creed, or to its interpretation, those with pastoral responsibility must have the authority to judge which of the conflicting opinions is in accord with the faith of the Church. According to the Catholic understanding of the matter, it is part of God's design that in every age of the Church there should be successors of the apostles, not, to be sure, as immediate recipients of revelation, but as authorised witnesses, with authority from Christ to preach and teach his word, and, when necessary, to settle questions that arise concerning the normative faith of the community. It is in this sense that Vatican II speaks of bishops as 'judges of faith' (LG 25). This of course does not mean that they are superior to the Word of God. A passage of *Dei Verbum* expressly denies this. It is a passage worth studying in detail, for the light which it throws on the notion of a pastoral teaching authority. The text is as follows (DV 10, my translation):

> Now this Magisterium is not above the Word of God, but serves it, teaching only what has been handed on, listening to it devoutly, guarding it conscientiously, and explaining it faithfully, by divine commission and with the help of the Holy Spirit. From this one deposit of faith it draws everything which it presents for belief as divinely revealed.

Practically each phrase here deserves some comment.

'... *not above the Word of God but serves it* ...' The authority of the magisterium is not an authority over the Word of God but over human interpretations of it, especially over those which are in conflict with the faith of the Church. It is an authority within the community of faith; a ministry to the Word, and to the people who have accepted this Word. It is a service to the unity of the Church in the profession of the true faith.

'... *teaching only what has been handed on* ...' The term 'what has been handed on' is used here with the same inclusive meaning which it had previously in DV 8, where the Council says: 'Now what was handed on by the apostles includes everything which contributes to the holiness of life and the increase in faith of the People of God.' In other words, it means the whole 'sacred deposit of the Word of God, which is committed to the Church' (DV 10). It is extremely significant that Vatican II says that it is to the *Church* (and not just to the magisterium) that the whole deposit of the Word of God has been entrusted. Likewise, it is 'the Church, in her teaching, life and worship, that perpetuates and hands on to all generations all that she herself is, all that she believes' (DV 8). This is a salutary corrective of the notion found in earlier treatises on this subject, according to which the deposit of faith was entrusted uniquely to the successors of the apostles, and is handed on primarily, if not exclusively, in the official teaching of the magisterium.[9]

'... *listening to it devoutly* ...' This phrase tells us that before the bishops can be preachers of the Word they must first be hearers of the Word; before they can belong to the 'teaching church' (*ecclesia docens*) they have to belong to

31

the 'learning church' (*ecclesia discens*). And since the 'sacred deposit of the Word of God has been entrusted to the Church', it follows that the bishops have to listen devoutly to this Word as it is handed on from generation to generation 'in the teaching, life and worship of the Church'. They cannot isolate themselves from the Church and listen only to themselves. An important part of their listening to the Word of God, then, will be to 'consult the faithful' as Cardinal Newman put it in his famous article;[10] another important part will be their listening to the exegetes and theologians who spend their lives studying the Word of God.

'. . . *guarding it conscientiously* . . .' This phrase suggests the special concern of the magisterium, and the reason why it tends to be generally 'conservative'; its primary function is not to penetrate into the depths of the mysteries of faith (the task of theology), but rather to safeguard the priceless treasure of the Word of God, and to defend the purity of the faith of the Christian community.

'. . . *and explaining it faithfully* . . .' Here the adverb 'faithfully' again suggests that the primary concern of the magisterium is fidelity to the original deposit of faith. Bishops are to explain the Word of God, but they do not take upon themselves the specific function of theologians, whose role it is to seek a deeper understanding of the faith, making use of knowledge gained from philosophy and other human sciences in the process.

'. . . *by divine commission* . . .' This is a reference to the source of the teaching authority of bishops. Vatican II expresses the Catholic belief that by virtue of their episcopal ordination and their hierarchical communion with the head and other members of the episcopal college, bishops share in the succession of this college to the apostolic college in teaching authority and pastoral rule in the Church (*Lumen gentium* 22). Hence they share the divine command to 'make disciples of all nations and teach them to observe all that Christ commanded them' (cf. Mt 28:20).

'. . . *and with the help of the Holy Spirit* . . .' While the Holy Spirit dwells in all the faithful, and 'arouses and sustains the supernatural sense of faith which characterizes the People as a whole' (*Lumen gentium* 12), Catholics believe that the sacrament of episcopal ordination, which confers on bishops the function of pastoral magisterium, is a divine pledge of a special assistance of the Holy Spirit in the fulfilment of their teaching role. We leave to a later chapter the consideration of the biblical and historical grounds of this belief, and the consequences of this special help of the Holy Spirit, especially in regard to the question of infallibility.

'... it draws from this one deposit of faith everything which it presents for belief as divinely revealed.' We have already insisted on the point that the 'deposit of faith' does not consist in a collection of propositions. The word 'deposit' suggests the fact that God's self-revelation to mankind is definitive in the Christ-event, and that this definitive Word of God is a treasure entrusted to the Church, to which nothing further will be added. Whatever the faithful can be called upon to believe as Word of God must be really contained (although not necessarily in explicit terms) in what the apostolic Church received and handed on.

An objection to the notion of hierarchical teaching authority

I shall conclude this chapter by briefly considering an objection that is sometimes raised against the very notion of a hierarchical teaching authority. The objection is that hierarchical authority is a juridical concept, which has no place where teaching is concerned, since teaching has to do with truth, and only the truth itself has authority over the mind. Hierarchical authority cannot make something to be true by imposing it as obligatory for belief.

Of course, if something is not true, no authority can make it to be true. But there are several considerations to be kept in mind, which help to explain the legitimate role of authority where assent to revealed truth is concerned.

The first point is that the truth of most of what God has revealed is not intrinsically evident to us; we have to 'take it on faith'. When we give intellectual assent to an article of faith whose truth is not evident to our mind, our act of faith is a free assent, which means that our free will is involved, choosing to believe. Furthermore, we have to rely on the testimony of witnesses to know what God has revealed. Here again we do not have the kind of evidence that forces our minds to assent; so again our free will has a part to play in our choice to accept their testimony.

It is this role of our free will in the decision to believe which leaves room for the legitimate exercise of teaching authority. Of course it cannot be a purely arbitrary authority; it has to be an authority which commends itself to us as reasonable to accept. As far as most Christians are concerned, it is reasonable to accept the authority of the apostles, since they were commissioned by Christ himself to bear witness to what he had revealed to them. As far as Catholics are concerned, it is also reasonable to accept the authority of the bishops when they declare something to be obligatory for our faith, because we believe that they share in the mandate which Christ gave to the apostles. Furthermore, we believe that along with this mandate, the bishops share in the promise of a special assistance of the Holy Spirit, which, while it provides an absolute guarantee of the truth of their teaching only in certain rather rare cases, gives reason for confidence in their guidance of the faith of the Church, and thus makes it reasonable for us to be disposed to accept their teaching authority even when it is not infallible. This does not rule out the possibility of legitimate dissent to non-infallible teaching, but neither does the possibility of legitimate dissent in particular cases rule out the reasonableness of respecting the teaching of the magisterium as an authoritative and generally reliable witness to the 'mind of the Church' on matters of faith and morals.

In this chapter I have been simply presenting what I believe to be the common Catholic understanding of what is meant nowadays by 'the magisterium'. I have said that I would return to the question of the exegetical and historical justification of the Catholic position. It is this question that the next chapter will take up. To sharpen the question, I shall look at it in the light of Hans Küng's contention that the arguments typically used to justify the Catholic theory of episcopal magisterium 'have feet of clay'.

3.

Biblical and Historical Basis for the Teaching Authority of Bishops

According to Hans Küng, 'the statements (of Vatican II) about an infallibility of the college of bishops, based on the traditional, unhistorical theory of a direct and exclusive apostolic succession of the bishops, exegetically, historically, theologically, have feet of clay.'[1]

While I am not immediately concerned with the question of infallibility, I quote this sentence from Küng's book because it shows that his critique is directed not just at the doctrine of papal or episcopal infallibility, but at the foundation of this doctrine in the Catholic theory of an authoritative teaching function of bishops, based on their claim to apostolic succession. To my way of thinking, the most radical questions that Küng raises in his book on infallibility are found in the last section of his final chapter, which has the subheading: 'A teaching office?'[2] Like the question mark in the title of the book, the question mark in this subheading is a hint of what Küng's own answer is going to be. Let us first briefly recall the teaching of Vatican II on the teaching office of bishops, and then see how Küng answers his question.

At the risk of some repetition, I shall present the teaching of Vatican II in a catena of quotations, some of which have been seen already.

'By divine institution bishops have succeeded to the place of the apostles as shepherds of the Church' (LG 20).

'Episcopal consecration, together with the office of sanctifying, also confers the offices of teaching and of governing' (LG 21).

'The order of bishops is the successor to the college of the apostles in teaching authority (*magisterium*) and pastoral rule' (LG 22).

'As successors of the apostles, bishops receive from Him (Christ) the mission to teach all nations and to preach the gospel to every creature' (LG 24).

(Bishops) 'are authentic teachers, that is, teachers endowed with the authority of Christ, who preach to the people committed to them the faith they must believe and put into practice' (LG 25).

'Bishops, teaching in communion with the Roman Pontiff, are to be respected by all as witnesses to divine and Catholic truth. In matters of faith and morals, the bishops speak in the name of Christ and the faithful are to accept their teaching and adhere to it with a religious assent of soul' (LG 25).

'When gathered together in an ecumenical council, they (the bishops) are teachers and judges of faith and morals for the universal Church. Their definitions must then be adhered to with the submission of faith' (LG 25).

Thus far the teaching of Vatican II in its Dogmatic Constitution on the Church. Another important statement is found in the declaration made by the Theological Commission of the Council on 6 March 1964: 'In view of conciliar practice and the pastoral purpose of the present Council, this sacred Synod defines matters of faith or morals as binding on the Church only when the Synod itself openly declares so. Other matters which the sacred Synod proposes as the doctrine of the supreme teaching authority of the Church, each and every member of the faithful is obliged to accept and embrace according to the mind of the sacred Synod itself, which becomes known either from the subject matter or from the language employed, according to the norms of theological interpretation.'[3]

I think this statement is particularly significant, because it shows that the bishops gathered at Vatican II saw what they were doing there as a concrete instance of the exercise of their authoritative teaching office, with a claim on the assent of all the Catholic faithful, even though they did not invoke their power to define any new dogmas with infallibility. Hence, in what follows, rather than think of episcopal magisterium in the abstract, we can think of it as embodied in the teaching authority of the bishops at the Second Vatican Council. Thus, if the doctrine of this Council about the teaching office of bishops 'has feet of clay', so does the authority of the Council itself.

Let us now see how the answer which Hans Küng gives to his question: 'A teaching office?' compares with the above teaching of Vatican II.

Bishops, successors of the apostles by divine institution?

According to Küng, 'it is true that there was church leadership from the very beginning, whether through the apostles or through other charismatic ministries. But it must be traced back, not to "divine institution", but to a long and complex historical development.'[4] While, according to Küng, the fact that 'the leadership of the community fell to the episkopoi and presbyters in the course of historical development' (p. 84) excludes a theory of divine institution for the episcopate, he does recognise this development as 'legitimate and pastorally appropriate' (p. 86). Hence there is a sense in which bishops can be described as successors of the apostles: 'Within the apostolic succession of the church as a whole, there is a particular apostolic succession of church leaders or pastors, in as much as they carry on the special apostolic function of church founding or church leadership, without themselves being apostles' (227-8). I would call attention to the fact that when Küng speaks of the role of the bishops as 'legitimate' and 'appropriate', he consistently speaks of it in terms of 'leadership'. We must now see what he says about the question of their teaching function in the Church.

Bishops, successors to the apostles in teaching authority?

Küng's first reply to this question is given in the context of his discussion of the historical development of the episcopate, where he says:

> Nor, on the basis of the development briefly outlined here, would it be possible to prove that the bishops are the sole (or sole 'authentic') teachers in the Church. According to the New Testament, all are called to proclaim the word. And although the leadership of the community, which fell to the episkopoi and the presbyters in the course of historical development, has to be exercised primarily through the word, this cannot in any case mean the absorption of the other charisms and ministries of proclamation. In 1 Corinthians 12, Paul defends himself expressly against individuals craving to monopolize everything and em-

phasizes *alongside* the apostles two other groups: 'second to prophets, third to teachers' (1 Cor 12:28), to whom in the Didache the episkopoi and deacons still seem to take second place for the celebration of the Eucharist. Along with a special succession of the apostles there is also a special succession of prophets and teachers: we shall not discuss here what this means when translated into modern terms, but it will be taken up again later in connection with the obscure concept of the teaching office. (p. 84)

The final section of his book, with the subtitle: 'A teaching office?', is the elaboration of the thesis suggested in the paragraph just quoted. Briefly put, his thesis is that bishops are the legitimate (though not divinely instituted) successors of the apostles in their role of pastoral leadership, but since, besides apostles, there were also prophets and teachers in the New Testament Church, succession in leadership cannot include succession in the function of teaching, since this would mean the monopolising of distinct charisms. The successors of the New Testament teachers in today's Church are the theologians, not the bishops.

Lest I be accused of distorting Küng's views, I shall quote a few of the key passages of his treatment of the question of a teaching office for bishops.

In the modern ecclesiastical sense of 'magisterium' the bishops, who are the leaders of the Church, are therefore supposed to be also her teachers. At the same time, it is apparently presupposed that teaching takes place through an office or authority ('teaching office' as a kind of parallel to 'home office' or 'foreign office'). But this also raises the problem: is it then so obvious that there is in the Church a teaching office as an authority, that the bishops and particularly the Roman pontiff in personal union are leaders of the Church and teachers of the Church? It will not be disputed that the bishops — in this respect anyway not distinct in a dogmatic sense from the presbyters — are leaders of the Church. But it cannot be claimed with equal certainty that they are also teachers in the Church and still less — as textbook theology states — the sole authentic teachers in their dioceses and — together with the Pope — in the Church as a whole. (p. 223)

Is the *Church leader* automatically also *Church teacher*? (p. 227)

If by 'teaching office' of the bishops (and the pope) is meant, not the proclamation of the gospel, but the official regulation of all teaching, so that the Church leaders would be the sole authority for teaching and thus the Church leaders would also be the Church teachers, then the objection must be raised that such a limiting, canalizing, and monopolizing of the charisms in a hierocracy of pastors clearly contradicts the New Testament message and the New Testament Church. (p. 230)

It means giving to ministry an absolute value in an unbiblical way when a leader considers himself simultaneously as apostle, prophet and teacher, and so wants to be everything in one . . . (p. 230)

. . . if we rightly speak of a succession of the apostles in the different pastoral ministries, [it is important] to speak with the same right of a succession of the prophets and teachers. . . . The question is easier to understand if, in accordance with present-day usage, we speak of theologians instead of teachers. (p. 231)

The leaders who do not want to hear the theologians in the Church . . . will claim, although the gifts are diverse, to be not only successors of the apostles, but also successors of the teachers. There *can* be pastors who are also teachers, but this — according to Paul — is not the rule. (p. 232)

Pastors and teachers in the Church, leaders and theologians, have their own charism, each his own vocation, each his own function. The ministry of leadership and the ministry of teaching must be seen in this functionality (p. 233). Certainly leaders and teachers in the Church have their special task: bishops and priests leadership, theologians scholarship. (p. 237-8)

Finally, in Küng's theory, it is only in an emergency situation that the bishops take over the teaching role normally reserved to theologians: when 'heresy shakes the Church to her foundations', and 'it is a question of the existence or non-existence of the Church of the gospel'. In such an emergency, the bishops 'in co-operation with all theologians of good will – will come together and, trusting in God's Spirit, say clearly what is the Christian faith and what is not' (p. 239).

I hope I may be pardoned for such a long series of quotations, but it seemed necessary to let Küng speak for himself. I shall now offer my own reflections on particular points of Küng's theory where I believe further clarification is called for.

Are bishops successors of the apostles 'in a direct and exclusive sense'?

Several times Küng refers to what he terms the 'unhistorical theory of a direct and exclusive apostolic succession of the bishops'. Against the idea of 'direct' succession he insists that the episcopate is the product of a complex historical development in the post-apostolic period. Against the idea of 'exclusive' succession of bishops he makes two points: that the whole Church, and not just the bishops, is in apostolic succession, as sharing the apostolic mandate to proclaim the gospel; and that presbyters also inherit the apostolic role of pastoral leadership in the Church.

My observation on this is that I do not believe that the teaching of Vatican II that 'bishops have succeeded to the place of the apostles as shepherds of the Church' depends on a theory of 'direct and exclusive' succession. I also would label as 'unhistorical' a theory of direct apostolic succession according to which either Christ himself explictly instituted the episcopate, or the apostles, before they died, established a single bishop in each of the churches which they had founded, and formally designated such bishops as their successors. I do not know of any serious Catholic scholar today who would not agree that the episcopate as we know it is the term of a historical development in the post-apostolic period.

As far as the claim to 'exclusive' succession is concerned, again I see no problem in agreeing that the whole Church is in apostolic succession, insofar as all Christians share the apostolic mandate to proclaim the good news of Christ to the world; Vatican II states this in several places, cf. the Decree on the Apostolate of the Laity,[5] and the statement in the Decree on the Ministry and Life of Priests, n.2: 'There is no member who does not have a part in the mission of the whole body.'

Nor is there any reason to deny that presbyters, as well as bishops, succeed in a real sense to the pastoral ministry of the apostles; cf. the following statement in the Decree on Ministry and Life of Priests, n.2: 'Since in their own measure priests participate in the office of the apostles, God gives them the grace to be ministers of Christ Jesus among the people.'

However, I do not believe that the teaching of Vatican II on the apostolic succession of bishops depends on any claim to 'direct and exclusive' succession that would call for a denial of the points to which I have expressed agreement. It suffices that bishops have inherited the apostolic ministry of pastoral leadership with a fullness that others have not, so that the relationship between bishops and priests is analogous to the relationship, as far as their ministry is concerned, between the apostles and the *episkopoi* and *presbuteroi* of the New Testament.

Is the apostolic succession of bishops 'of divine institution'?

It would seem that in Küng's view there is an obvious contradiction between the claim that the apostolic succession of bishops is of divine institution, and the admission that the episcopate, as we know it, is the term of a post-New Testament development. Küng dwells at some length on the details of the historical process by which the episcopate is thought to have emerged, but he nowhere tells us why this necessarily rules out a theory of divine institution. I am tempted to suggest an analogy with people who take it for granted that if you can demonstrate the theory of biological evolution you have automatically ruled out the divine creation of man.

Presumably Küng assumes that any theory of divine institution necessarily means a claim that Christ himself explicitly determined the hierarchical structure of his Church in all its details, including the monarchical episcopate. It is true that Vatican II, in *Christus Dominus* n. 20, does say: 'The apostolic office of bishops was instituted by Christ the Lord', but I do not think even this statement, while open to misunderstanding, has to be understood as committing the Council to the idea that Christ explicitly instituted the episcopate.

The notion of divine institution, as applied to such elements of Church structure as the episcopate, is one that no Catholic

41

scholar nowadays interprets in a simplistic sense that would require the explicit determination of all such structures by Christ before his ascension, or even their full development before the death of the last apostle. It is now generally recognised that Christ did not draw up a 'blueprint' for his disciples to follow in the organisation of the Church. Indeed it is apparent from the New Testament (e.g. in the appointment of the 'Seven' in Jerusalem)[6] that the apostles made decisions about Church structures as the need arose, and that they felt guided by the Spirit in such decisions. It is quite consistent with the development which we see taking place in the New Testament itself, that in the post-New Testament period such development continued, as the churches experienced the need of a focal point of unity in each local church: a point of unity that previously had been supplied by the founding apostle or apostolic missionary. If, while the founding apostle was still alive, there was not the felt need of a single pastoral leader in each local church, it is reasonable to surmise that such a need was felt afterwards, when the apostle was no longer there to maintain unity. In any case, the fact is that within a century or so after the death of the apostles, practically every Christian church of which we have any information was being led by a single bishop. It is also a fact that these bishops were being universally recognised as the successors of the apostles in their role of pastoral leadership. There is no evidence of any resistance to the system of episcopal leadership except from the gnostics and other sects.

Can we then speak of 'divine institution'? Most Catholic scholars think that we can. Obviously not in a simplistic sense. But in the sense that we have good reason to believe that this development, which is consistent with what was already taking place in the New Testament Church, was guided by the Holy Spirit and was part of God's design for his Church.

In support of the claim that this development was consistent with what was already taking place in the New Testament Church, we can appeal to the following factors. First, the New Testament Church clearly understood that the pastoral charge given to the apostles of 'making disciples, baptising, teaching people to observe all that Jesus had taught them' was to continue to the end of this age. Surely this is the sense of the final verses of the Gospel of Matthew. Therefore, while in many respects the original apostles could have no successors, for in many ways their role was unique and untransmissible, their pastoral ministry was to continue, and that meant that others had to succeed them in this respect. Secondly, within the New Testament we see provision being made for the carrying on of the apostles' ministry by those who would survive them. Whether the Letters to Titus and Timothy were written by St Paul or not, they are a clear witness to this development taking place within the time of the New Testament. And, while it would be anachronistic to describe Titus and Timothy as local bishops in the modern sense, they do suggest the beginning of the development from the original founding apostle to the later local bishop. Thirdly, we can detect in other places in the New Testament indications of a tendency to the emergence of a single leader in each local church. The role of James in the church of Jerusalem, as suggested by Acts 21:8, would be a case in point. Perhaps also Diotrephes of 3 John 9; perhaps also the fact that the word *episkopos* occurs only in the singular in the Pastoral Epistles.[7]

If the dating generally accepted for the letters of Ignatius of Antioch is correct,[8] then before all the books of the canonical New Testament were written, the threefold hierarchy of one bishop, a college of presbyters and a number of deacons, was already established in Syria and parts of Asia Minor. And by the third quarter of the second century, every church that we have information about, with the exception of Alexandria, had a single bishop. On the basis of the following facts: that this development took place within so short a time, in the whole Church, without any resistance on the part of presbyters or people; that these bishops were accepted as the legitimate successors of the apostles; and that their role has undoubtedly been beneficial for the life of the Church — the conclusion is drawn that this development must have been guided by the Holy Spirit, and must have been, part of God's design for his Church. It is in this sense that I would claim that it is of 'divine institution'. I do not claim to have provided a strict exegetical or historical 'proof' of this conclusion. I agree that it depends on what one is prepared to believe about the guidance of the Church by the Holy Spirit, and what significance one attributes to universal reception by the Church. My position is that what the whole Church receives, whether doctrine (as Word of God), writings (as canonical Scripture) or bishops (as successors of the apostles) must indeed be what the Church accepts them to be.

Are bishops not only pastors but also teachers in the Church?

According to Vatican II, 'the order of bishops is the successor to the college of the apostles in teaching authority (*magisterium*) and pastoral rule' (LG 22). According to Hans Küng, bishops can be said to be successors to the apostles in pastoral rule, but not in teaching, since the New Testament distinguished between apostles and teachers, and the successors of the New Testament teachers are not the bishops but the theologians. While some Catholic writers now prefer to speak of two *magisteria* in the Church, Küng insists that there is only one: that of theological scholarship.

Let us look at his argument more closely. First, a comment on his statement that 'it would be impossible to prove that the bishops are the sole (or sole "authentic") teachers in the Church' (p. 84). I do not know of anyone who claims that bishops are the sole teachers in the Church. With regard to the claim that they are the sole 'authentic' teachers, the meaning of such a claim depends on the sense of the word 'authentic'. As has been pointed out above, the word 'authentic' as applied to the *magisterium*, is to be understood to mean 'having hierarchical authority'. It cannot be taken to mean simply 'authoritative', and much less can it be taken to mean 'genuine' or 'trustworthy'. Obviously, even in the sense in which Vatican II does actually claim that bishops are the sole authentic teachers in matters of faith and morals, Küng will not agree, but at least it is important to know that Vatican II is not making the absurd claim that bishops are the only genuine teachers in the Church, or the only ones who can teach with any kind of authority at all.

What about Küng's thesis that if bishops are the successors of the New Testament leaders they cannot also be the successors of the New Testament teachers, since this would amount to a 'limiting, canalizing and monopolizing of the charisms in a hierocracy of pastors that clearly contradicts the New Testament message and the New Testament Church' (p. 230)?

The first question I would raise about this thesis concerns Küng's identification of teaching in the Church with the work of the university professor of theology. If indeed 'teaching' can only be understood as the communication of the fruits of scholarly research, then one could agree that only theologians can be teachers in the Church. As far as I can see, this is in fact the supposition of his thesis. He consistently identifies 'teachers' as 'theologians', and describes their function as 'scholarly reflection: scholarship by investigation' (p. 238).

But surely university professors of theology are not the only ones who can be rightly called teachers in the Church. What about catechists, what about those who teach Christian doctrine in schools, what about parents who are the teachers of the faith in the 'domestic church'?

In any case, it is obvious that Küng denies that bishops (at least those who are not also professional theologians) can be said to do any real teaching in the Church. My question, then, is simply: what were the bishops doing at Vatican II? Does Küng accept the documents of this Council, especially its 'dogmatic constitutions', as examples of teaching or not? Would he claim that it was only the theologians called to be *periti* who did any real teaching during the four years of the Council?

It seems to me that the very fact of the Second Vatican Council, its history and its documents, provide tangible proof that there is a genuine kind of teaching in the Church which is distinct from and different from the work of the university professor of theology. To use the language of St Thomas, there is a *magisterium cathedrae pastoralis* in the Church as well as a *magisterium cathedrae magistralis*. There is a kind of teaching that the bishops at Vatican II proved they were capable of doing (admittedly with the help of theologians); surely the bishops were exercising a genuine *magisterium* there, even though few of them were professional theologians.

Küng insists that there are distinct charisms in the Church, and of course he is right. But he seems to believe that there is only one kind of charism of teaching: the charism of theological scholarship. I would say that there are at least two distinct charisms of teaching in the Church: the charism of scholarly teaching such as theologians exercise in the univer-

45

sity lecture hall, and the charism of pastoral teaching, such as the bishops exercised at the Second Vatican Council. Indeed, the success of this council was due in large measure to the happy collaboration of these two charisms, each making its own distinctive contribution.

Küng is right, of course, in insisting that there should be no monopolising of all the charisms by any one person or class of persons. But the question is whether it is possible, and even appropriate, for the charisms of pastoral leadership and pastoral teaching to be found in the same person.

Küng claims that 'for Church leaders to be also Church teachers would contradict the New Testament message and the New Testament Church' (p. 230). His 'proof-text' for this thesis is 1 Cor 12:28: 'God has appointed in the Church first apostles, second prophets, third teachers.' Küng consistently assigns to the apostles the role of leadership; they have the 'special apostolic function of Church founding and Church leadership' (p. 228). He nowhere speaks of their ministry as also involving teaching. He seems to take for granted that it was only those called *didaskaloi* who did any teaching in the New Testament Church. Indeed, although the few references in the New Testament to such *didaskaloi* tell us hardly anything about what or how they taught, Küng confidently tells us that 'the teachers are those who may take endless pains to find the tradition, the teaching and the correct interpretation of the original Christian message. . . . while the prophet makes his announcement in a more intuitive fashion, the teacher will reflect and develop the message in a more theological and systematic way' (p. 231). Even in the time of the New Testament, the teachers were already theologians!

It would seem that, as Küng reconstructs it, in the New Testament Church the apostles founded and ruled the churches, but the *didaskaloi* did all the teaching. As the *didaskaloi* were not apostles, neither could the apostles be teachers. The charisms of leadership and teaching could not be united in the same persons, not even in the apostles. How does this theory square with the New Testament evidence? It strikes me that it does not square with it at all.

All one has to do is read the letters of St Paul — say, his letter to the Romans — to know that an apostle could have a stupendous charism of teaching, along with his charism for

46

church leadership. There are numerous references in the New Testament to St Paul as 'teacher', and to his ministry as 'teaching'. He speaks of his own ministry as 'teaching' in 1 Cor 4:17; Rom 6:17 and 16:17; 2 Th 2:15 and Col 1:28. In the Acts he is described as engaged in teaching at 11:26; 15:35; 18:11; 20:20; 21:21; 28:31. For the author of the Pastoral Letters he is *the* teacher: 1 Tim 2:5-7; 2 Tim 1:1; 3:10.

There are also references to a teaching ministry on the part of other apostles. In Acts 2:42 we are told that those who received the word on the first Christian Pentecost 'devoted themselves to the apostles' teaching'. At Acts 4:2 it is Peter and John who are teaching the people; at Acts 5:21 and 42 it is 'the apostles' who teach, both in the temple and at home. Matthew's Gospel could hardly have concluded with Jesus giving the apostles their mandate to 'make disciples . . . teaching them to observe all that I have commanded you', if the apostles were not known to have carried on a ministry corresponding to this command.

I conclude: while in the early Church there were teachers (*didaskaloi*) who were not apostles, and perhaps were not among the church leaders, one can hardly deny that there were Church leaders, namely at least some of the apostles, who had the twofold charism and ministry of leadership and teaching.

Furthermore, there is evidence that in the later period of the New Testament Church, the combination of pastoral leadership and teaching in the same person was looked upon as something quite normal. For instance, in Eph 4:11 it is noteworthy that while each of the other ministries has its own definite article, the 'pastors and teachers' are joined by the same article. J. Fitzmyer remarks on this that the teachers 'seem to be identified with or at least related to the shepherds (pastors), being linked by one definite article.'[9] In the address of St Paul to the elders or *episkopoi* of the church of Ephesus, (Acts 20:17-35) the warning he gives them in vv. 28-31 suggests that they are to have care for the purity of doctrine, to be alert against those who would spread false teaching, and to speak with authority if need should be.

When we come to the Pastoral Letters, to quote J. Fitzmyer again, 'Here the function of the teacher is clearly predicated of the delegates of the apostle and of those whom they appoint as *episkopoi*.'[10] Timothy and Titus, who are assigned a role of pastoral leadership over the churches of Ephesus and Crete, are also repeatedly reminded of their obligation to teach. Timothy is told: 'Command and teach these things' (1 Tim 4:11). 'Till I come, attend to the public reading of scripture, to preaching, to teaching' (1 Tim 4:13). 'Take heed to yourself and to your teaching' (1 Tim 4:16). 'Be unfailing in patience and teaching' (2 Tim 4:2). And Titus likewise: 'But as for you, teach what befits sound doctrine' (Tit 2:1).

It is even more significant that the men whom Timothy and Titus are to appoint as presbyters and *episkopoi* in these churches are also to combine the roles of leadership and teaching. Among the qualifications which are required in candidates for the episcopate is that a man be *didaktikos*: 'an apt teacher' (1 Tim 3:2). While all of the presbyters had a role of leadership, some also had a ministry of teaching: 'Let the elders who rule well be considered worthy of double honour, especially those who labour in preaching and teaching' (1 Tim 5:17). Timothy is instructed: 'What you have heard from me before many witnesses entrust to faithful men who will be able to teach others also' (2 Tim 2:2). Likewise, Titus is told that among the qualifications of an elder or *episkopos* is that 'he must hold firm to the sure word as taught, so that he may be able to give instruction in sound doctrine and also to confute those who contradict' (Tit 1:9).

J. Fitzmyer thus sums up the evidence we have seen:

> In the Deutero-Pauline letters, then, we have a clear picture of a number of emergent details regarding the function of teaching in different local churches. The author himself clearly writes as a *didaskalos* guaranteeing the 'sound doctrine', and he relates the teaching of it to the office of *episkopos*, who is to be concerned for it and for the judgment and confutation of what is opposed to it. . . . This does not mean, of course, that such officials are the only teachers in the (local) Christian community, but the Deutero-Pauline letters suggest that concern and wariness for sound doctrine rest with such appointees.[11]

Now it is true that we cannot presume that the kind of church organisation reflected in the Pastoral Letters was found in all the local Christian communities of the same period. The Johannine literature gives us quite a different picture. Here the stress is on the role of the Holy Spirit, guiding the Church into all the truth (cf. Jn 16:13), and on the anointing which all the faithful receive, which teaches them about everything, so that they have no need that anyone should teach them (cf. 1 Jn 2:26-7). Of course we cannot overlook the fact that the author of 1 John is actually teaching by his letter, so he can hardly have meant that they take too literally his statement that they had no need that anyone should teach them. In any case, we have enough evidence from the Pauline letters, Acts and the Pastorals, of a close association between the ministry of pastoral leadership and the ministry of teaching in the New Testament churches, to justify the conclusion that the union of these two ministries in the same persons not only does not contradict the New Testament message, but is altogether in accord with what was actually taking place in many of the New Testament churches.

In view of this, it is no surprise when we find the bishops of the second century being recognised as successors of the apostles not only as leaders but also as Church teachers, and indeed as authoritative exponents of the genuine apostolic tradition. This does not mean, of course, that bishops were the only teachers in the second and third century churches. Justin Martyr was not a bishop, nor were most of the other early Christian apologists. Neither were such influential teachers as Tertullian, Clement of Alexandria, Origen or Lactantius. But there is abundant evidence that the bishops of this period exercised a twofold ministry of leading and teaching.

One striking witness to the union of the charisms of leadership and teaching in the same person is found in the account of the martyrdom of Polycarp, Bishop of Smyrna. The presbyters who wrote this account about the middle of the second century described their hero as 'the wonderful martyr, Polycarp, who in our days was an apostolic and prophetic teacher, bishop of the Catholic Church in Smyrna.'[12] At about the same time that Polycarp was martyred, Hegesippus was visiting the Christian churches on his way from the east to Rome. He tells us that in each church he found the sound apostolic tradition being handed down by the local

49

bishop.[13] A few decades later we have the great work of Irenaeus of Lyons against the gnostic heretics. One of Irenaeus' major themes is that the true apostolic doctrine is to be found not in the 'ravings' of the gnostics, but in the sober teaching of the bishops in the churches. He describes the bishops as 'those whom the apostles left as their successors, to whom they handed on their own role of teaching' (*quos et successores relinquebant, suum ipsorum locum magisterii tradentes*).[14]

It hardly seems necessary to multiply quotations from the writings of Irenaeus, Tertullian and others of this period to prove the point that from the late second century on, the bishops who ruled the churches were also exercising a role of pastoral *magisterium*. I do not believe that Küng would dispute this fact. What he questions is not the fact that bishops assumed the role of *magisterium*, but that they did so legitimately, rather than by usurping a charism that by rights belonged to the successors of the New Testament *didaskaloi*.

And my question is: what theological significance are we to attribute to the fact of the universal *reception* by the Christian churches, of bishops as both pastors and teachers? What is the significance of the fact that the Christian churches everywhere did recognise in their bishops the legitimate successors of the apostles in the twofold pastoral ministry of leading and teaching? Was the whole Church mistaken about this? Could it have been?

Now I do not believe that we can safely argue from the abiding presence of the Holy Spirit in the Church 'guiding it into all the truth' (Jn 16:13), to the conclusion that every historical development in church organisation has necessarily been legitimate or beneficial. On the other hand, when we are talking about the universal reception of bishops as authoritative teachers whose decisions on matters of faith were recognised as binding on the faithful, we are talking about the reception by the Church of a *norm* of its faith.

As we have seen in our first chapter, it has always been recognised that the faith of the Christian community is normative for the faith of its individual members. A profession of this normative faith has always been required of candidates for baptism, and perseverance in this faith is a condition for continued membership in the community. Now in a community with a normative creed, it is obvious that there must

50

be some authority in the community that can settle disputes about the terms of the creed or its interpretation. While the apostles were still alive this was evidently their prerogative. It is a matter of historical fact that during the course of the second century this function was taken over by the bishops. It is also a matter of historical fact that the whole Christian Church recognised and accepted the bishops as the authoritative witnesses to apostolic tradition, who had the authority to judge whether a particular doctrine was in conformity with this tradition or not, and consequently the authority to define the terms in which the community was obliged to profess its faith. In other words, the whole Church accepted the teaching of bishops as *normative* for its faith.

Now I do not see how a Church that is indefectible in its faith could have been mistaken when it determined what was going to be the norm of its faith. I believe that the argument is just as valid concerning the significance of the universal reception of the teaching of the bishops as normative, as it is concerning the universal reception of certain writings as normative for Christian faith. We do not know who wrote many of the books of the New Testament, but we believe that the Church could not have been mistaken when it accepted these and not other writings into its canon of Scripture, because we believe that the Church could not have made a mistake in determining the very norm of its faith. An erroneous decision about the very norm of faith would inevitably have led the Church into incalculable errors in particular matters of faith.

If our confidence that the Holy Spirit must have guided the second and third century Church in its discernment of the writings that were going to be normative for its faith, justifies our acceptance of the New Testament as inspired Scripture, it seems to me that we are justified in being equally confident that the Holy Spirit must have guided that second and third century Church in its recognition of its bishops as the rightful and authoritative teachers whose decisions about matters of Christian doctrine would be normative for its faith. I do not see how anyone who denies either of these points could still maintain that the Holy Spirit keeps the Church indefectibly in the truth.

4.

The Bearers of the Pastoral Teaching Office

It must be obvious from what has already been said that to the question: 'Who have pastoral teaching authority in the Church?' the answer I shall give is: the bishops do. But since it makes a difference whether one is talking about a single bishop or the whole episcopal college, whether this college is gathered in council or dispersed, and whether the single bishop in question is the bishop of Rome or some other, the question requires a somewhat differentiated answer. In this chapter I shall take as my point of departure the teaching of the Second Vatican Council regarding the magisterium. The principal *locus* of this teaching is n.25 of the Council's Dogmatic Constitution on the Church, so it would be advisable for the reader to refresh his or her memory of that section of *Lumen gentium* at this point, and to keep it handy for reference.

The context of Lumen gentium n. 25

Chapter Three of *Lumen gentium* is entitled: 'The Hierarchical Structure of the Church, with Special Reference to the Episcopate'. Section 25 is the first of three sections of this chapter in which the Council describes the threefold ministry of teaching, sanctifying and ruling which it had already named as the pastoral function of bishops in the Church. In n. 20 the Constitution describes bishops as 'teachers of doctrine, priests of sacred worship, and officers of good order'. In the following section it describes the effects of episcopal consecration as follows:

Episcopal consecration, together with the office of santifying, also confers the offices of teaching and of governing. . . . For from tradition, which is expressed especially in liturgical rites and in the practice of the Church both of the East and of the West, it is clear that by means of the imposition of hands and the words of consecration, the grace of the Holy Spirit is so conferred, and the sacred character so impressed, that bishops in an eminent and visible way undertake Christ's own role as Teacher, Shepherd and High Priest, and that they act in His person.

In both places where the Council speaks of the threefold ministry of bishops, it names the role of teacher in the first place. Thus it is no surprise that this is the role taken up in the first of the three sections (25, 26, 27) which the Council devotes to the ministry of bishops. It begins with a description of the teaching function of bishops in their own dioceses.

The teaching function of the bishop in his own diocese

Among the principal duties of bishops, the preaching of the gospel occupies an eminent place. For bishops are preachers of the faith who lead new disciples to Christ. They are authentic teachers, that is, teachers endowed with the authority of Christ, who preach to the people committed to them the faith they must believe and put into practice. By the light of the Holy Spirit, they make that faith clear, bringing forth from the treasury of revelation new things and old (cf. Mt 13:52), making faith bear fruit and vigilantly warding off any errors which threaten their flock (cf. 2 Tim 4:1-4). Bishops, teaching in communion with the Roman Pontiff, are to be respected by all as witnesses to divine and Catholic truth. In matters of faith and morals, the bishops speak in the name of Christ and the faithful are to accept their teaching and adhere to it with a religious assent of soul. . . . The individual bishops do not enjoy the prerogative of infallibility . . .

I suggest that one can distinguish three qualities which this text attributes to the magisterium of the individual bishops: it is pastoral, authoritative, and fallible.

Pastoral

The teaching function of bishops as described in the above text is clearly different from that of university professors of theology. The bishop's role is to preach the gospel, to lead new disciples to Christ, to make the faith bear fruit, to ward off errors which threaten their flock, and to witness to divine truth. The bishop's church is called a 'cathedral', because it houses his *cathedra*, the chair which is the symbol of teaching authority. His, however, is the *cathedra magisterii pastoralis*, not the university chair of the professor.

Authoritative

The Latin word is *authenticum*, which I have already suggested should not be translated as 'authentic' but as 'authoritative', since the immediately following phrase tells us that in this context it means: 'endowed with the authority of Christ'. A little later we are told that 'in matters of faith and morals the bishops speak in the name of Christ'. This teaching authority involves the corresponding obligation on the part of the faithful 'to accept their teaching and adhere to it with a religious assent of soul'. This obligation is a consequence of the fact that the faith of the community is normative for the faith of the individual who wishes to be a member of it, and that the bishop is the official witness and spokesman of the faith of the community.

Since the bishop's authority to teach depends on his being the witness of the faith of the Church, it is subject to several important conditions and limitations. Its object is limited to 'matters of faith and morals'. (We shall examine this term more closely in a later chapter). Its exercise depends on the local bishop's 'teaching in communion with the Roman Pontiff'. Earlier in Chapter Three of *Lumen gentium*, when the Council declared that episcopal consecration confers the offices of teaching and of governing, it added immediately: 'These, however, of their very nature, can be exercised only in hierarchical communion with the head and members of the college' (LG 21). The obligation, therefore, on the part of the faithful to accept the teaching of their local bishop and give their assent to it, is conditioned by the degree to which his teaching does truly reflect communion in doctrine with the whole college and its head. For example, a bishop who happens to believe in the immaculate conception of St Joseph cannot oblige the faithful of his diocese to share his belief in that regard. History provides more than one example of resistance on the part of the faithful to a bishop who attempted to impose unorthodox beliefs on his portion of the flock. This brings us to the third characteristic of the magisterium of individual bishops. It is not infallible.

Fallible

The admission of the council that 'individual bishops do not enjoy the prerogative of infallibility', following upon the statement that 'the faithful are to accept their teaching and adhere to it with religious assent of soul', raises the question how anyone can be obliged to give his assent to a teacher who is not speaking infallibly. This question will arise even more acutely when we come to treat of the ordinary, non-infallible magisterium of the Roman pontiff, so I shall postpone discussion of it until then. In any case, it is clear that as far as the obligation to give internal assent to the teaching of a local bishop is concerned, the question can legitimately be raised whether his teaching on a particular point is consonant with the faith of the Church as reflected in the teaching of the pope and the rest of the episcopal college. Since this faith is also reflected in the unanimous teaching of Catholic theologians, one could hardly be obliged to assent to a bishop who wished to impose as obligatory for belief, an opinion which Catholic theologians generally termed a matter of free discussion in the Church.

The teaching authority of the episcopal college dispersed throughout the world

The statement of Vatican II about the teaching authority of the dispersed episcopal college focuses on the conditions under which its teaching would be infallible.

Although the individual bishops do not enjoy the prerogative of infallibility, they can nevertheless proclaim Christ's doctrine infallibly. This is so, even when they are dispersed around the world, provided that while maintaining the bond of unity among themselves and with Peter's successor, and while teaching authentically on a matter of

55

faith or morals, they concur in a single viewpoint as the one which must be held conclusively.

For the present I intend to prescind from the question of infallibility, and simply consider the episcopal college as a subject of teaching authority when it is not gathered in an ecumenical council.

First, we recall the statement of Vatican II to the effect that 'the order of bishops is the successor to the college of the apostles in teaching authority and pastoral rule' (LG 22). From this the Council draws the corollary that 'the episcopal order, together with its head, the Roman pontiff, and never without this head, is the subject of supreme and full power over the universal Church' (LG 22). Without doubt this means that the college enjoys supreme teaching authority as well as supreme pastoral authority in the Church.

Now according to Vatican II, the episcopal college enjoys supreme authority not only when it is gathered in ecumenical council, but also when dispersed throughout the world (LG 22). Hence we can also speak of its supreme teaching authority even when it is not gathered in council. The teaching authority which the episcopal college exercises when it is not gathered in ecumenical council and is not defining a dogma of faith, is called its 'ordinary and universal magisterium'. It is called 'ordinary' to distinguish it from the solemn or extraordinary act of defining a dogma of faith. It is universal in that it involves the teaching authority of the whole college, including, of course, that of its head.

According to the First Vatican Council, Catholics are obliged to believe not only the dogmas of faith which have been solemnly defined, but also what is taught as divinely revealed by this 'ordinary and universal magisterium' (D-S 3011). If one asks for examples of such doctrines which are part of obligatory Catholic faith but have never been solemnly defined, I would suggest some of the articles of the baptismal creed, which have been part of the profession of faith required of candidates for membership in the Church from the earliest centuries, but have never been the subject of controversy, and have therefore never been the matter of solemn definition by any council or pope. The Church has never defined that 'Jesus is Lord, and that God has raised him from the dead', but these are far more basic articles of our faith than many dogmas that have been solemnly defined.

The subject, then, of this ordinary and universal magisterium, is the college of Catholic bishops including the bishop of Rome. Its teaching authority is 'supreme' only insofar as it is truly 'collegial'; its authority cannot be understood merely as the sum of the teaching authority of the individual bishops. Under certain conditions, its teaching enjoys the prerogative of infallibility; we shall return to this aspect of the question later on.

The teaching authority of ecumenical councils

We can begin by recalling what Vatican II tells us about ecumenical councils. *Lumen gentium* n. 22, having stated that the episcopal college together with its head the Roman pontiff is the subject of supreme and full power over the universal Church, goes on to say: 'The supreme authority with which this college is empowered over the whole Church is exercised in a solemn way through an ecumenical council. A council is never ecumenical unless it is confirmed or at least accepted as such by the successor of Peter. It is the prerogative of the Roman Pontiff to convoke these councils, to preside over them, and to confirm them.' Then, with regard to the teaching authority of ecumenical councils, *Lumen gentium* n. 25 says: 'This (teaching) authority (of the bishops) is even more clearly verified when, gathered together in an ecumenical council, they are teachers and judges of faith and morals for the universal church. Their definitions must then be adhered to with the submission of faith.'

What is an 'ecumenical' council?

Our first remark concerns the meaning of the word 'ecumenical'. It is derived from the Greek word *oikoumene*, which means 'the inhabited world'. The adjective 'ecumenical', then, means 'of the whole world', or 'universal'. As applied to councils, it means 'of the whole Church', as distinguished from provincial or regional councils.

In the present century the word 'ecumenical' has come to have a new meaning: the one, that is, which it has in the term 'ecumenical movement'. As Vatican II explains this term at the beginning of its *Decree on Ecumenism*, the ecumenical movement is a 'movement for the restoration of unity among *all* Christians,' which is promoted by those who 'long that there may be one visible Church of God, a Church truly *universal* and sent forth to the *whole world*.' The words I have stressed here indicate the reason why the word 'ecumenical' has been judged appropriate to describe this movement.

In view of the way the term is now being used, it is easy to see why many people would deny the term 'ecumenical' to such councils as Trent, Vatican I and Vatican II, on the grounds that they were simply councils of the Roman Catholic Church. Many would question the ecumenicity of all the western councils in which the bishops of the Eastern Christian Churches have not taken part. And some would deny the ecumenicity of any council which did not express the communion and common witness of all the Christian Churches.

What, then, is an 'ecumenical council' in the eyes of the Catholic Church? First of all, the Catholic Church has never explicitly defined what is meant by the term 'ecumenical council', nor has it ever drawn up a definitive list of such councils. However, the Christian Churches of both East and West recognise seven councils of the ancient Church as ecumenical: Nicea (325), Constantinople I (381), Ephesus (431), Chalcedon (451), Constantinople II (553), Constantinople III (681), and Nicea II (787). If we look to these seven councils in order to determine what is required for ecumenicity, we have to admit that no very clear or simple criteria emerge. If we recall the statement of Vatican II that we quoted above, we can say that the first condition laid down there has been fulfilled in each case: these seven councils have all been confirmed or at least accepted by the successor of Peter. But in no case did the Roman pontiff convoke them or preside over them; it was the Roman emperor who convoked them, and generally it was his legate who presided. If then we look to the universality of these councils in terms of actual participation, we find that practically all the bishops who took part in them were of the East, while the whole Western Church was represented by a few legates of the Bishop of Rome. In fact, there were no representatives of the Western Church at all at the First Council of Constantinople, which received its ecumenical status only in virtue of its subsequent reception by the West.

If then we take these seven councils as paradigmatic for the notion of ecumenicity, we have to give primary importance not to the question of who convoked them, presided over them, or participated in them, but to their *reception* by the universal Church, as expressing the communion of all the churches, and witnessing to their common faith.[1]

However, even with regard to this criterion of reception, we have to recognise the fact that some of these ancient councils had to wait for decades before being universally received, and in many cases their doctrinal decisions were never accepted by some sectors of the Christian world (thus the Arians rejected Nicea, the Nestorians Ephesus, and the Monophysites Chalcedon). In hardly any case can we speak of an absolutely universal reception. This fact gives greater importance to the reception of all these councils by Rome and by all the churches in communion with Rome. Indeed, I think one would have to say that this is the essential criterion on which the ecumenicity of a council rests in the modern Catholic understanding of the matter.

However, we must admit that this criterion of ecumenicity, which would justify taking the Councils of Trent and of the Vatican to be ecumenical, is a relatively modern idea, for until the sixteenth century the idea persisted in the Western Church that only those councils in which both East and West had taken part deserved the title 'ecumenical'. It was Bellarmine and Baronius who first included the medieval western councils in the list of ecumenical councils.[2] It is worth noting that in his letter commemorating the seventh centenary of the Second Council of Lyons (1274), Pope Paul VI described it as 'the sixth of the general synods held in the west', but nowhere in that letter spoke of it as an 'ecumenical council'.[3]

I see no reason for denying that a future council which would manifest restored communion between East and West, with the full participation of Orthodox Bishops, would be a qualitatively more ecumenical council than any that has been held since the beginning of the Great Schism. However, I think that to be consistent with the doctrine of Vatican II, one has to say that the Councils of Trent and the Vatican were ecumenical councils. For, according to *Lumen gentium*, the authority of an ecumenical council is essentially the authority of the episcopal college. ('The supreme authority with which this college is empowered over the whole Church is exercised in a solemn way through an ecumenical council': (LG 22). But membership in this college requires hierarchical communion with the bishop of Rome. ('One is constituted a member of the episcopal body by virtue of sacramental consecration and by hierarchical communion with the head and members of the body': LG 22). It follows that a council in which the college of bishops in communion with the bishop of Rome exercises its supreme pastoral and teaching authority is an ecumenical council. But Trent, Vatican I and Vatican II were clearly such. Indeed, Trent and Vatican I exercised the supreme teaching authority of the episcopal college to its fullest extent, by solemnly defining dogmas of faith. Vatican II chose not to do so, but it had the authority to do so, if it had wished.

The assent required by the teaching of ecumenical councils

Vatican II distinguishes between two ways in which an ecumenical council can exercise its teaching authority, and between two different levels of obligation to give assent to its doctrines.

Lumen gentium speaks of conciliar *definitions*, and says that they must be adhered to with the submission of faith; the Theological Commission speaks of conciliar teaching that does *not* 'define', and of the obligation to accept such teaching. Let us look more closely at these distinctions.

When we speak of a council as 'defining' a doctrine, the word 'define' does not mean to give the exact meaning of a term, but rather to give a definitive judgment on a question. The root word *finis* means 'end' or 'limit'; when a council 'defines' a doctrine, it puts an end to freedom of opinion on the matter, and sets limits to the communion of faith, because what is defined becomes part of the *normative* faith of the community.

Lumen gentium says that when the bishops are gathered together in an ecumenical council 'they are teachers and judges of faith and morals for the universal church. Their definitions must then be adhered to with the submission of faith' (LG 25). Vatican I had spoken of such definitions as 'solemn judgments', and declared that what is proposed in such solemn judgments as having been revealed by God, must be believed with 'catholic and divine faith' (D-S 3011). However, when *Lumen gentium* says that such definitions must be adhered to 'with the submission of faith', it does not specify 'divine faith'. The reason given by the Theological Commission involves its intention not to exclude the possibility that a council might define a truth which is not strictly revealed, but is required for the defence or explanation of revealed truth.[4] In such a case, the faithful are called upon to *believe* that what is defined is *true* — and hence one can speak of 'faith' — but it is not 'divine faith', because what is defined is not proposed as *God's* Word. 'Divine faith' is given to what is divinely revealed. For it is the Word of God, not the word of the council as such, which calls for the 'submission of divine faith'. The council witnesses to the Word of God when its definition is a solemn judgment that something is part of divine revelation. Only what is divinely revealed can become a 'dogma of faith', that is, an article of the normative faith of the community. The authority of the council, exercised to its full extent in the solemn definition of a dogma of faith, calls for our unconditional 'yes' to the council when it tells us: 'This is God's Word'. But then our 'yes' of *faith* is given to God's Word, and to God himself who has spoken it.

The Theological Commission of Vatican II spoke of a kind of conciliar teaching other than solemn definitions, and of the assent such teaching requires, in its Declaration of 6 March 1964. Its statement is as follows:

> In view of conciliar practice and the pastoral purpose of the present Council, this sacred Synod defines matters of faith or morals as binding on the Church only when the Synod itself openly declares so. Other matters which the sacred Synod proposes as the doctrine of the supreme teaching authority of the Church, each and every member of the faithful is obliged to accept and embrace according to the mind of the sacred Synod itself, which becomes known either from the subject matter or from the language employed, according to the norms of theological interpretation.[5]

When the council chose to teach but not to define a doctrine, it chose not to set limits to the communion of faith by determining that what it was teaching would henceforth be part of the normative faith of the community.

However, there is still an obligation to accept this kind of teaching, because even here the council is exercising its 'supreme teaching authority'. This obligation is evidently not of the same degree for everything in the council documents, for this depends on the 'mind of the Synod'. One indication of the mind of the Synod can be seen in the variety of titles given to the documents of Vatican II. Two are called 'dogmatic constitutions'[6], one is simply called a 'constitution',[7] one is a 'pastoral constitution',[8] others are 'decrees',[9] others still are 'declarations'.[10]

Another indication of the mind of Vatican II is the use of the phrase 'docet sancta Synodus', which is employed rather rarely, and in each case introduces an important doctrinal statement.[11] Another is the use of the word 'credimus' or 'creditur', when it is clear that this is equivalent to saying: 'It is the belief of the Catholic Church that . . .'[12]

In view of the obligation to accept the doctrine of Vatican II out of respect for its 'supreme teaching authority', the question arises as to the consequences of the rejection of its teaching. Since this council chose not to define any new dogmas, it would not be heretical to deny any of its teachings unless the matter were already a dogma of Catholic faith. However, rejection of the work of the council as a whole, or of its principal contributions to the renewal of Catholic life and thought, would surely have the effect of alienating a person from the mainstream of the Catholic Church today.

The teaching authority of the Roman pontiff

Since I have just been speaking of the teaching authority of an ecumenical council, the simplest way to describe the teaching authority of the Roman pontiff is to say that according to Vatican I and II, the pope himself, in his role as 'supreme teacher of the universal Church' (LG 25) has the same teaching authority which an ecumenical council has, including the authority to define dogmas of faith. When a pope issues such a solemn definition he is said to be speaking *ex cathedra*. But just as Vatican II did, the pope can propose doctrine to be held by the faithful without intending to define the issue; in this case there is the same kind of obligation to adhere to his teaching as there is to the teaching of Vatican II. The text of *Lumen gentium* on this point is almost identical with the statement of the Theological Commission which I have already quoted regarding the obligation to accept the teaching of the Council. It is my intention in a later chapter to discuss more fully the nature of this obligation to adhere to doctrine proposed by this 'ordinary magisterium' of the pope. For the present I wish to consider the authority which Vatican I and II ascribe to the pope to speak *ex cathedra*, i.e. to pronounce definitive judgments on matters of faith, which have the same binding force for Catholics as the solemn definitions of an ecumenical council. For the present I also wish to prescind from the question of the infallibility which is predicated of such solemn judgments; this will also be the subject of a later chapter.

The question I wish to discuss here concerns the recognition by the Church of the pope's authority to make definitive decisions about matters of faith. How ancient is such recognition? How universal? On what grounds is it based?

Recognition of papal teaching authority during the first millennium

An adequate treatment of this topic would require another book at least, so I am obviously not going to go into much detail. But I shall mention some of the salient factors.

We have already seen that by the end of the second century the pastoral and magisterial role of bishops was generally recognised throughout the Christian Church. Irenaeus, writing about the year 185, gives us the list of the bishops who had handed on the apostolic tradition in Rome by their unbroken succession from the Apostles Peter and Paul. For Irenaeus, the criterion of orthodox faith was agreement with the tradition handed down in the churches that had been founded by the apostles. The church of Rome was not the only such church, but, being the one which had preserved the teaching of the greatest of the apostles, Peter and Paul, he saw it as the pre-eminent witness to genuine apostolic tradition. Irenaeus, who was not a Roman himself, drew the conclusion that every church that claimed to follow the genuine apostolic tradition would have to be in agreement with the tradition handed down in Rome.[13]

Given the contemporary recognition of the role of bishops as pastors and teachers in the Christian churches, the idea of looking to the church of Rome as criterion of apostolic tradition inevitably focused attention on the bishops of Rome as the primary exponents of this tradition. If appeal was made to Rome to determine whether a particular doctrine was in conformity or not with apostolic tradition, naturally it was the bishop of Rome who was expected to give the answer. The initial recognition of the authority of the bishop of Rome to judge questions of doctrine was based on his role as official witness to the apostolic tradition handed down in the church of Rome: the church where the greatest of the apostles, Peter and Paul, had made the ultimate confession of Christian faith by martyrdom.

Of course there were other churches of apostolic origin, whose bishops were also official witnesses to apostolic tradition, so the role of the bishop of Rome in that respect was not unique. Indeed, the ultimate criterion of genuine tradition was seen not in the isolated witness of any one church alone, but in the concordant witness of all the apostolic churches. As long as the bishops everywhere were teaching the same doctrine, there was no need to look to the teaching of any particular one as a standard of orthodoxy. Unanimity was accepted as the surest guarantee of truth.

The question of a special teaching authority of the bishop of Rome arose when there was no longer unanimity among the bishops on important questions concerning the faith. When differences on doctrinal issues threatened to divide the churches, the need was acutely felt of some criterion by which it could be determined which of the contending parties was in accord with the genuine apostolic tradition. To the extent that in such cases agreement with Rome was seen as a touchstone of orthodoxy, its bishop came to be looked upon as an authoritative arbiter of disputes about the faith.

Now there is no questioning the fact that during the first millennium, appeals to the bishop of Rome for judgments concerning doctrinal disputes came not only from churches like those of North Africa, which looked to Rome as the source of their own apostolic tradition, but also from the apostolic churches of the East. Such bishops as Athanasius and Cyril of Alexandria, and Flavian of Constantinople, appealed to the bishop of Rome to pronounce his judgment on the disputes that were dividing the churches of the East in their day.[14] It would be tempting to take such appeals to Rome as evidence of a universal recognition of the authority of the bishop of Rome to make definitive pronouncements on matters of doctrine for the whole Church. But the reality is more complex than that. Modern Catholic scholars insist on the necessity of distinguishing between the Roman view of papal authority to decide doctrinal disputes for the whole Church, and the attitude of the bishops of other churches, both of the East and of the West.

Cyprian and Stephen (c. 250)

An early instance of such a conflict of views can be seen in the rejection by Bishops Cyprian of Carthage and Firmilian of Caesarea, of the authority of Pope St Stephen I to impose the Roman doctrine concerning the validity of baptism in heretical sects, on the churches of Africa and Asia Minor.[15] We do not have the text of Stephen's letter, but from what Firmilian says it seems clear that the Pope had based his authority on the fact that he held the 'chair of Peter'.[16] This evidently did not give him the right, in the eyes of Cyprian and Firmilian, to demand that they accept his teaching as definitive.

St Augustine (417)

It is significant that St Augustine, who accepted the Roman doctrine on heretical baptism against what had been the tradition of the African church, said that Cyprian would surely have changed his opinion if the matter had ever been decided *by a plenary council*.[17] Augustine obviously recognised that for Cyprian 'Roma locuta est, causa finita est' would not have sufficed. Indeed, one can question whether this phrase (which Augustine did not actually use) accurately expresses his own mind. There is no doubt about the fact that for St Augustine, the ultimate criterion of orthodoxy is the judgment of the whole Church: 'securus iudicat orbis terrarum'.[18] In his view, doctrinal issues were best settled in plenary councils: 'quorum est in ecclesia saluberrima auctoritas'.[19] When the question of Pelagius was handled in two regional councils, held in Carthage and Mileve in 416, the decision of these councils was sent to Rome for confirmation; when the reply was received from Rome, Augustine was satisfied that the African decision was indeed the teaching of the *catholica*, the universal Church, and he could say 'causa finita est'.[20] It is not at all certain that he meant that the teaching authority of the bishop of Rome, by itself, had decided the issue. In another reference to this question he appealed to the apostolic Roman see *along with others*.[21] Again, Augustine said to Julian of Eclanum: 'Your cause is finished by a competent decision of bishops in common'.[22] For Augustine the surest test of orthodoxy is the 'consent of the universal Church'.[23]

The attitude of the eastern church, as shown in the ecumenical councils

Apart from the question of Pelagianism, practically all the major doctrinal disputes in the first millennium were carried on in the East, where the ecumenical councils by which they were eventually settled, were also held. The clearest manifestation of the Roman claim to possess definitive teaching authority for the universal Church, and the most reliable index of the extent to which papal teaching was accepted as definitive by the bishops of the eastern churches, is seen in the history of the ecumenical councils of the first millennium. This question has been thoroughly researched by W. De Vries, whose findings I shall briefly summarise here.[24]

Nicea (325)

At the first ecumenical council, Pope Sylvester was represented by two priests whom he sent as his legates. There is nothing to indicate that the papal legates played a role of any significance in the decisions of this council. The signing of the decrees by the papal legates was taken as sufficient evidence of the agreement of Rome, and thus of the whole western church, and there is no evidence that any further confirmation by Pope Sylvester was requested.

Constantinople I (381)

We have already had occasion to mention the fact that there were no representatives of the western church at the

Second Ecumenical Council, which was actually intended to be only an eastern synod. Hence there is no question of papal teaching authority in connection with that council. It does not seem to have occurred to the eastern bishops to request confirmation of the conciliar decrees by Rome.[25]

Ephesus (431), Chalcedon (451) and Constantinople III (680-681)

On the basis of De Vries' study, it is possible to see a common pattern in these three councils which decided the major christological disputes. The following factors are common to all three of these councils:

1. Christological disputes were dividing the great churches of the East from one another.

2. The emperors were supporting the side that would eventually be declared heretical.

3. The proponents of the view that would eventually be declared orthodox appealed to Rome for support.

4. The popes, after consultation with a Roman synod, issued their doctrinal decision, and condemned the contrary opinion as heretical.

5. The emperors, usually new ones more favourable to the orthodox view, summoned an ecumenical council.

6. The popes agreed, usually somewhat reluctantly, to the summoning of the council, but insisted that the doctrinal issue had already been settled by their own decree.

7. The papal legates came to the council with instructions to insist on the council's acceptance of the papal decision, and in each case made strong statements of the papal authority to decide questions of faith for the whole Church.

8. The eastern bishops listened politely to the papal legates, but insisted on a full conciliar discussion of the issue, on the grounds that only the council could give the ultimate decision that represented the mind of the universal Church.

9. After such discussion, the councils did in each case decide in agreement with the papal teaching, condemning those whom the pope had condemned.

10. In each case, the popes made a significant contribution to the settlement of the issue, and their position in the dispute was confirmed by the council; but there remained a deep difference regarding the definitiveness of the papal

intervention. In the view of Rome, the papal decision ought to have been accepted without further discussion and simply ratified by the council; in the view of the eastern bishops who made up the vast majority at all these councils, the council itself had every right to test the papal teaching in the light of Scripture and tradition, and only after full discussion of the issue, come to its decision, which, in their view, would be the really definitive one.

So there was a basic difference between Rome and the East on the question *why* the council should accept the papal teaching. The Roman view was that it should accept the pope's decision because, as successor to Peter, he had received from Christ the authority to decide questions of faith for the universal Church. The eastern bishops were ready to accept the papal teaching when they were satisfied that it was consonant with Scripture and tradition. Without doubt their acclamation: 'Peter has spoken through Leo', in their intention, meant not that Pope Leo had spoken with Peter's authority, but that Leo's teaching reflected genuine apostolic tradition.[26]

The Second Council of Constantinople (553)

Of all the ecumenical councils, this is the one which witnessed the most radical challenge to papal authority on the part of the eastern episcopate. No doubt this is largely due to the fact that this was also the only council in which the eastern bishops were united among themselves and with the emperor against the pope. The initiative for this council came from the Emperor Justinian's determination to placate and reconcile the Monophysites by condemning three long-dead bishops: Theodore of Mopsuestia, Theodoret of Cyr, and Ibas of Edessa, whom the Monophysites accused of Nestorianism. The western church saw this move as a retreat from the orthodoxy of Chalcedon, and strongly condemned Pope Vigilius' initial acquiescence to the emperor's demand. When Vigilius saw how violent was the reaction of the West to his first decree, he withdrew it, whereupon Justinian summoned a council and had Vigilius forcibly brought to Constantinople to take part in it. The eastern bishops were ready to do the emperor's bidding, but Vigilius forbade the council to proceed to the condemnation of the 'Three Chapters', reserving the case to his own judgment. He then issued his *Constitutum* in which he rejected the idea of condemning the three long-dead bishops, but did censure some of their writings. The council, under the domination of the emperor, declared Vigilius excommunicated for defying the ecumenical council, and proceeded without him to condemn the 'Three Chapters'. The council could hardly have more strongly expressed its rejection of the papal claim to definitive teaching authority.

However, emperor and council still recognised the need of papal confirmation to give ecumenical status to the conciliar decrees, and Justinian continued to put pressure on the pope until eventually he capitulated and issued his second *Constitutum*, confirming the action taken by the council. Vigilius' successors on the papal throne felt obliged to uphold the decisions of the council, but they did so at considerable cost to the prestige of the papacy and to the unity of the western church, since it took well over a century for the popes to reconcile large portions of the West to what was seen by many as a betrayal of the Council of Chalcedon.

The Second Council of Nicea (787)

This seventh ecumenical council was summoned to restore the unity of the eastern church, which had been broken by the quarrel over the veneration of sacred images. In the view of the eastern bishops, this schism could only be resolved by an ecumenical council, especially since the veneration of images had been condemned as idolatrous by the council held at Hieria in 753. The fact that Pope Hadrian II had issued his decision in favour of the veneration of images was not accepted by them as sufficient to settle the issue definitively. Needless to say, the Roman view was that the pope's dogmatic statement about the matter should have been accepted by the council without further discussion. However, as before, the eastern bishops insisted on a full examination of the question, in the light of Scripture and tradition, before rendering their decision. It is true that at this council a few eastern bishops expressed their readiness to accept the papal decision as final on the grounds of the pope's authority as successor to Peter. But the majority insisted that they must first satisfy themselves that the pope's teaching agreed with apostolic tradition. In their view, such examination, even of papal teaching, was an inalienable right of the ecumenical council, and only its decision would be final.

The attitude of the western church during the first millennium

Following De Vries' study of the ecumenical councils, we have seen that there was a real difference, during the first millennium, between the Roman conception of papal teaching authority, and the attitude of the eastern bishops toward that claim. Congar's study of the ecclesiology of the High Middle Ages shows that in this period there was also a difference between the Roman view, and the attitude of many of the leading bishops of the western church regarding the doctrinal authority of the bishop of Rome. Here is how Congar describes the situation in the ninth century.[27]

> Of course everybody knew that the Roman See was the *sedes Petri* . . . and one drew the consequence, as did the *Libri Carolini*, that one had to refer to the church of Rome or to its Pope for 'cases concerning the faith', and to ask their help 'in times of need for the corroboration of the faith.' . . . But it does not seem that one thought of the Roman magisterium along the lines of a *juridical* type of doctrinal *authority*. . . . When doctrinal authority was explicitly attributed to the Pope, it was a question rather of a religious quality which Rome owed to the fact that it is the place of the martyrdom and tombs of Peter and Paul. . . . In the end, the real magisterium was less that of an authority attached to superior rank, than that of Tradition, of which the bishops had the custody, and which the church of Rome had had the grace to preserve well. The Roman see, the see of Peter, was the place of the orthodox faith. Hincmar invoked, against Gottschalk, the faith of the Roman church — but its *faith* and its *tradition*, not its judgment. The real magisterium was that of Tradition, which the councils recognize and proclaim.

The recognition of papal teaching authority in the West during the second millennium

The attitude towards papal teaching authority which was typical of the eastern bishops, and also of many western bishops, during the first millennium, survived in the West in the form of conciliarism, and later on, of gallicanism. But the predominant trend in the western church, from the time of

70

its break with the East in 1054, was towards the general acceptance of what had previously been the characteristically Roman concept of papal teaching authority. This is but one aspect of the development towards a monarchical theory and practice of the papacy which has characterised western Christianity during the second millennium. It is the task of historians to identify and evaluate the various factors that contributed to this development. Among them must surely be numbered the introduction of material from the 'False Decretals' of Pseudo-Isidore into the influential *Decretum* of Gratian (the 'Denzinger' of its day).[28] This collection of 240 decretals, 115 totally forged, 125 partly so, attributed to Roman bishops of the early Church statements and decrees that were favourable to a centralised and strongly juridical exercise of the papacy. It seems certain that these forgeries did not originate in Rome, and that they were accepted there as genuine in good faith. Their effect was to lend an aura of antiquity and venerability to the ideas of such monarchically-minded popes as Nicholas I, Gregory VII and Innocent III.

For documentation of the acceptance of the Roman view of papal teaching authority, I shall limit myself to two witnesses from the second half of the thirteenth century: St Thomas Aquinas, and the Second Council of Lyons. St Thomas treats this question in the *Summa Theologiae*, where his question is whether it pertains to the Supreme Pontiff to draw up a creed (2a 2ae, q.1, a.10). His initial reply (the 'sed contra') is as follows:

> Formulation of a creed takes place at a general council. Such a body can only be convened by authority of the Supreme Pontiff, as is established in the *Decretals*. The drawing up of a symbol of faith, therefore, comes under papal authority.[29]

He then proceeds to give his full reply in the body of the article:

> As pointed out already (art. 9 ad 2), a new statement of the creed is required as a defence against the incursion of errors. Revision of the creed, therefore, engages the competence of the one to whom it belongs by right to settle authoritatively what is of faith, to the end that all hold to this with steadfast faith. This comes under the Pope's

authority, *to whom*, the *Decretum* declares, *serious and more difficult questions for the Church are referred.* [30] So our Lord declared to Peter, whom he instituted as chief pontiff, *I have prayed for thee, Peter, that thy faith fail not, and thou, being once converted, confirm thy brethren* (Lk 22:32). The reason is that there must be one faith for the entire Church: *That you all speak the same thing, and that there be no schisms among you* (1 Cor 1:10). This norm could not be followed unless every question arising out of faith were resolved by the one having care over the whole Church, whose decisions therefore are followed by the whole Church. A new version of the creed, then, falls to the sole authority of the pope, just as do all other matters affecting the whole Church, e.g. the convoking of a general council and other matters of the sort.

We should also take note of his reply to the objection that the Council of Ephesus had forbidden the drawing up of new creeds:

2. Proscription and sentence by a council are directed against private persons, who have no right to make pronouncements on the faith. Such conciliar judgments do not take away from a subsequent council the power to formulate a new version of the creed, one embodying not a different faith, but the same faith more explicitly. This has in fact been the practice of the councils, namely for a later one, because of a need caused by the rise of a heresy, to amplify the declarations of an earlier one. Consequently, this is a matter for the pope, by whose authority a council is convened and its decisions confirmed.

A few years after St Thomas wrote this question of his *Summa*, the Second Council of Lyons, under Pope Gregory X, included the following statement in the Profession of Faith which it imposed on the Emperor Michael Palaeologus:

This same holy Roman Church holds the supreme and full primacy and sovereignty over the whole Catholic Church, which it truthfully and humbly acknowledges that it received from the Lord himself in blessed Peter, the prince and head of the apostles, whose successor is the Roman Pontiff. And just as he is obliged, above all others, to defend the truth of the faith, so it is by his judgment that questions that arise concerning the faith must be decided. (D-S 861)

I think it important to call attention to the terms used in these texts to describe the specific exercise of teaching authority which they attribute to the pope. I mean such terms as: 'to issue a definitive judgment about matters regarding the faith' (*sententialiter determinare ea quae sunt fidei*); 'a question arising about the faith be decided by him who presides over the whole Church' (*quaestio fidei exorta determinetur per eum qui toti Ecclesiae praeest*); 'by his judgment questions that arise concerning the faith must be decided' (*si quae de fide subortae fuerint quaestiones, suo debent iudicio definiri*). This language indicates: 1) that the object of this magisterium is understood to be matters of Christian faith; 2) that the specific exercise of this magisterium is to 'determine with finality' or to 'issue definitive judgments' on questions arising about the faith; and 3) that the intended result is the unity of the whole Church in orthodox faith: (*ut sic eius sententia a tota Ecclesia firmiter teneatur*).

Another observation that should be made concerning the text of St Thomas that has been quoted above, is that while he attributes to the pope the authority to make definitive pronouncements on questions of faith, he clearly recognises that the pope normally does this by promulgating dogmatic decisions that are arrived at by councils. The *sed contra* and the reply *ad secundum* make this quite apparent. Further confirmation is had in his *De Potentia* q.10, a.4, ad 13, where he is speaking of the authority of a later council to clarify the creed of a previous council.

Just as a later council has the authority to interpret the creed established by an earlier one, and to add something to clarify its meaning . . . so also the Roman Pontiff can do this by his own authority, for it is by his authority alone that a council can be convoked and its decisions confirmed, and to him appeal can be made from a council. All this is evident from the Acts of the Council of Chalcedon.

Nor is it necessary, in order to provide such a clarification, that a universal council be convened, since conflicts of

73

war can sometimes make this impossible, as we read happened in the case of the seventh council, when the Emperor Constantine said that because of imminent wars he could not convoke all the bishops, but still those that did assemble settled some problems that had arisen concerning the faith, following the judgment made by Pope Agatho . . .

Several points are noteworthy in this text. It is again evident that St Thomas saw the doctrinal authority of the pope normally exercised in association with that of a council. Furthermore, he saw it as exceptional (e.g. because of wartime conditions) that this not be a *universal* council; however, even in the instance he gives, the decision was still made by a council together with the pope.[31]

In his discussion of the teaching of St Thomas on this point, Congar observes that Thomas attributes the formulation of a new creed to the authority of the pope *working in concert with a council*. He insists: 'The thirteenth century did not set council against pope; it saw them rather conjoining their authority; that of the pope had its proper origin, its supreme degree.'[32] Congar also notes that Thomas's view on this question was undoubtedly much influenced by the practice of the medieval 'papal' councils, especially the Fourth Lateran (1215), whose dogmatic decree *Firmiter* (D-S 800-802) was looked on as a decree of Pope Innocent III.[33]

While, as Congar says, 'the thirteenth century did not set council against pope', the following centuries did witness such a conflict, with the conciliarist theory dominant at the Councils of Constance and Basel, and the papalist position prevailing at the Council of Florence and generally thereafter in Roman Catholicism. The authority of the pope to define dogmas of faith without summoning a council to deliberate with him was exercised by Pope Pius IX in 1854, was defined as Catholic dogma by Vatican I, and exercised again by Pope Pius XII in 1950.

In my opinion the dogma of Vatican I does not prevent a Catholic from agreeing with St Thomas and other great theologians of the thirteenth century,[34] that it is the *normal* thing that papal authority to define dogmas of faith should be exercised in association with a council of bishops, rather than by the pope acting alone. It is true that after Vatican I some people thought that there would be no further need of holding councils, and perhaps the definition of the Assumption in 1950 may have confirmed that idea for some. But the unexpected decision of Pope John XXIII to summon the Second Vatican Council, and the teaching of that Council on the collegial structure of Church authority, including the role of the bishops to be 'teachers and judges of the faith', has gone far to bring modern Catholic thinking back to a position more like that of St Thomas and the theologians of the thirteenth century.

It is not a question of denying the pope's *authority* to define a dogma without calling a council to deliberate on the question, to say that the principle of collegiality suggests that he should choose to exercise his authority in this way only when exceptional circumstances warrant it. One does not question his power to act if one suggests how such power is most appropriately used.

However, I can well understand that a question can be put to me at this point: if you do not question papal authority to define dogmas in the way that Popes Pius IX and Pius XII did, how do you justify your belief that they have such authority? Do not the biblical and historical arguments for such papal claims, as Hans Küng would say, 'have feet of clay'?

Now obviously an adequate discussion of the arguments from Scripture and Tradition for the Catholic understanding of papal authority in matters of faith would take far more space than I can give it here. I shall limit myself to indicating some of the results of recent ecumenical discussion of this question.[35]

First, to speak of a biblical basis for papal authority does not mean claiming that the New Testament texts usually cited in favour of papal primacy should convince any unprejudiced exegete of the truth of the Catholic position. This position involves an understanding of the full implications of the 'petrine ministry', at which the Catholic Church arrived only after many centuries of experience of the ministry exercised by the bishops of Rome.

Perhaps one could say that the biblical basis for the papacy consists in the reasons that justify speaking of this as the 'petrine ministry': that is, as the ministry on behalf of the unity of the Church in faith and communion, that finds its

75

model in the role which the New Testament attributes to Peter. I say 'the role which the New Testament attributes to Peter', because recent ecumenical discussion of 'Peter in the New Testament' has shown that in the course of the period during which the books of the New Testament were being written, there was a growing interest in and appreciation of Peter's role of leadership, with special attention to his role as first witness to Jesus as Messiah and Son of God (Mt 16: 16-17), and as the Risen Lord (1 Cor 15:5; Lk 24:34; Acts 2: 36 etc.). New Testament scholars now speak of a 'trajectory' of the images associated with Peter, i.e. of the tendency for Peter's role to be given greater prominence as one moves from the earlier to the later contributions to the New Testament.[36] Such a trajectory through the New Testament is homogeneous with the ongoing development of the 'petrine ministry' of the bishops of Rome during the post-New Testament period.

In view of the fact that the New Testament shows Peter in the role of first and chief witness to faith in Jesus as the Christ and the Risen Lord, it is all the more significant that the primacy of the Church of Rome is derived from its being chief witness to the apostolic tradition based on the teaching of Peter and Paul and their ultimate confession of faith by martyrdom. I have expressed my opinion that the initial recognition of the authority of the bishops of Rome as arbiters of doctrinal disputes was based on their role as official witnesses to the apostolic tradition handed down in the Church of Rome. This developed into the understanding, shared by the East as well as the West, that questions concerning the faith could not be decided without the participation of the bishop of Rome.

It is undeniable that the undivided Church of the first millennium recognised the bishop of Rome as the occupant of the 'chair of Peter', and on that account attributed to him a primary role in the settling of disputes about the faith. Their understanding and appreciation of the 'petrine ministry' on behalf of the unity of the Church in the true faith, developed in the light of the positive role which the bishops of Rome played in maintaining the genuine apostolic tradition when the faith was threatened by heresies. Even the blunder committed by Pope Honorius did not substantially weaken respect for the doctrinal authority of the Roman See.[37]

It is true, as we have seen, that it was only the western church, after its separation from the East, that accepted the authority of the popes to define dogmas of faith. The Catholic view is that this development of the western church's understanding of the doctrinal authority involved in the 'petrine ministry', is homogeneous with the development that had already taken place during the first millennium, even though the East did not arrive at this stage of the development before 1054, and of course did not share it after that.

How can we be confident that the Catholic understanding of papal doctrinal authority is a correct insight into what is implicit in the 'petrine ministry'? I would say that our confidence is ultimately based on our belief that the Church of Christ is indefectible in its faith, and that it subsists in the Catholic Church. When the Catholic Church accepted papal authority to define dogmas, it was making a judgment about a norm of its faith. A Church that is indefectible in its faith cannot be mistaken about the very norm of its faith.

I would immediately point out that such an argument cannot be used to justify every historical development of the papacy that has taken place in the Catholic Church during the second millennium. Indeed, I agree with Joseph Ratzinger when he observes that one of the unhappy results of the isolation of the western church from the East after 1054 was the loss of the distinction between the *patriarchal* and the strictly *papal* roles of the bishops of Rome.[38] The disappearance of this distinction contributed greatly to the growth of a theory and practice of the papacy which, in terms of the centralised exercise of jurisdiction by Rome over the whole Catholic Church, has gone far beyond what the papacy, as 'petrine ministry', necessarily calls for or justifies. We do not have to believe, for instance, that the 'petrine ministry' of the bishop of Rome really includes the power to depose kings and to release subjects from their oaths of allegiance to them — nor even that it means that the pope ought to name the bishop of every diocese in the Church.

However, we do believe that the 'petrine ministry' is rightly understood as a ministry for the unity of the whole Church in the true faith, and that as such it involves the authority, when circumstances warrant it, to pronounce a definitive judgment whether a particular teaching is consonant or not with the faith which St Peter taught and died for at Rome.

The First Vatican Council defined it to be a dogma of Catholic faith, that when a pope pronounces such a definitive judgment, he is gifted by the Holy Spirit with 'that infallibility with which the divine Redeemer wished his Church to be endowed in defining doctrine of faith and morals' (D-S 3074). So we must now take up the question of infallibility.

5.

The Infallibility of the Magisterium in Defining Dogmas of Faith

Explanation of terms

By 'the magisterium' here I mean the episcopal college together with its head, the bishop of Rome. The term: 'in defining' limits the question to those solemn judgments which can be made either by an ecumenical council or by the pope speaking *ex cathedra*. I shall return later on to the question of the infallibility of the 'ordinary universal magisterium', i.e. of the episcopal college dispersed throughout the world, when it unanimously teaches a doctrine of faith as definitively to be held.

The term: 'in defining dogmas of faith' limits the present question to those solemn judgments in which the supreme teaching authority (ecumenical council or pope) exercising its magisterium in the highest degree, definitively pronounces some truth to have been divinely revealed, and henceforth to be an article of the normative faith of the Catholic community. I prescind here from questions concerning a 'secondary object of infallible magisterium', e.g. whether the magisterium could infallibly define some non-revealed proposition to be true, and if so, what kind of matter would be included in such a secondary object. As I understand it, a non-revealed proposition even if it could be infallibly defined to be true, could never be defined as a 'dogma of faith', because only what is in itself divinely revealed can be an object of divine faith. I shall return in a later chapter to the question of the secondary object of infallibility. For the present, suffice it to say that it is only the infallibility of the magisterium in defining dogmas of faith which is itself a dogma of Catholic faith. The Church has never defined the infallibility of the magisterium with regard to non-revealed truths, nor has it ever defined the limits of such a secondary object of infallibility.

Finally the key term of this chapter: infallibility. As I understand it, to believe that the magisterium is infallible in defining dogmas of faith is to believe that when an ecumenical council or pope definitively proclaims something to be divinely revealed, the Holy Spirit assists the magisterium in such a way as to guarantee that what is defined is true. Infallibility means that the Holy Spirit sees to it that the magisterium does not solemnly oblige the faithful to believe something as divinely revealed which really is not contained in God's Word. It involves the assurance that a proposition in which the magisterium definitively proposes some aspect of revelation for belief, while it remains a human proposition, with the limitations inherent in any human attempt to express divine truth, will be a true proposition. Infallibility does not exempt the defined proposition from any limitation which is compatible with its being true.

Of course a belief in infallibility presupposes the possibility of true propositions concerning matters of divine revelation. A proposition is the *meaning* of a statement; to say that a proposition is true is to say that what a statement *means* is true. Infallibility guarantees the truth of the proposition. It does not guarantee that the statement in which the proposition was enunciated was a fully adequate expression of the divine reality which it was intended to express. Nor does it guarantee that it will always be an appropriate or easily intelligible expression of that meaning.

As I understand it, belief in the infallibility of the magisterium does not postulate the existence of a class of 'infallible propositions' which would be intrinsically more perfect than other true propositions. Infallibility is correctly predicated not of the propositions as such but of the teaching authority in the exercise of its teaching function. To my way of thinking, a *true* proposition can be *infallibly taught*, if there is a divine guarantee that this teacher, in this exercise of his teaching function, has spoken the truth. The matter is more properly expressed adverbially than adjectivally; not: 'this kind of proposition is infallible', but: 'this teacher has spoken infallibly'.

I believe that it is a mistake to base a theory of infallibility on the premise that only a certain special kind of proposition could be an 'infallible proposition'.[1] This is one of the problematic aspects of the theory of Hans Küng in his book *Infallible? An Inquiry*. He presumes that an 'infallible proposition' would have to be exempt from such limitations as: 'always falling short of reality, always (being) open to misunderstanding, only translatable up to a point, constantly changing, easily ideology-prone, never absolutely to be clarified'.[2] He evidently thinks that accepting the infallibility of the magisterium means postulating a kind of 'infallible proposition' which would be exempt from limitations to which human propositions are inevitably subject, and he logically concludes that no human proposition can be 'infallible'.

But I do not see why, in order to believe that the magisterium, under certain particular conditions, speaks infallibly, one has to claim that the defined proposition is exempt from any limitation that is compatible with its being true. If one grants that propositions about matters of faith can be *true*, I do not see what more is required, as far as the intrinsic nature of the proposition is concerned, to be able to say that in this case the magisterium has spoken infallibly. All that this adds is a guarantee, provided by the assistance of the Holy Spirit, that the solemnly defined proposition is true, and will always be true. This is what is meant when defined propositions are said to be 'irreformable'. Here one must recall the distinction between a proposition and a statement: a proposition is the meaning which a statement is intended to express. The term 'irreformable' cannot be predicated of dogmatic *statements* as such, because it is impossible to formulate a statement about revealed truth which would not be open to different and possibly better formulation. But a proposition can be said to be irreformable if what is meant is irreversibly true. It might become necessary to express this meaning differently, in order to make it intelligible to a new culture or a new mentality, because every formulation of a meaning is necessarily conditioned by a historical and cultural context which makes it less well adapted to a different context. But to say that a proposition is irreformable means that it will remain true even when reformulated. In my opinion, a better expression than 'irreformable' would have been 'irreversible', or 'irreversibly true'.

81

I agree, then, with many critics of Hans Küng's book, that his argument that there can be no such thing as an 'infallible proposition' has really missed the mark.

The really fundamental question raised by Hans Küng's critique of the Catholic doctrine of infallibility is whether the sources of Christian faith provide adequate grounds for the belief that the Holy Spirit does in fact assist the magisterium in such a way as to guarantee that it will not solemnly define, and thus oblige the faithful to believe as a dogma of faith, any proposition which is not true.

Hans Küng believes, as do a great many Christians, that the Church will always be maintained in the truth by the Holy Spirit. The question is: *how* does the Holy Spirit keep the Church in the true faith? Or even more precisely: what has God revealed to us about how the Holy Spirit does this? Is it enough to believe that the Holy Spirit will maintain the Church in the truth despite the errors which the magisterium makes even in its most solemn dogmatic decisions — by seeing to it that the Church at large will detect such erroneous 'dogmas' and reject them? Or do the sources of Christian faith justify the Catholic belief that the magisterium enjoys such assistance of the Holy Spirit that it will not solemnly define erroneous propositions as dogmas of faith in the first place? This is the question to which we must now turn our attention.

Are there adequate grounds for belief in an infallible magisterium?

In approaching this question, it is sobering to recall the following facts: that explicit belief in the infallibility of ecumenical councils does not appear in Christian literature until the ninth century; that the infallibility of the pope has never been a matter of faith for the Christians of the Eastern Orthodox tradition; that explicit belief in the infallibility of the pope appears in western Christianity only in the last quarter of the thirteenth century; and that the doctrine of the infallibility of the pope was much contested in the West from the thirteenth to the nineteenth century, and became universally accepted in the Roman Catholic Church only when it had been defined by the First Vatican Council in 1870.

These facts suggest that the doctrines of conciliar and papal infallibility cannot be very clear and obvious in Scripture or early Christian tradition. In view of this history, it can hardly be claimed that the scriptural texts usually cited in favour of the infallibility of the magisterium provide a simple and easily convincing proof of the thesis. The texts are convincing, it would seem, only to those who are disposed to accept the doctrine. Therefore one must be realistic, and not expect that there is a scriptural 'proof' of conciliar or papal infallibility that will convince everyone 'of good will' who hears it.

We have to reckon with the fact that with regard not only to papal infallibility but even to conciliar infallibility, we are dealing with the controversial problem of the development of doctrine. What makes the problem more complex in this case is that the development of belief in conciliar and papal infallibility presupposes the development, in the Church's ongoing life, of the very institutions we know as ecumenical councils and the Roman papacy. It is obvious that we do not find these institutions already existing as such in the New Testament Church. They are the result of a centuries-long historical development, which we believe to be the divinely-guided, and in that sense *de iure divino*, actualisation of seminal factors already present in the New Testament.

This is not the place to try to justify the Catholic belief that such institutions as ecumenical councils and the Roman papacy, even though they are the result of post-New Testament developments of Church structure in which many contingent factors and human decisions played their part, are still realisations of Christ's will for his Church. What concerns us here is the evident fact that there could be no question of faith in the infallibility of ecumenical councils or the papacy until these institutions themselves had become matters of Christian experience and until their authority to decide questions of faith for the whole Church had become generally recognised.

As we shall see, the historical evidence points to the conclusion that Christians came to believe in the infallibility of the dogmatic decisions of ecumenical councils only after having had repeated experience of the salutary effects which conciliar decisions had had in settling doctrinal disputes and safeguarding the orthodox faith. It was in reflecting on the consistently good fruit which these decisions had borne that the Church became convinced that this could only be explained by the assistance of the Holy Spirit. Similarly, belief in papal infallibility developed in the western church because it was there that the authority of the pope to decide questions of faith for the whole Church came to be generally accepted. It should not surprise us, then, to observe that it is only towards the end of the first millenium that we find explicit belief in the infallibility of ecumenical councils, and only late in the second that the doctrine of papal infallibility became universally accepted by Roman Catholics, and then only by them. I suggest that the best way to approach this question is to see how these beliefs developed in the faith-consciousness of the Church.

The development of belief in the infallibility of ecumenical councils

For the development of this belief during the first millennium I rely on the study which H.J. Sieben has done on the idea of the council in the early Church.[3] Obviously it will be impossible to do more here than indicate some of the major conclusions which Sieben draws from his careful examination both of conciliar documents and of the theological literature of the period.

The first point to be noted is that whatever can be described as a 'theology of the councils' in the writings of this period was the fruit of reflection on the councils that had actually taken place. In retrospect it was recognised that certain councils, such as those of Nicea and Chalcedon, had been vehicles of the apostolic *paradosis*, in that they had handed on the apostolic faith in its purity, even when they had had to formulate it in new terms. Furthermore, it was observed that the councils which had been the most effective in eliminating heresies and strengthening the Church in the orthodox faith were the ones which had not only manifested the consensus of a very large number of bishops taking part in them, but had also been most universally received, not only in the East, where they took place, but also in the West, represented by the church of Rome.

A theory about the special significance of 'ecumenical councils' was the fruit of reflection on the fact that certain great councils had brought the Christian faith safely through the crises caused by heresies, and in doing so had clarified the meaning of the basic articles of the creed. As Sieben puts it, these 'ecumenical' councils were seen to have achieved a two-fold consensus: a 'vertical' consensus with Scripture and Tradition, and a 'horizontal' consensus in the faith of the whole contemporary Church. This two-fold consensus guaranteed the truth of the doctrine proposed by these councils, since no one doubted that what the whole Church accepted as faithful to Scripture and Tradition had to be true.

As Sieben points out, there was general recognition of the authority of these great gatherings of bishops to make doctrinal and canonical decisions binding on the whole Church, and many of the writers of this period, reflecting on the providential role which such councils as Nicea and Chalcedon had played in maintaining the purity of the apostolic faith through the crises caused by various heresies, expressed their belief that this could only have happened by virtue of a special assistance or even inspiration given by the Holy Spirit. But Sieben did not find any of the Fathers arguing in an *a priori* way from the authority of these councils to make dogmatic decisions for the whole Church, to the conclusion that they must enjoy the divine assistance that would guarantee infallibility to their decrees. Rather, it was commonly understood that the claim of a council to have been divinely guided in its decisions was beyond question only when its doctrine had been received by the whole Church, as consonant with Scripture and Tradition.

According to Sieben, the first writer explicitly to attribute infallibility to the decisions of ecumenical councils was a ninth-century monk and bishop, Theodore Abu Qurra (A.D. 820/5), who wrote the first systematic treatise on the councils. He argued from Acts 15 that ecumenical councils were a divine, not merely ecclesiastical institution. As the apostles could say of their conciliar decision: 'It has seemed good to the Holy Spirit and to us' (Acts 15:28), so could the bishops gathered in ecumenical councils rely on the assistance of the Holy Spirit. Indeed, it was the Holy Spirit who sanctioned the authority of these councils, and demanded that the faithful accept their decisions. Now since the Holy Spirit could not require the acceptance of false doctrine, Theodore Abu Qurra concluded that the Holy Spirit must ensure that the doctrine promulgated by ecumenical councils is true.

Of course, he was aware that a crucial question still remained to be answered: on what grounds are certain councils reckoned as 'ecumenical', while others are not? By his day, the answer to this question in the East was that the criterion of ecumenicity was the consensus of the Pentarchy: i.e. of the five great patriarchal sees. Agreement at the council itself, or at least subsequent reception of its decisions, by the bishops of the five patriarchal sees (Rome, Constantinople, Antioch, Jerusalem and Alexandria) was seen as evidence of the consensus of the whole episcopate. And, as Abu Qurra saw it, the consensus of the episcopate, proposing a doctrine to be believed by all the faithful, enjoyed the assistance of the Holy Spirit that would guarantee the truth of its teaching.

The consensus of the Pentarchy was undoubtedly the operative criterion of ecumenicity at the Second Council of Nicea (787). As the consent of the Bishop of Rome had always been taken to signify the consent of the western church, so now the consent of all five Patriarchs was taken to signify the consent of the universal Church. But this relatively simple criterion of ecumenicity was challenged by the Frankish theologians of the Carolingian period, who insisted on the necessity of consulting and obtaining the consent of all the bishops, and not relying exclusively on the consent of the five patriarchal sees. They also called for a much more rigorous proof from Scripture and Tradition than had been offered by the Second Council of Nicea for its doctrine on the veneration of images.

As Sieben points out, the bishops of Spain likewise considered themselves qualified to examine and judge the decisions taken at Nicea II in the light of Scripture and previous conciliar doctrine. Only when they had satisfied themselves, in their own synods, that the decisions of Nicea II met these tests, did they 'receive' the decrees of the council of 787.

From the independent attitude shown by these western bishops regarding the decrees of Nicea II, we can see that in the ninth century the idea was still very much alive that a council was truly ecumenical only when it manifested the 'horizontal' consensus of the whole episcopate, and that all bishops were entitled to express their judgment whether a conciliar decision met the criterion of 'vertical' consensus with Scripture and Tradition. In none of the great councils of the first millennium had all the bishops actually taken part. The reception of the council's decrees by the bishops who had not been present at it, was still being seen as an integral element of the ecumenicity of the council itself. Of course it was realised that absolute unanimity could not be required, because so often the bishops whose doctrines had been condemned by a council refused to accept its decision. No doubt it was this fact that led to such emphasis being put on the consent of Rome and the other great patriarchal sees.

Perhaps it would not be an over-simplification to say that by the end of the first millennium a council's dogmatic decisions were recognised as infallibly true when it was certain that the council itself was fully ecumenical, and that a council was recognised as fully ecumenical when its decisions had been received by the universal episcopate. The basic supposition, of course, was that the whole Church cannot be led astray in its faith, which it would inevitably be if the whole episcopate could err in what it solemnly obliged all the faithful to believe. Again, this was not a purely *a priori* conviction; it was the fruit of the experience which the Church had had, from the first to the second council of Nicea, that the councils which actually achieved the consensus of the whole episcopate had performed an incalculable service for the faith of the Church. It was the common conviction that this could only be explained as the effect of a special guidance or even 'inspiration' of these councils by the Holy Spirit.

Views of Orthodox theologians

At this point, before going on to speak of the further development of the ideas of conciliar and papal infallibility in the West, it might not be out of place to say a few words about how the Orthodox look on the question of ecumenical councils, and their infallibility. We have already seen that at the Seventh Council (Nicea II) the consensus of the Pentarchy was the operative criterion of ecumenicity. For the Orthodox, this criterion is still in effect: which means, of course, that in their view there has been no ecumenical council since 787, and can be none until communion is restored between Rome and the Orthodox churches. It is true that about twenty Greek archbishops took part in the Council of Ferrara-

Florence (1438-1445), and signed its decrees, but the subsequent repudiation of that council by the church of Constantinople rules out its claim to ecumenicity in the eyes of the Orthodox.

With regard to the infallibility of ecumenical councils, Orthodox opinion has been divided ever since A. Khomiakov proposed his theory of *sobornost* (catholicity) in the middle of the last century. According to this theory, only the faith-consciousness of the whole Church enjoys the assistance of the Holy Spirit which ensures its remaining in the true faith. The bishops, even gathered in an ecumenical council, have no claim to such assistance of the Holy Spirit as would guarantee the truth of their dogmatic decrees. The bishops can only witness to what is already the faith of the Church, and it is only when their teaching is confirmed by its reception by the faithful that it has any dogmatic authority.

While Khomiakov's view has had wide acceptance, especially among Russian Orthodox theologians, it is rejected by many, especially of the Greek Orthodox, who see it as an innovation which does not reflect the traditional eastern position regarding the magisterial authority of bishops.[4] These Orthodox theologians hold that the ecumenical councils of the first millennium, representing the dogmatic consensus of the whole episcopate, enjoyed the assistance of the Holy Spirit which ensured the truth of the doctrines they solemnly defined. They reject the idea that the whole body of the faithful is the *only* locus of the guidance of the Holy Spirit to the faith-life of the Church.

Later development in the West

While the idea persisted in the West until the sixteenth century that only those councils could be called 'ecumenical' in which the churches of both East and West had taken part, it was less than a century after the definitive rupture of communion between Rome and Constantinople that Pope Callistus II summoned the first of what became a series of general councils of the Western Church (First Council of the Lateran, 1123). This and the next six general councils: Lateran II (1139), Lateran III (1179), Lateran IV (1215), Lyons I (1245), Lyons II (1274) and Vienne (1311-12), are characterised as the medieval 'papal councils', because of the predominant role which the popes played in them.[5] Most of these councils were primarily engaged in enacting legislation for the reform of the Church and the settlement of the outstanding problems of Christian society. From the time of Pope Gregory VII it was accepted that the pope was the supreme legislator for the universal Church, and by now the 'universal Church' was identified with western Christendom. The decrees of these councils were promulgated as decisions made by the reigning pope 'with the approval of the sacred council'. Even though the assembled bishops, abbots and other clerics who took part in them seem to have had a consultative rather than a fully deliberative voice in the proceedings,[6] the fact that the decisions were made by the pope with the approval of a general council gave them a special solemnity. The unquestioned fact that they were made 'with the authority of the universal Church', combined with the axiomatic belief that the universal Church could not err in faith, justified the conclusion that when such conciliar decrees determined points of faith, they could not be erroneous. We find St Thomas arguing this way concerning the creed: since it was promulgated with the authority of the universal Church, and since the universal Church cannot err in faith, nothing in the creed can be incorrect (2a, 2ae, q.1, a.9).

A new question arose in the fourteenth century, when the only solution available for the disastrous situation caused by the 'western schism' was the exercise of authority over the rival claimants to the papal throne by a general council acting without the pope. The question raised by the Council of Constance was whether the authority of the universal Church resided in a general council made up of bishops, abbots, doctors of theology and canon lawyers, conceived of as a kind of ecclesiastical parliament, distinct from and ultimately superior to the executive, the pope.

The claim that a general council could define dogmas of faith altogether independently of the bishop of Rome had the weight of the tradition of the great councils of the first millennium against it. The evident excesses to which the conciliarist position led at the Council of Basel brought about a reaction in favour of papal authority, which was firmly asserted at the Council of Florence. From this time on there has been no doubt in the Catholic Church about the fact that a general council consists essentially of the pope acting together with the college of bishops; that such a council can define dogmas 'with the authority of the universal Church', and that when it does so, it speaks with infallibility. At Vatican I the infallibility of '*the Church* in defining doctrine of faith or morals' — by which undoubtedly was meant the infallibility of ecumenical councils, since otherwise the Church does not 'define doctrine' — was taken to be so undisputed a dogma of faith that this council did not bother explicitly to define it, when it attributed this same infallibility to the pope speaking *ex cathedra* (D-S 3074). And this brings us to the next question.

The development of Catholic belief in papal infallibility

In the previous chapter, surveying the development of the recognition of papal authority to make definitive decisions for the whole Church in matters of faith, we have seen that whereas the popes themselves, from the fifth century at least, had no doubt about their definitive teaching role, neither the eastern churches, nor many of the leading bishops of the West, outside of Italy, shared the Roman view during the first millennium. After 1054 there was even less readiness on the part of the East to accept such authority on the part of the Bishop of Rome, so the further development towards the recognition of papal teaching authority and eventually of papal infallibility is a uniquely western phenomenon.

We quoted two witnesses of the late thirteenth century to the acceptance of papal authority to define dogmas of faith: St Thomas Aquinas and the Second Council of Lyons. While both clearly state that the pope has definitive teaching authority, neither of them goes so far as to say that the pope is infallible in his dogmatic definitions. However, Yves Congar, quoting the same text of St Thomas (2a 2ae, q.1, a.10), remarks: 'If the Pope has the power "to decide matters of faith authoritatively, so that they may be held by all with unshaken faith," then clearly the dogma of Vatican I necessarily follows.'[7] By what reasoning? Congar does not spell it out, but it seems pretty clear that the argument would be that if the pope could err when exercising such authority, the whole Church would inevitably be led into error in its faith. In other words, once the Church had recognised in the pope the same kind of dogmatic authority it already attributed to ecumenical councils, the same reason for believing conciliar definitions to be infallible would also apply to papal definitions. Congar concludes: 'Thus it is legitimate to see, here in article 10, a first statement of what would soon become the theological idea, and six centuries later, the dogma, of the infallibility of the pontifical magisterium.'[8]

I would call the reader's attention to the word 'soon' in the above quotation. St Thomas died in 1274, and by the year 1283 the Franciscan John Peter Olivi had written his *quaestio*: 'Whether the Roman Pontiff is to be obeyed by all Catholics as an infallible (inerrabili) standard in faith and morals.'[9] Brian Tierney has shown that Olivi had 'an axe to grind' in proposing what was then his novel theory of papal infallibility.[10] For he was deeply apprehensive that a future pope would depart from the teaching of Pope Nicholas III, who, in his Bull 'Exiit' of 1279 had asserted that the Franciscan way of life was inspired by the Holy Spirit, and that the Franciscan renunciation of all property, both individually and in common, was the very way of perfection which Christ has taught by word and example.

Olivi's intention, in proclaiming the infallibility of papal teaching, was to show that just as popes were bound by the dogmatic decisions of ecumenical councils, so they were also bound by the dogmatic decisions of previous popes. And just as a pope who contradicted a dogma defined by an ecumenical council would thereby betray himself as a heretic and automatically cease to be a legitimate pope, so also would a pope who contradicted the infallible teaching of Nicholas III about evangelical poverty. It seems that Olivi anticipated that the great mass of Catholics would accept the teaching of the 'heretical' pope who would contradict Pope Nicholas, in which event he and the little flock of faithful followers of St Francis would constitute the true Church. Perhaps one could see a modern parallel in the insistence of 'traditionalist' Catholics on the infallibility and irreformability of the liturgical decrees of Pope Pius V (the Tridentine mass, etc.) as a justification for their rejection of the liturgical reform instituted by the Second Vatican Council and Pope Paul VI. In any case, it can hardly be said that Olivi's ideas about papal infallibility really anticipated those of the First Vatican

Council. However, within a half-century there appeared another *quaestio* on papal infallibility: this time from the pen of a Carmelite, Bishop Guido Terreni, who so closely anticipated the doctrine of Vatican I that in the judgment of B.M. Xiberta, the Carmelite scholar who edited his work, 'if he had written it after Vatican I he would have had to add or change hardly a single word'.[11]

I would sum up Terreni's argument as follows. Taking as his major premise the universal conviction that the Church cannot be led astray in its faith, and as his minor premise the teaching of St Thomas (to which he explicitly refers, citing 2a 2ae, q.1, a.10) that 'it belongs to the authority of the Roman Pontiff to determine definitively (*sententialiter*) questions about faith so that they may be held by all with unshaken faith', he concludes that in such determinations of matters of faith for the whole Church, the pope cannot err.[12] Needless to say he recognises that infallibility is not a human achievement, but is due to a special assistance of the Holy Spirit; the same Holy Spirit who protects the unerring faith of the Church also prevents the pope from leading it into error in faith. Terreni is very clear and explicit about the difference between an error that would concern only the pope's personal faith, and an error that would concern the faith of the whole Church. He admits (with medieval theologians generally) that a pope could fall into heresy in his private opinions, but he insists that the Holy Spirit would prevent a heretical pope from issuing a decision that would oblige the faithful to follow him in his heresy.

The word in Terreni's vocabulary which corresponds to the term *definire* of Vatican I is *determinare*, which he sometimes qualifies with the adverb *sententialiter*. According to Terreni, such a 'determination' in a matter of faith involves 'the authority of the universal Church, which resides in the supreme pontiff'.[13] He is very clear in holding that questions which the pope can 'determine' for the whole Church have to be concerned with the faith, for it is only the *faith* of the whole Church which is protected from error. He does not use the expression *res fidei et morum* of Vatican I, but it seems likely that he would have included revealed morality among matters of faith.

Xiberta has good reason to assert that this fourteenth century Carmelite strikingly anticipated the dogma of Vatican I. However, Terreni does use a phrase which the minority of Vatican I would like to have seen in the definition of papal infallibility, but which the majority adamantly refused to allow: namely, that the pope cannot err when he determines a question of faith *cum consilio dominorum cardinalium* (with the advice of the cardinals, or having consulted the cardinals).[14] Xiberta maintains that with this phrase Terreni simply intended to distinguish between the pope's solemn pronouncements as head of the Church, and the opinions that he held as a private individual.[15] Tierney agrees that this seems to be the correct interpretation, since it is clear that Terreni understood the supreme teaching authority to reside in the pope, and not in the corporate body of pope-and-cardinals.[16] He seems to have taken it for granted that the pope would not issue a definitive statement in a matter of faith without having consulted his cardinals. And it is only in such definitive statements that he believed the pope to be infallible.

So the dogma of 1870 was already being taught in 1330, but the five and a half centuries that intervened were not a time during which this doctrine enjoyed peaceful possession of the field. It was soon to receive a major setback with the papacy's loss of prestige during the western schism (1378-1417), and the triumph of conciliarism at the Council of Constance (1414-1418). Even after the demise of the radical form of conciliarism, more moderate conciliarist ideas continued to have their influence, most notably in the 'Articles of the Gallican Clergy' of 1682. According to the fourth of these articles, 'In questions of faith the Supreme Pontiff has a principal role, and his decrees pertain to each and every church, but his decision is not irreformable unless it obtains the consent of the Church.' (D-S 2284) In the context of Gallicanism, the term 'the consent of the Church' means 'the consent of the episcopate'; definitive teaching authority, and hence infallibility, was attributed to the whole episcopate, including of course the Bishop of Rome, but was denied to the pope defining doctrine on his own authority.

Meanwhile, there were not lacking able defenders of papal infallibility both before and after the Council of Trent, among whom can be named such theologians as Juan de Torquemada, Cajetan, John Driedo, Thomas Stapleton, Robert Bellarmine,

Francisco Suarez, and the theological faculty of Louvain. But one can certainly not speak of steady progress towards unanimity on the question of papal infallibility between the Council of Trent and Vatican I.[17] Indeed, at the beginning of the nineteenth century an attitude of doubt or denial regarding papal infallibility was prevalent not only in France but in much of Northern Europe and North America as well. One influence here was the fact that the Sulpicians propagated a gallican approach to this question in the seminaries where they educated priests for France, Ireland and the United States.[18]

A good deal of attention has been given in the past few years to the factors which contributed to the change of attitude that took place in the course of the nineteenth century, resulting in the fact that by 1870 the great majority of Catholic bishops were ready to define papal infallibility as a dogma of faith. There is a general consensus that non-theological factors played at least as important a role here as the strictly theological ones. Prominent among the former was the widely shared hope that a strong affirmation of the spiritual authority of the Holy See would provide a remedy for the many evils of the day that were looked upon as the fruit of the liberalism and free-thinking stemming from Protestantism and the French Revolution. Yves Congar, for instance, sees Catholic ecclesiology between the French Revolution and Vatican I as 'under the sign of the affirmation of authority'.[19]

During the eighteenth century most of the defenders of papal infallibility had been Italians (P. Ballerini, F.A. Zaccaria, A. Muzzarelli, M. Cappellari)[20] – which accounts for the name 'ultramontane' given to this current of thought by those living north of the Alps. The remarkable fact is that the nineteenth century witnessed such a rapid and widespread acceptance of 'ultramontanism' among Catholics in France, Germany, Austria and England. H.J. Pottmeyer has studied this development in great detail, showing the variety of motives that led nineteenth-century Catholics to see the best hope for the future of the Church to lie in the spiritual sovereignty of the pope, and his spiritual sovereignty best expressed in his prerogative of infallibility.[21]

There is no denying the fact that non-theological factors played an important part in the development that led to the definition of papal infallibility in 1870. Nor is there any denying that the ecclesiology underlying ultramontanism was of the type that Congar has aptly termed 'hierarchology', rather than a genuine theology of the Church.

On the other hand, as Congar also points out, one cannot say that Vatican I actually defined the kind of papal monarchy that was typical of ultramontane ecclesiology. While, for instance, it is true that the extreme papalist, Joseph de Maistre, helped to prepare minds to accept papal infallibility, Congar insists: 'It was absolutely not his mediocre version of things, so alien to the tradition of the Church, that was made into dogma.'[22]

No doubt it is important for our understanding of the dogma of papal infallibility to know how it came to be defined, and to be aware of the all too human factors that contributed to the triumph of the 'infallibilists' at Vatican I. A.B. Hasler has attributed this triumph to the unfair pressures put on the bishops by Pope Pius IX, to the point that the council's decision was not truly free.[23] While few of his reviewers were convinced that he had proved his thesis, there is no doubt about the fact that undue pressures were applied, and that some of the tactics employed by the leaders of the majority (like the stacking of the *Deputatio de Fide* with 'infallibilists') were far from admirable.

At this point I would invoke the judgment of John Henry Newman, who on the one hand publicly deplored the tactics used to get the doctrine solemnly defined, and on the other hand was satisfied that the extremists had not succeeded in getting *their* version of infallibility ratified by the council; he therefore had no difficulty in accepting the Vatican dogma as true in the form in which it was actually defined.[24]

It is my impression that the attitude of most Catholic theologians today would resemble that taken by Newman. Few would want to subscribe to the ultramontane ecclesiology of the nineteenth century; fewer perhaps would be satisfied with the arguments from Scripture and Tradition which are offered in the fourth chapter of *Pastor aeternus* (D-S 3063-3070). And yet, as Newman was, they are convinced of the truth of the dogma itself, being satisfied that one can accept the dogma without having to accept the theology or the exegesis of those who defined it, because it is not these that were defined. This view, which I share, is that the dogma of papal infallibility, far from being an invention of nineteenth-century ultramontanists or intelligible only against the background of their identification of papal sovereignty with papal infallibility, is thoroughly consistent with the understanding of the 'petrine ministry' to which a theologian of the stature of St Thomas Aquinas had already arrived in the thirteenth century.

As I see it, the dogma of papal infallibility is grounded in two distinctively Roman Catholic beliefs:

1. That the Roman Catholic Church, in which the Church of Christ subsists, is indefectible in its faith, and therefore will never be led into contradiction with the truth of the Gospel by those whose definitive judgments on matters of faith Catholics are ready to accept as binding on their faith;

2. That while such definitive judgments are normally the fruit of the deliberation of the whole episcopate with the pope, the 'petrine ministry' on behalf of the faith and communion of the whole People of God includes the function, when circumstances warrant it, of pronouncing definitive judgments on matters of faith, which are equally as binding as the decisions of ecumenical councils.

Or, to put it more briefly: believing that the pope has authority from God to guide them in their faith, Catholics are confident that God will not permit such authority to oblige them to believe anything that is contrary to the Gospel.

There are two ways that one might evade the conclusion that follows from these premises: one would be to question the pope's authority to make definitive decisions on matters of faith; the other would be to argue that an erroneous definition on the part of the pope would not lead the Church into error, because the Holy Spirit would bring it about that the whole Church would recognise his teaching as erroneous and reject it.

The first approach is that of most of our separated brethren, whether, like most Protestants, they do not admit any definitive teaching authority in the Church, or, like many Orthodox and Anglicans, they recognise such authority in the great ecumenical councils, but deny it to the pope.

The second approach is that of Hans Küng, who sees no grounds for the claim of infallibility for the pope (or for the ecumenical councils, for that matter), since the Holy Spirit can maintain the Church in the truth by leading it to reject the erroneous teaching which pope or council could propose even in their most solemn pronouncements.

The question he raises has to do with our understanding of the way that the Holy Spirit maintains the Church in the truth. The traditional Catholic view is that the Holy Spirit does this both by arousing and sustaining the supernatural sense of faith in the whole People of God (LG 12), and by conferring on those called to ministry in the Church the charisms necessary for the effective carrying out of their office. Since Catholics have come to believe that the petrine ministry includes a teaching office with authority to guide the faith of the whole Church, they also believe that the Church's charism of infallibility is present in a special way in the Roman pontiff when he makes a definitive statement about the faith. This is a kind of abiding assistance, which comes into play in a particular way to guarantee that the pope will not oblige the faithful to give their assent of faith to a teaching that is alien to the Gospel.

Hans Küng's theory about the way the Holy Spirit maintains the Church in the truth seems to me to call for a more extraordinary, almost miraculous, kind of intervention of the Holy Spirit, that would be needed in the emergency situation that would be caused by the solemn definition of a false teaching, which the faithful would then have to detect and refuse to believe. It suggests to me a notion of the Spirit's work as that of controlling and repairing damage already done, rather than that of simply seeing to it that such damage was not done in the first place.

Of course Hans Küng and others will argue that the popes have made mistakes in the exercise of their teaching authority, and that nonetheless the Holy Spirit has maintained the Church in the true faith, and the papal errors have been eventually corrected. To this I would reply that Catholic theologians and historians who defend the doctrine of papal infallibility are aware of the fact that popes have made mistakes in the exercise of their teaching function, but they are satisfied that in no case has a pope ever solemnly defined as a dogma of faith a proposition that was incompatible with the truth of the Gospel. It is true that prior to Vatican I some of the overzealous promoters of the doctrine of papal infallibility seemed to want the Council to declare that the pope could never make a mistake in the exercise of his official teaching function. They wanted a definition of papal infallibility that would, for instance, have required Catholics to believe that every proposition in Pope Pius IX's 'Syllabus of Errors' (D-S 2901-2980) had been infallibly judged and condemned. But no Catholic theologian today would agree that this is what Vatican I actually defined. The dogma of papal infallibility would be historically untenable without a distinction not only between the pope's personal opinions and his offical teaching, but also between his solemn definitions and other teaching which, while public and official, still falls short of being dogmatically definitive.

It is sometimes objected by critics of the doctrine of papal infallibility that this distinction is an artificial contrivance that would not have been understood by earlier popes and hence cannot be used to distinguish between their 'ordinary' and their 'extraordinary' magisterium. For instance, Brian Tierney described this distinction as an example of 'equivocations' which he says modern Catholic theologians have 'brought into play precisely in order to distinguish the very rare infallible pronouncements from the mass of fallible ones in which they are embedded'. He adds: 'This particular development of modern theology seems to have no precise antecedents in medieval thought.'[25]

To this I would reply that the terms used by St Thomas, Guido Terreni and other medieval theologians seem to me to show that they understood the difference between a definitive and a non-definitive exercise of teaching authority. What does Tierney make of such an expression as *sententialiter* (or *finaliter*) *determinare* quae sunt fidei, ut ab omnibus inconcussa fide teneantur'? In the context St Thomas is thinking of nothing less solemn than the new formulation of a creed: something that throughout the first millennium had been seen as the exclusive prerogative of ecumenical councils. Surely this is not your ordinary, everyday exercise of a teaching function. I think there is good reason to believe that St Thomas, Guido Terreni and others of their time understood that not every papal statement on a question of doctrine would have been intended to 'determine the question definitively, so as to oblige all to hold it with unshaken faith'.

98

In any case, it is certainly the official teaching of the Catholic Church, confirmed by both Councils of the Vatican, that the 'charism of infallibility' comes into play not in every exercise of hierarchical teaching authority, but only when certain very definite and exacting conditions are fulfilled. It is generally recognised that the minority group at Vatican I performed an invaluable service by insisting on the recognition of these conditions, and bringing it about that some of them were explicitly mentioned in the formula by which papal infallibility was defined. Other conditions were in fact acknowledged by proponents of the definition of papal infallibility, but were not included in the formula.[26] Vatican I was of course directly concerned with the conditions for papal infallibility, but there are also particular conditions that have to be fulfilled for a conciliar act to be recognised as infallible.

Actually there are two different questions that have to be raised here: 1) what conditions are objectively required for an infallible conciliar or papal definition? and 2) how can we know, in any particular case, that all of these conditions have been fulfilled? Since these are distinct questions, let us take them separately.

Conditions required for an infallible definition

We can distinguish three sets of such conditions: (1) those that concern the *subject* (the definer); (2) those that concern the *object* (the matter defined); (3) those that concern the *act* of defining.

1. *Conditions concerning the subject.* Catholics are agreed that only the bearer of supreme and universal teaching authority in the Church can solemnly define a dogma of faith. However, there are two ways of describing the bearer of this authority. Between Vatican I and Vatican II it was customary to speak of *two* 'inadequately distinct' subjects of supreme authority in the Church: namely, the pope, and the ecumenical council. These are 'inadequately distinct' from one another, because the supreme authority of an ecumenical council necessarily includes the authority of the pope. It is obviously absurd to speak of two *supreme* authorities so distinct from one another that they could possibly be in conflict. Another, more recent way of speaking about this, preferred by Karl Rahner and others, is to say that there is really

only one subject of supreme teaching authority in the Church, namely the whole episcopal college (necessarily including its head, the pope), but there are two ways in which the authority of this one subject can be exercised. According to Rahner, when the pope defines a dogma without summoning an ecumenical council (as Pius IX and Pius XII did) he is acting in his capacity as head of the episcopal college, and exercising the authority of which the whole college is the subject. To do this, he does not require any authorisation from the rest of the body, nor does his act juridically depend on the consent of the body for its validity.[27] It seems to me that either of these explanations would be consistent with the teaching of Vatican II. When, in what follows, I speak of the pope as 'subject' of an infallible exercise of magisterium, I do not intend to reject Rahner's explanation of how this is to be understood.

Let us then consider the conditions that concern the episcopal college as subject of an infallible dogmatic definition. Now it is true that this college, when exercising its ordinary magisterium throughout the world, can, under certain conditions, teach infallibly (we shall treat this question in the following chapter). However, the pronouncing of a solemn dogmatic definition is an extraordinary exercise of magisterium, in which the episcopal college deliberates upon and judges a question of faith in a strictly collegial way. Until now, this has been possible only when the bishops have been actually gathered in ecumenical councils. So, historically, the condition required for the episcopal college to be the subject of an infallible dogmatic definition has been that it be assembled in an ecumenical council. We have already discussed the criteria on the basis of which certain councils are recognised as ecumenical.

At this point the question can be raised whether, in the future, it might be possible for the episcopal college to exercise such deliberation and judgment in a strictly collegial way, without being physically gathered in one place. Given the recent advances in methods of global communication, it does not seem out of the question that the kind of common deliberation required for a strictly collegial decision might be possible without an actual assembly of the bishops in a conciliar *aula*.

100

Another question is whether a group of bishops elected and authorised by their fellow bishops to represent the whole episcopate could, together with the pope, be the subject of supreme teaching authority, capable of defining a dogma of faith. In view of the fact that in the ecumenical councils of the first millennium the whole western episcopate was represented by only two or three bishops, legates of the bishop of Rome, it would not seem impossible for the authority of the whole episcopal college to be exercised by a body of its elected representatives. Such a body would have to be authorised to make decisions together with the pope with fully deliberative voice. In this respect it would have to be different from the 'Synod of Bishops' established by Pope Paul VI in 1965, which, as constituted, is a purely advisory organ for the pope, with merely consultative voice.

Whatever one might say about these two questions we have just raised, it is certain that in order for the episcopal college to be the subject of a dogmatic definition, the bishops have to be exercising their function as 'judges of the faith' (LG 25) in a truly deliberative way. This necessarily includes the condition that the bishops be free to express their own judgment: in other words that they not be under such pressure or coercion as would deprive them of genuine freedom in expressing their views. It is well known that critics of Vatican I, both in the last century and more recently, have charged that the pressure put on the bishops by Pope Pius IX was such that the deliberations of that council were not truly free. As far as I know, no defender of Vatican I has questioned the major premise of their argument: namely, that the episcopate has to be free from coercion in order to be a subject of the deliberative decision-making required for a conciliar definition of faith.

Let us now look at the conditions that concern the Roman pontiff as subject of an infallible dogmatic definition. The condition explicitly laid down at Vatican I is that the Roman pontiff be 'exercising his supreme apostolic authority as pastor and teacher of all Christians' (D-S 3074). In other words, while the pope can speak as a private theologian, or simply as bishop of Rome, it is only in his capacity as head of the universal Church that he can define a dogma of faith.

Other conditions that are not explicitly stated here are

nevertheless implied. For instance: the Roman pontiff who defines a dogma of faith must be a pope of whose valid election there is no doubt. He must not have lost the papacy by openly falling into heresy or schism (something that such staunch defenders of the papacy as Torquemada, Cajetan, Bellarmine and Suarez considered a possibility to be reckoned with). Furthermore, he must make his decision to define while of sound mind and free of coercion. Otherwise he could hardly be said to be truly exercising his supreme teaching authority.

2. *Conditions concerning the object.* I shall speak very briefly on this question here, since I intend to treat it at length in the next chapter. Since we are dealing in the present chapter with the question of the infallibility of the magisterium in defining dogmas of faith, the object has to be a truth that is capable of being so defined. Now only a truth that has been revealed to us by God 'for the sake of our salvation' (DV 11) can be defined as a dogma of faith. In other words, the object of solemn definition as dogma has to be a 'doctrine of faith or morals' which is in itself formally contained in the 'deposit of revelation'. We shall explain these terms more fully in the following chapter.

3. *Conditions that concern the act of defining.* We have already seen that the term 'to define' in the present context means to give a definitive judgment which puts an end to freedom of opinion on a question and decisively establishes some truth as an element of the normative faith of the community. For an act of the magisterium to constitute a dogmatic definition, it must be evident that it is intended as such a definitive judgment, obliging the faithful to give their assent of faith to the doctrine so defined.

Such a definitive judgment can also be expressed negatively, by the solemn condemnation of an opinion as heretical. When it is clear that the term 'heresy' is intended to mean that the condemned opinion is in contradiction to a truth of faith, the contradictory of the heresy is thereby defined as a dogma of faith.

When we look to the conditions that must be fulfilled for an infallible dogmatic definition to be made by the pope, we come to the question that most deeply divided the bishops at the First Vatican Council. The question was whether the consultation and consent of the episcopate was a condition on which the infallibility of a papal definition would depend, and which should therefore be named as such a condition in the formula by which papal infallibility was to be defined. The *Deputatio de Fide* (representing the majority view at the Council) adamantly refused to allow such a condition to be inserted into the formula of definition; indeed at the last moment it added a phrase that explicitly ruled out the dependence of papal definitions on the consent of the Church, saying that such definitions are 'irreformable of themselves and not from the consent of the Church' (D-S 3074). What did they intend by this much-controverted phrase?

This is a good example of the necessity of interpreting magisterial statements in the light of the historical factors which reveal the mind of their authors. It is historically certain that what the majority of Vatican I intended by this phrase was the definitive repudiation of the fourth of the 'Articles of the Gallican Clergy' of 1682, which said that a doctrinal decision made by the pope would be irreformable only if it obtained the consent of the Church (D-S 2284). There is no doubt about the fact that the 'Church' in this Article really means 'the episcopate'. The precise target at which Vatican I aimed was the idea of such a juridical dependence of papal definitions on episcopal approval that there could be a legitimate appeal from a papal definition to the judgment of the rest of the episcopal college, which could conceivably reverse the Pope's decision. To admit such juridical dependence of papal definitions on episcopal approval would amount to denying primacy and infallibility to papal magisterium and attributing it uniquely to the magisterium of the whole episcopate.[28]

It is most important, however, to observe that while Vatican I's 'ex sese, non autem ex consensu Ecclesiae' rules out the juridical dependence of papal definitions on episcopal consent, it does not, and indeed cannot rule out a real dependence of papal definitions on the faith of the Church. For the pope can define as a dogma of faith only what is contained in the deposit of revelation. Now *Dei Verbum* tells us that 'the sacred deposit of the Word of God has been entrusted to the Church' (DV 10), and it is the Church which 'in her teaching, life and worship perpetuates and hands on this deposit to all generations' (DV 8). If, then, before he can define anything as divinely revealed, the pope must 'listen to the Word of God' (DV 10), and if this Word of God has been 'entrusted to the Church' (DV 10), and is handed on ' in her teaching, life and worship' (DV 8), it follows that before the pope can define a dogma he must listen to the Church, and that he can define as dogma only what he finds in the faith of the Church. The pope has no source of revelation that is independent of the faith-life of the Church. As Vatican I had already said, the Holy Spirit is promised to him not so that, by the Spirit's revelation he might proclaim new doctrine, but rather that with the Spirit's assistance he might guard and explain the revelation handed down from the Apostles (D-S 3070).

From this it follows that the pope simply cannot define a dogma of faith without having in some real way consulted the faith of the Church, for he can define as a dogma only something that has been and is being handed on in the teaching, life and worship of the Church. But to say this is not the same thing as to prescribe exactly what form this consultation must take in order to satisfy juridically established conditions. It is not the same thing as to lay down, as an indispensable condition for a valid papal definition, that the pope have previously consulted the whole episcopate, or have ascertained the prior consensus of all the faithful on this point of doctrine. For there are as many ways of consulting the faith of the Church as there are ways that the deposit of revelation has been handed on in her teaching, life and worship. These include Sacred Scripture, the writings of the Fathers and Doctors of the Church, the sacred liturgy, the decrees of councils, the works of theologians, traditional beliefs and practices, etc. All of these reflect the faith of the Church in various ways, and therefore to say that the pope must consult the faith of the Church before defining a dogma does not mean that necessarily, and in every case, he must have consulted and obtained the agreement of all the bishops, or ascertained the fact of a universal consensus of the faithful, before proceeding to define a dogma of faith.

The magisterial role of the pope cannot be reduced to merely announcing the results of a Church-wide opinion poll. There have been times in the past and may be again in the future when a considerable portion of the faithful has been led into error, usually by erring bishops, and then it has been the role of the supreme teaching authority to pronounce a decisive judgment in order to resolve the dispute and lead the faithful to a consensus in the truth. The Sacred Congregation for the Doctrine of the Faith has made this point in its Declaration *Mysterium Ecclesiae* of 1973, saying: 'However much the Sacred Magisterium avails itself of the contemplation, life and study of the faithful, its office is not reduced merely to ratifying the assent already expressed by the latter; indeed, in the interpretation and explanation of the written or transmitted Word of God, the Magisterium can anticipate or demand their assent.'[29]

It is true that in regard to some doctrines that have been defined as dogmas of faith, the universal consensus of the Catholic faithful has in fact provided the only sufficient grounds for certitude that these particular doctrines were really contained in the deposit of revelation. This was the case with regard to the doctrines of the Immaculate Conception and Assumption of the Blessed Virgin Mary. In these cases it was indispensable that the pope first ascertain the fact of such a *consensus fidelium* before proceeding to define these doctrines, and he could hardly have done this otherwise than by consulting all the bishops, who are the authorised witnesses to the faith of their flock.

Furthermore, given the ease of world-wide consultation provided by modern means of communication, a pope could hardly be said in the future to have fulfilled his grave obligation to make use of every suitable means available to him in the preparation of an *ex cathedra* definition, if he neglected to consult the episcopal college about the doctrine he contemplated defining. However, one cannot lay down the morally unanimous consent of the episcopate as a condition absolutely to be fulfilled prior to a papal definition, because ascertaining the fact of such prior consensus would not in every instance be the only way of consulting the faith of the Church, and secondly, because this would eliminate the possibility of a decisive act of the papal magisterium that might be needed to overcome a threat to the Church's unity in the faith, and bring about a consensus, or restore one that had been lost.

We have answered the question: what conditions are required for an infallible definition of a dogma of faith? We must now answer the question: how can we know, in a particular case, that all these conditions have been fulfilled? Can we always know this *a priori*?

A priori infallibility?

A certain amount of confusion about the notion of '*a priori* infallibility' has been caused by the neglect of the distinction between the actual fulfilment of the conditions required for an infallible definition, and our verification of the fact that all such conditions have been fulfilled. As I understand it, to say that when certain conditions are fulfilled, a council or pope speaks infallibly, means that, in virtue of the divine assistance attached to such an exercise of their teaching office, there is an *a priori* guarantee that the solemnly defined proposition will be true. I do not see how we could correctly speak of infallibility (as distinct from mere inerrancy) if it did not mean such 'immunity from error', given all the conditions objectively required for a solemn dogmatic definition. This means also that the infallibility of an act of defining dogma cannot depend on conditions that can be fulfilled only after the fact. For instance, I do not see how one could consider subsequent reception of a dogma by the Church as a condition on which the infallibility of the magisterium in making that definition would objectively depend. It seems to me that in order to maintain the infallibility of the teaching authority of the Church 'in defining doctrine' (*in doctrina definienda*: Vat. I, D-S 3704) one has to hold that when all the conditions required for a dogmatic definition are fulfilled, the defined dogma is infallibly true, *prior to* its reception by the Church. In this sense, I think it is correct to speak of '*a priori* infallibility'.

However, it is quite a different question when one asks: how can we *know*, in a particular case, that all the conditions required for an infallible definition have actually been fulfilled? According to the 1983 Code of Canon Law, 'No doctrine is understood to have been dogmatically defined unless this is manifestly the case' (Can. 749, §3). Now we have just been considering a rather large number of conditions that have to be fulfilled, regarding the subject,

106

the object, and the act of defining, in order that an act of the magisterium be rightly termed an infallible definition. According to Avery Dulles, 'For some the very essence of infallibility consists in the *a priori* assurance that if certain easily verifiable conditions are fulfilled, the definition may be regarded as unquestionably true.'[30] I agree with his judgment that this is an oversimplification. I would say that the attitude he describes is mistaken on two points: it presumes that the conditions for an infallible definition are always easily verifiable, and that we can always have an *a priori* assurance that they are fulfilled.

Let us recall, for instance, some of the conditions required for an infallible conciliar definition. Regarding the subject: it has to be an ecumenical council. Now it is a fact that historically the recognition of certain councils as ecumenical, and the non-recognition of others, has been *a posteriori*: i.e. on the basis of their reception by the whole Church. Regarding the act of defining: we have seen that the bishops have to exercise their function as judges of the faith in a truly deliberative way, free of any undue pressure or coercion. This might not always be easily verifiable. Furthermore, for an act of the magisterium to constitute an infallible definition of a dogma of faith, it has to be clearly intended as a definitive judgment, obliging the faithful to give their unconditional assent of faith to the doctrine so defined. Now one of the most difficult tasks which positive dogmatic theology has to perform is to determine precisely which statements of ecumenical councils have fulfilled all the conditions required to constitute such definitions of dogmas of faith. To take the Council of Trent, for example: the recent studies by Piet Fransen on the meaning of such terms as 'faith', 'dogma', 'heresy', *'anathema sit'* etc., in the Tridentine decrees, have shown how gravely mistaken it would be to take the use of such terms at Trent as certain proof of the intention to define something as a dogma of faith in the modern sense of that term. Fransen rightly insists that it calls for careful historical research to identify dogmatic definitions in the *acta* of past councils.[31]

The same would be true of the problem of identifying all the dogmatic definitions that have been made by popes. At least prior to modern times, in the exercise of magisterium by councils and popes, it can hardly be maintained that the conditions required for infallible definitions have been easily verifiable, and they certainly were not always so *a priori*. What about the future exercise of conciliar and papal magisterium? Can we say that at least from now on, the presence of all the conditions required for an infallible definition will always be easily verifiable, so that we can have an *a priori* assurance that the defined proposition will be true? It is likely enough that the intention to define will be more easily verifiable in future statements of the magisterium than it has been in many statements of the past.

But the crucial question here is: will the intention to define, explicitly stated by a council or a pope, provide *of itself* the evidence that all the conditions required for an infallible definition are fulfilled? Or, to put it more concretely, when the pope says: 'I define . . .', does he implicitly define, with the same infallibility, that all the conditions required for a dogmatic definition are fulfilled? For example, does he thereby define the fact that he is of sound mind, free of coercion, and that the question falls within the proper sphere of infallible magisterium? Does the fact that the pope has used an *ex cathedra* formula in making a particular statement, absolutely rule out any question as to whether all the conditions objectively required for an *ex cathedra* definition of faith were actually fulfilled in that act?

I am inclined to agree with a number of Catholic theologians who give a negative answer to this kind of question.[32] I would say that when a pope clearly expresses his intention to define a question, there is a good *presumption* that all the conditions objectively required for an *ex cathedra* statement are present. But it seems to me that one cannot rule out the possibility that this presumption might have to yield to contrary evidence. What would constitute evidence that some necessary condition for an *ex cathedra* definition had been lacking? I do not see how one could quarrel with the answer which Bishop B.C. Butler has given to this question. Noting that according to *Lumen gentium* (n. 25) 'a genuine *ex cathedra* definition will always be received by the Church with the assent of faith', the Bishop goes on to say: 'It follows, of course, though Vatican II does not say so, that if a definition failed in the end to enjoy such a "reception" on the part of the Church, this would prove that the definition had not in fact met the stringent requirements for an *ex cathedra* pronouncement.'[33]

If eventual ('in the end') non-reception of a conciliar or papal statement is evidence that an infallible definition has not actually taken place, we must also ask what positive significance should be attributed to the reception by the Church of decisions taken by the magisterium.

The significance of 'reception' by the Church of magisterial decisions

The statement of *Lumen gentium* to which Bishop Butler referred, follows the discussion of the infallibility which both ecumenical councils and popes enjoy in making solemn definitions. The text continues with the statement: 'To the resultant definitions the assent of the Church can never be wanting, on account of the activity of the same Holy Spirit, whereby the whole flock of Christ is preserved and progresses in unity of faith' (LG 25). This statement calls for several observations, in the light of the history of the reception of the definitions of the great ecumenical councils.

First, hardly any council called to settle a doctrinal dispute has had its decision accepted by all the parties to the dispute. In most instances some portion of the Church has refused to accept the condemnation of its views, and has separated itself from the main body of the Church. Secondly, even on the part of those who eventually assented to the conciliar decision, a general reception of the new dogma has sometimes taken a considerable length of time. For instance, it took about fifty years for the Nicene dogma of the consubstantiality of the Word to be generally accepted by those who rejected the Arian heresy. Thirdly, the 'whole flock of Christ' which is said to be preserved in unity of faith, has to be understood in a rather limited sense. Historically, it can only mean that portion of the Christian community which, after each crucial doctrinal decision, has actually accepted the definition and stayed in communion with the bishops who made it. When this idea is applied to such councils as Trent and Vatican I, it becomes obvious that here it is the Roman Catholic Church alone that is being described as 'the whole flock of Christ.'

Now it seems to me that this is a way of speaking that is

not fully consonant with the attitude expressed elsewhere in the documents of Vatican II with regard to the ecclesial status of other Christian communities. So the question must be raised: if we no longer claim an exclusive identification between the Church of Christ and the Roman Catholic Church, so that we no longer think of the Catholic Church as 'the whole flock of Christ', can we any longer consider the reception of a dogma by the Catholic Church, sufficient proof that the magisterium has spoken infallibly in defining this dogma, if in fact it is rejected by practically all other Christian churches?

I have already expressed my opinion that a truly ecumenical consensus would be the most satisfying basis for a judgment that all the conditions for infallibility have been fulfilled, and that in the future it is probable that more attention will be paid to the beliefs of other Christians in the preparation of dogmatic definitions than has been the case in the past. But I do not believe it would be consistent with the teaching of Vatican II to hold, as some theologians now do,[34] that ecumenicity of reception should be recognised as a requirement for infallibility of teaching.

My first objection to this idea is that it seems to ignore the fact that hardly any important dogmatic decision taken by the great councils of the first millennium was received by all sectors of the Christian Church. Secondly, it is my understanding of the mind of Vatican II that when it says that the Church of Christ 'subsists in the Catholic Church', it means to affirm that the inalienable properties of the Church of Christ also 'subsist' in the Catholic Church. But among such properties is indefectibility in the true faith. I do not think there can be any doubt about the fact that when Vatican II speaks of the 'unerring quality' of 'universal agreement in matters of faith and morals' (LG 12), it intends to attribute such infallibility to the universal consensus of the Catholic bishops and faithful on such doctrines as the Immaculate Conception and Assumption of the Blessed Virgin Mary. Hence I do not see how, consistently with the teaching of Vatican II, one could require ecumenicity of reception as a requirement for infallibility.

Rather, I would say that the reception of the dogmas of Vatican I by the Catholic Church can rightly be taken as the ultimate confirmation of the truth of these dogmas. If one

110

believes that the Holy Spirit maintains the Church of Christ in the true faith, and if one further believes that the Church of Christ 'subsists in the Catholic Church', then one can be satisfied, as John Henry Newman was, with the reception of the dogma of papal infallibility by the Catholic bishops who had opposed the definition, and by the Catholic faithful generally, as final confirmation of the fact that an infallible definition had taken place at Vatican I.[35]

If one asks: how can we have infallible certitude that all the conditions required for an infallible definition are present in any particular case? — I would reply: the evidence of this which itself enjoys infallibility is the reception of the defined dogma in the faith-consciousness of the Church. Subsequent reception does not confer infallibility on the act of the magisterium, but it provides infallible confirmation of the fact that an infallible definition has taken place.

The sentence of *Lumen gentium* which speaks of the assent of the faithful to dogmatic definitions, ascribes this to the activity of the Holy Spirit. So a further question is:

How does the Holy Spirit bring about the assent of the Church?

In the past century, treatises on this question generally spoke of the 'passive infallibility' of the 'learning Church', in contrast to the 'active infallibility' of the 'teaching Church'. In this framework, the activity of the Holy Spirit which assured the assent of the faithful to the decisions of the magisterium was seen primarily as inspiring in the faithful attitudes of docility and trusting obedience, with the formal authority of the office-holders as the principal motive for assent to their definitions.

More recent studies of the notion of reception of magisterial decisions on the part of the faithful pay more attention to the activity of the Holy Spirit in stirring up and maintaining the 'supernatural sense of the faith', by which believers recognise the truth-content of what is authoritatively proposed for their belief.[36] The role of the faithful is seen to be not merely passive obedience to formal authority, but an active sharing in the process by which the whole People of God 'clings without fail to the faith once delivered to the saints, penetrates it more deeply by accurate insights, and applies it more thoroughly to life' (LG 12).

111

The reception of magisterial decisions by the faithful is a logical consequence of the fact that the magisterium can only define as dogma what it finds in the deposit of faith which was entrusted to the Church (DV 10), and is handed on in the 'teaching, life and worship' of the Church (DV 8). The magisterium has to draw from the faith-consciousness of the Church whatever it proposes as revealed truth. So the response of the faithful to the teaching of the magisterium has the effect of closing a circle: from the faith of the Church, to the official teaching, back to the faith of the Church.[37] When the magisterium expresses the Church's faith in new terms, the role of the Holy Spirit is to assist the faithful to recognise their traditional faith in the new formulation given it by the dogmatic definition. 'Reception', then, is not a matter of blind obedience to formal authority, but of the divinely-assisted recognition of the truth of what is taught.

The non-reception of papal infallibility by other Christians

I cannot conclude this chapter without offering some reflections on the evident fact of the non-reception of the Vatican dogma of papal infallibility by the rest of the Christian world. I shall say something, at least briefly, about the reasons for this, its significance, and its implications for the prospects of Christian reunion.

If reception means the recognition of one's traditional faith in the newly defined dogma, then it is reasonable to expect that a dogma will not be received by those whose previous faith-consciousness did not embrace the doctrine that is defined. Roman Catholics were prepared to accept the dogma of papal infallibility because they believed in the authority of the pope to make definitive decisions for them on matters of faith, and were confident that the Holy Spirit would not permit such authority to lead the whole Church into error. But this confidence was the fruit of a development which took place in the western Church after its break with the East: a development which was not shared by eastern Christians, who continued to look to the councils as the only bodies qualified to define dogmas of faith. Indeed, a result of the deepening alienation between East and West during the centuries that followed the schism was the tendency on the part of eastern bishops and theologians to attribute less doctrinal authority to the bishop of Rome than their predecessors had acknowledged him to have when they appealed to Rome during the doctrinal controversies of the first millennium. Another factor in the rejection of papal infallibility by the Orthodox in modern times has been the influence of Khomiakov's theory of *sobornost*, which attributes infallibility uniquely to the whole community's consensus in faith, rejecting the idea of any infallible magisterium whether conciliar or papal.

With regard to the non-reception of the Vatican dogma by the Protestant world: first of all, one must recall that at the time of the Reformation the doctrine of papal infallibility had not yet achieved an undisputed consensus within the Catholic Church itself. On the other hand, the fact that Luther saw the rejection of his theses by Rome as the rejection of the pure Gospel truth of justification by faith, led him to conclude that the pope was abusing his authority to forbid the preaching of the Gospel. Understandably, this destroyed any confidence in papal magisterium on the part of those who accepted Luther's teaching as a genuine insight into the meaning of the Gospel. Furthermore, the insistence of Luther on the sinful nature of every human institution led to the rejection of the idea of an infallible magisterium; God alone, and his Word, could be taken as infallible.

That these ideas still provide the basic motivation of the non-reception of papal infallibility on the part of modern Lutherans can be seen in statements made by the Lutheran participants in the Lutheran-Catholic dialogue in the United States. This dialogue has shown that Lutherans who are prepared to recognise that there is a reasonable basis for accepting a 'petrine ministry', to be exercised by the bishop of Rome for the unity of the whole Christian Church,[38] still find it impossible to accept the idea of an infallible papal magisterium. The following quotations indicate their reasons for rejecting this doctrine.[39]

Lutherans think that Catholics have overconfidently identified the locus of the work of the Spirit with a particular person or office. (p. 32) Contemporary Lutheran thought, emphasizing the sinfulness of all human institutions and instruments, finds it difficult to recognize any episcopal see, church office, person, or officeholder as gifted with such unfailing assistance from the Spirit as to preclude error in teaching. (p. 40) Lutherans reacted against the terminology of papal infallibility primarily because they thought it contradicted their basic conviction of the fallibility of all ecclesiastical institutions and orders. To speak of the pope or any of his pronouncements as infallible suggested to them the usurpation of the place which only Christ and the Word of God could occupy in the Church's teaching ministry. (p. 61) We thus return to the emphasis on God's promises, which is expressed in the affirmation that only the Word of God found in Scripture is 'infallible and unalterable.' (p. 67)

The two statements on 'Authority in the Church' which have been published by the Anglican-Roman Catholic International Commission (ARCIC), show that Anglicans too, who can go a long way towards recognising the legitimacy of a universal primacy of the bishop of Rome, still have grave reservations about the Vatican dogma of papal infallibility. The following quotations from the *ARCIC Final Report*[40] bring out the reasons why they find it difficult to accept this doctrine.

Anglicans find grave difficulty in the affirmation that the pope can be infallible in his teaching. . . . special difficulties are created by the recent Marian dogmas, because Anglicans doubt the appropriateness, or even the possibility, of defining them as essential to the faith of believers (p. 65). The Church's teaching authority is a service to which the faithful look for guidance especially in times of uncertainty; but the assurance of the truthfulness of its teaching rests ultimately rather upon its fidelity to the Gospel than upon the character or office of the person by whom it is expressed (p. 94). If the definition proposed [by the pope] for assent were not manifestly a legitimate interpretation of biblical faith and in line with orthodox tradition, Anglicans would think it a duty to reserve the reception of the definition for study and discussion (p. 95). The dogmas of the Immaculate Conception and the Assumption raise a special problem for those Anglicans who do not consider that the precise definitions given by these dogmas are sufficiently supported by Scripture. For many Anglicans the teaching authority of the bishop of Rome, independent of a council, is not recommended by the fact that through it these Marian doctrines were proclaimed as dogmas binding on all the faithful (p. 96). Anglicans do not accept the guaranteed possession of such a gift of divine assistance in judgment necessarily attached to the office of the bishop of Rome by virtue of which his formal decisions can be known to be wholly assured before their reception by the faithful (pp. 96-7).

One observation I would make on the reasons given by the Lutherans and the Anglicans in these dialogues for rejecting papal infallibility, is that they confirm the idea that reception of a dogma presupposes that one recognises in it an explication of what one already, at least implicitly, believed. On the contrary, it is quite understandable that a Catholic dogma will not be received by Christians to whom it seems 'not to be a legitimate interpretation of biblical faith, or in line with orthodox tradition', or to whom it seems even to 'contradict some basic conviction' of their own faith.

One conclusion that follows from this is that continued ecumenical dialogue is necessary on the 'basic convictions' that made it possible for Catholics, and impossible for other Christians, to accept papal infallibility as a dogma of their faith. As I suggested earlier in this chapter, the 'proofs' for this doctrine from Scripture and Tradition will be convincing only to those who are already disposed to believe it because, at least implicitly, it is already part of their faith.

What then are the implications of the non-reception of papal infallibility by other Christian churches, with regard to the prospects of Christian reunion? The question has already been raised, and will surely have to be taken seriously in the future: will the explicit reception of the dogma of papal infallibility by the separated Churches be a requirement necessarily to be met before full ecclesial communion can be restored between Rome and those Churches? This is not a question of the admission of an individual Christian to full communion with the Catholic Church — but of the restoration of full communion between Churches. One thing seems clear: if the restoration of communion is going to depend on the explicit reception of the dogma of papal infallibility, the prospects of restored communion are rather remote.

But it seems to me that a good case can be made for the view that Rome should not require of the Orthodox Churches, for example, as far as their acceptance of Roman primacy is concerned, more than was expected of the eastern Churches in full communion with Rome during the first millennium. In its Decree on Ecumenism, Vatican II describes this state of full communion in the following terms (UR 14):

> For many centuries, the Churches of the East and of the West went their own ways, though a brotherly communion of faith and sacramental life bound them together. If disagreements in belief and discipline arose among them, the Roman See acted by common consent as moderator. . . . Therefore, this sacred Synod urges all, but especially those who plan to devote themselves to the work of restoring the full communion that is desired between the Eastern Christians and the Catholic Church, to give due consideration to these special aspects of the origin and growth of the Churches of the East, and to the character of the relations which obtained between them and the Roman See before the separation, and to form for themselves a correct evaluation of these facts.

I see in this statement of Vatican II an encouragement for those who envision the possibility of a restored communion between Rome and the Orthodox Churches that would be modelled on the 'brotherly communion of faith and sacramental life' which bound them together during the first millennium, rather than on the kind of relationship that presently binds the 'Uniate' eastern Churches to Rome. This view takes seriously the fact that the Vatican dogma was the culmination of a western development in the theory and practice of the papacy in which the East did not share. Not having shared in this development, eastern Christians can hardly be expected to be psychologically prepared to accept its end result. Might it not, then, be sufficient for the restoration of ecclesial communion if the Orthodox Churches were to accept papal infallibility as a development in the understanding of the meaning of the Roman primacy which is compatible with Orthodox Christian faith, without being obliged explicitly to profess it as an article of their faith?

Cardinal Ratzinger, for one, thinks that it ought to suffice.

116

Speaking of the conditions that would have to be fulfilled before ecclesial communion could be restored between Rome and the Orthodox, he has written:

> As far as the doctrine of the primacy is concerned, Rome must not require more of the East than was formulated and lived during the first millennium. When Patriarch Athenagoras, on the occasion of the visit of the Pope to the Phanar on July 25, 1967, addressed him as 'the successor of Peter, the first in honor among us, the one who has the presidency of love,' we hear from the mouth of this great Church leader the essential content of the first millennium's statement about the primacy — and Rome must demand no more than this. Reunion could take place on this basis: that for its part the East should renounce attacking the western development of the second millennium as heretical, and should accept the Catholic Church as legitimate and orthodox in the form which it has found through this development, while, for its part, the West should acknowledge the Church of the East as orthodox and legitimate in the form which it has maintained.[41]

Papal infallibility and the 'hierarchy of truths'

In its Decree on Ecumenism, the Second Vatican Council has urged Catholic theologians who are engaged in ecumenical dialogue to 'remember that in Catholic teaching there exists an order or "hierarchy" of truths, since they vary in their relationship to the foundation of the Christian faith' (UR 11). It is important, first of all, to note that the place of a doctrine in this 'hierarchy of truths' is not determined by whether it has been dogmatically defined or not. Inevitably, however, the fact that papal infallibility was the object of solemn definition by Vatican I tended to exalt its importance in the eyes of many Catholics. But the sober fact is that it is far from being among the truths at the very foundation of our faith. It would be a gross misunderstanding to think that the certitude of our Catholic faith somehow depends on the infallibility of the pope. It would be an even grosser mistake to think that we put our hope for salvation in holding correct doctrine, and that our assurance that we hold correct doctrine depends on papal infallibility. If this were the case, there

117

would be some justice to the charge that we Catholics put our hope for salvation in the infallibility of the pope, rather than in the mercy of God. But of course this would be a caricature.

Actually, our belief in the infallibility of the pope is a fairly remote consequence of our foundational belief that Jesus is the Lord, and that 'he loved the Church and gave himself up for her' (Eph 5:26). Belief in Christ's eschatological victory and his universal Lordship is the foundation of our belief that the Church which is his body and bride, and the flock of which he is the chief Shepherd (1 Pe 5:4), will never be led away from the truth of the Gospel by the one who has inherited the charge given to Peter to 'feed his lambs and feed his sheep' (Jn 21:15-17). Our difference with our separated brethren is not about these foundational beliefs, but about the understanding at which the Catholic Church has arrived, in the course of time, of what is involved in the charge given to Peter to feed the flock of Christ. As John Henry Newman put it, in his reply to Gladstone: 'What has the long history of the contest for and against the pope's infallibility been, but a growing insight through centuries into the meaning of those three texts to which I just now referred [the 'primacy texts'], ending at length by the Church's definitive recognition of the doctrine thus gradually manifested to her?'[42]

118

6.

The Infallibility of the Ordinary Universal Magisterium and the Limits of the Object of Infallibility

There are two questions here, but I shall treat them in one chapter, because I think the most practical way to discuss them is to apply them to the currently controverted question whether the sinfulness of artificial contraception has been infallibly taught by the ordinary universal magisterium. The answer to this question involves both the conditions under which a doctrine can be said to have been infallibly taught without being solemnly defined, and the limits of the object about which the magisterium can teach infallibly. Since Vatican II spoke to both of these issues, the current controversy also involves the question of the correct interpretation of the pertinent texts of the Council, and their application to this case. Let us begin by quoting the texts of *Lumen gentium* which deal with these issues; they are both in LG 25.

The statement on the ordinary universal magisterium is as follows:

> Although the individual bishops do not enjoy the prerogative of infallibility, they can nevertheless proclaim Christ's doctrine infallibly. This is so, even when they are dispersed around the world, provided that while maintaining the bond of unity among themselves and with Peter's successor, and while teaching authentically on a matter of faith or morals, they concur in a single viewpoint as the one which must be held conclusively.

The statement on the limits of the object of infallible magisterium is as follows:

> This infallibility with which the divine Redeemer willed

119

His Church to be endowed in defining a doctrine of faith and morals extends as far as extends the deposit of divine revelation, which must be religiously guarded and faithfully expounded.

It is the contention of J. Ford, G. Grisez and M. Zalba, among others, that for at least a century prior to 1962 the Catholic bishops throughout the world, in their authoritative teaching on morals, concurred on the grave sinfulness of artificial contraception as a viewpoint which all Catholics were bound to hold conclusively. They further hold that the morality of birth-control, even if it is not in itself formally revealed, still falls within at least the secondary object of infallible Church teaching. They conclude that the grave sinfulness of artificial contraception has been infallibly taught by the ordinary universal magisterium of the Catholic Church. Hence, they also conclude that Pope Paul VI had no choice but to confirm this infallible teaching in his encyclical *Humanae vitae*.[1]

Hans Küng agrees that according to the official Catholic doctrine on the infallibility of the ordinary universal magisterium, the sinfulness of artificial contraception has been infallibly taught. But he draws a very different conclusion from this. On the premise (which he takes to be self-evident) that this teaching of *Humanae vitae* is erroneous, he concludes that the official Catholic doctrine about the infallibility of the magisterium must be erroneous too.[2]

Karl Rahner and most other Catholic theologians agree neither with Ford and Grisez nor with Küng on this issue. They do not agree that according to the official Catholic doctrine on the infallibility of the ordinary universal magisterium, the sinfulness of artificial contraception has been infallibly taught.[3]

As I have already said, there are two questions involved here: the infallibility of the ordinary universal magisterium, and the limits of the object of infallibility. Let us begin with the first of these questions.

Ordinary magisterium

The term 'magisterium' in this context means the exercise of the teaching authority of the Catholic hierarchy. This teaching is exercised in a 'solemn' or 'extraordinary' way when a doctrine is *defined* by an ecumenical council, or by a Pope speaking *ex cathedra*. Any other exercise of the teaching authority of the bishops or the Pope is called 'ordinary'. Examples of such ordinary magisterium are the teaching by bishops in their own dioceses or in regional synods, and the teaching by Popes in their encyclical letters. Although the Second Vatican Council was an extraordinary event, its documents represent what we mean here by 'ordinary' teaching, since this council chose not to use the authority it had to define any new dogma of Catholic faith.

An increasingly important exercise of such ordinary magisterium of bishops is seen in the doctrinal statements which are issued by episcopal conferences. Prominent among such statements since Vatican II have been the documents issued by the combined conferences of the bishops of Latin America at Medellín and Puebla, and the recent pastoral of the conference of the bishops of the United States on nuclear warfare. Archbishop Hickey of Washington, D.C. spoke of the magisterial role of episcopal conferences at a meeting of the American bishops at Collegeville, in June 1982:[4]

> We have to ask if there is in fact a magisterium that is exercised by episcopal conferences. The council speaks of the magisterium of the whole college (either joined with the pope in council or teaching as one body dispersed in the world) and it speaks of the magisterium of the individual bishop in his local church. But the council does not speak of any magisterium of episcopal conferences. However, one would have to be quite blind and deaf to reality if he denied that the statements of episcopal conferences do have an effective impact on the pastoral life of local dioceses and beyond. How many have not relied on the pastoral letters of episcopal conferences to find pastoral solutions to burning moral issues? How many times are priests and people not referred to the teaching of our conference and of other conferences? Many of the pastoral letters of conferences play an important role in the life of the church. We have to admit, then, that the conference offers the most effective vehicle nationally for our teaching office. Its statements have impact through the media and through decisions and parochial applications in the life of our country. Our collective exercise of the teaching office is

necessary to answer specific challenges that arise for us from the collective life of the nation.

Important as this 'collective exercise of the teaching office' by episcopal conferences has come to be in the modern church, it obviously does not have the authority proper to the whole episcopal college together with the pope. If an episcopal conference takes a position which does not express the unanimous view of the participating bishops, the conference does not have the authority to require assent on that position from all the Catholics of the region which the conference represents. Perhaps Cardinal Ratzinger had this in mind when he raised the question whether episcopal conferences have a mandate to teach.[5] However, Archbishop Hickey's statement about the importance and effectiveness of this collective exercise of the bishops' teaching office surely reflects the reality of life in the Church today. His view is confirmed by the new Code of Canon Law, whose canon 753 attributes authoritative magisterium to Catholic bishops, whether they are teaching individually, or together in episcopal conferences and particular councils.

Universal ordinary magisterium

The term 'universal ordinary magisterium' refers to the concordant teaching of the whole Catholic episcopate together with the Pope, apart from the rather rare occasions when the bishops are gathered in an ecumenical council.

The first reference to this ordinary magisterium of the episcopate in the documents of the Holy See is found in the letter 'Tuas libenter' of Pius IX (21 Dec. 1863), in which he insisted on the obligation of Catholic teachers and writers to believe not only what has been expressly defined by ecumenical councils or by a pope, but also what is taught as divinely revealed by 'the ordinary magisterium of the Church dispersed throughout the world' (D-S 2879).[6] Not surprisingly, the First Vatican Council echoed this statement of Pius IX and gave it the weight of a conciliar definition, when it declared in its *Dogmatic Constitution on the Catholic Faith*: 'All those things are to be believed with Catholic and divine faith which are contained in the Word of God, written or handed on, and are proposed by the Church either by a solemn judgment or by its ordinary and universal magisterium as divinely revealed and to be believed as such'. (D-S 3011).

In this statement of Vatican I the term 'solemn judgment' refers to the act by which a doctrine is defined; hence the term 'ordinary' refers to the kind of teaching by which doctrines are not defined. It is also clear from the *Acta* of Vatican I that the term 'universal magisterium' refers to the teaching of the whole episcopate with the pope, and not to the teaching of the pope alone, even when this is directed to the universal Church.[7]

The question has been raised whether this statement of Vatican I defines the *infallibility* of the ordinary universal magisterium. It certainly does not do so explicitly, nor is it likely that it was the intention of the Council to define it implicitly in this Constitution, since questions about the magisterium were still to be treated in the Constitution on the Church. However, it might be said to follow as a theological conclusion from the obligation on all the faithful to believe what is taught by this magisterium, in view of the basic principle that the whole Church cannot err in its faith.

While the Second Vatican Council did not define the infallibility of the ordinary universal magisterium either (in fact, it chose not to define anything), it did explicitly state the conditions under which it is infallible. I have already quoted the pertinent text at the beginning of this chapter; now let us examine it in detail.

'Although the individual bishops do not enjoy the prerogative of infallibility, they can nevertheless proclaim Christ's doctrine infallibly.'

Since the first clause denies to individual bishops the prerogative of infallibility, the 'they' who can speak infallibly are evidently the bishops taken collectively: in other words, it is the *episcopal college as such* which enjoys the prerogative of infallibility. Now if the individual bishops are not infallible, the mere sum of them would not be infallible either. So in some real way, any infallible teaching by the bishops must involve a *collegial* exercise of their teaching authority. This of course requires the participation of the pope as head of the college.

'This is so, even when they are dispersed around the world . . .'

In other words, the episcopal college can teach infallibly not only when it is gathered in an ecumenical council, but also when dispersed around the world. But the problem is: how can the dispersed college teach in a collegial way? The following clauses provide the answer.

'. . . provided that while maintaining the bond of unity among themselves and with Peter's successor . . .'

The Latin term which is translated as 'bond of unity' is *communionis nexum*: 'bond of communion.' This undoubtedly refers to what is elsewhere in *Lumen gentium* called the 'bond of hierarchical communion' which links bishops with one another and with the pope. According to LG 22 this bond of hierarchical communion is a requisite for membership in the episcopal college. Since this involves acceptance of the authority of the pope as head of the college, it follows that the episcopal college to which Vatican II attributes infallible magisterium is the Roman Catholic episcopate. This is consistent with the position that such councils as Trent and Vatican I spoke infallibly when they defined dogmas of faith. However, the question may be raised whether it is consistent with the decision taken at Vatican II no longer to assert a total and exclusive identification between the Church of Christ and the Roman Catholic Church. I believe that it is, since this decision did not prevent the same Council from saying that the unity which Christ gave to his Church subsists indefectibly in the Catholic Church (UR 4, c). If the Church's unity in the faith subsists in the Catholic Church, one can also expect to find that the infallible magisterium which is intended to be the human agency of that unity also subsists in the Catholic Church. If infallible magisterium required the unanimity of all validly ordained bishops, the Church would have lacked such a magisterium since 1054.

'. . . and while teaching authentically . . .'

We have seen in an earlier chapter that the word translated here as 'authentically' would be better rendered as 'authoritatively', or 'with their pastoral authority'. It is a question not of what bishops might hold as private opinions, but of what they do when, as 'teachers endowed with the authority of

Christ, they preach to the people committed to them the faith they must believe and put into practice' (LG 25).

'. . . on a matter of faith or morals . . .'

This phrase is used to describe the object about which the magisterium can teach authoritatively and, in some instances, infallibly. Since our second question in this chapter concerns the exact limits of this object, I shall postpone discussion of it for now.

'. . . they concur in a single viewpoint . . .'

This 'concurring in a single viewpoint' is evidently what gives a *collegial* character to the teaching of the dispersed bishops. The question that arises is: how can it be demonstrated that on some point of doctrine which has never been solemnly defined or been the subject of a conciliar vote, the whole Catholic episcopate is authoritatively teaching the same thing?

It would not seem to be enough to say that Roman Catholic bishops do not contradict the official teaching of the pope, and that therefore it can be presumed that they are all teaching whatever the pope has taught (e.g. in his encyclicals). For it is possible that some ordinary papal teaching, while not openly contradicted, might be given a rather passive reception or might even be qualified by a significant number of bishops. Hence, to be able to say that the whole episcopal college concurs in a single viewpoint in its authoritative teaching, it is necessary to show that the bishops have come to agreement through exercising their function as 'judges of faith and morals' (cf. LG 25). Furthermore, they must concur in this single viewpoint: *'. . . as definitively to be held'* (*tamquam definitive tenendam*).

This phrase was not in the original draft of *Lumen gentium*, and is a very significant addition to the text. Since it has the ring of a technical theological term, it is helpful to see how this term is used in the standard manuals of ecclesiology. The manual which was probably most widely used in the decades prior to Vatican II was that of J. Salaverri, S.J. His explanation of the term is as follows: 'Definitive tenendam doctrinam docent episcopi qui summo suae auctoritatis gradu ad assensum irrevocabilem fideles obligant.'[8] I translate: 'The bishops teach a doctrine as definitively to be held when, with the

125

highest degree of their authority, they oblige the faithful to give irrevocable assent to it.'

In his commentary on this article of *Lumen gentium*, Karl Rahner gives to this phrase the same meaning which Salaverri gave to it. He says:

> The text states explicitly that there can be question of the infallible teaching of the ordinary magisterium . . . only when the unanimous teaching of the whole episcopate proposes a matter of faith or morals 'to be held definitively' (*tamquam definitive tenendam*). An absolutely strict and irreformable assent must be explicitly called for. . . . Hence not every doctrine taught unanimously by the whole episcopate is of itself infallible, even when it deals with faith or morals or intends to do so. (The draft of 10 November 1962, no. 30, pp. 29-31, did not contain the clause *tamquam definitive tenendam*, which is very important in judging the intention of the final text). Only unanimity thus determined is a criterion which we can use of the infallibility of the doctrine proposed. The text does not, of course, take up the difficult question, which can be of practical consequence at times, of how this specially qualified unanimity is to be ascertained by the faithful who are bound to believe.[9]

Rahner further elucidates this question in his article on 'Magisterium' in *Sacramentum Mundi*, where he says:

> When a dogma is to be taught by the ordinary magisterium of the whole episcopate, without conciliar or papal definition — as is quite possible — it is not enough that a doctrine be propounded with moral unanimity by the whole episcopate. It is further required that the doctrine be explicitly propounded 'tamquam definitive tenendam' (LG 25). Hence mere *de facto* universality of Church doctrine related to the faith is not enough. It has often been assumed in the past, with practical effects, that a doctrine is irreformable in the Church simply because it has been generally taught without clearly notable contradiction over a considerable period of time. This view runs counter to the facts, because many doctrines which were once universally held have proved to be problematic or erroneous, and is fundamentally unsound.[10]

126

One might ask why Rahner calls 'fundamentally unsound' the view that a doctrine is irreformable simply because it has been generally taught without clearly notable contradiction over a considerable period of time. If I am not mistaken, it is because this view does not make the important distinction between what are merely commonly held opinions in the Church, and beliefs to which the Church is irrevocably committed. It is only with regard to the latter that there are solid grounds for maintaining that the Church is infallible. And therefore it is only when the magisterium obliges the faithful to give irrevocable assent to its teaching that it can be said to teach infallibly.

It is time now to examine the second question raised by the claim that the sinfulness of artificial contraception has been infallibly taught by the ordinary universal magisterium: namely, the question of the limits of the object of infallible magisterium, and, in particular, the question of the so-called 'secondary object' of infallibility.

The object of infallible magisterium

I have quoted the key statement of *Lumen gentium* on this issue at the beginning of the chapter, but it is worth quoting again:

> This infallibility with which the divine Redeemer willed His Church to be endowed in defining a doctrine of faith and morals extends as far as extends the deposit of divine revelation, which must be religiously guarded and faithfully expounded.[11]

In this sentence we find first a generic description of the object of infallibility as 'doctrine of faith and morals'; this is then distinguished into a *primary object*: 'the deposit of revelation', and a *secondary object*, which, as we shall see, is intended by the clause: 'which must be religiously guarded and faithfully expounded'. Let us first consider what is meant by the term 'doctrine of faith and morals'.

Doctrine of faith and morals

This generic description of the object of pastoral teaching authority is used no less than five times in *Lumen gentium* 25, which also gives us an illuminating paraphrase of it, when it says that the role of bishops is to 'preach to the people committed to them the faith they must believe and put into practice'. This clearly corresponds to the term *res fidei et morum*, and indicates that while some matters of faith are simply to be believed, others are to be both believed and put into practice.

A primary source for the distinction between matters of 'faith' and matters of 'practice' is the description which the Council of Trent gives of the Gospel as 'fontem omnis et salutaris veritatis et morum disciplinae.'[12] Here the 'Gospel' (not meaning a book, but the whole Christian revelation) is described as the source of all saving truth, and of the practically untranslatable *disciplina morum*; in any case one must resist the temptation to translate it literally as 'moral discipline'. In the language of Trent, *disciplina* means instruction or teaching; and *mores* includes far more than what we call 'morals'; actually it includes everything that the Gospel reveals about the Christian way of life: how to live, how to pray, how to worship God . . .[13] Perhaps the English word that comes closest to the Tridentine sense of *mores* is 'practices', so that *res fidei et morum* would be better translated 'matters pertaining to (Christian) faith and practice.' I insert the word 'Christian' to bring out the fact that for Trent, not only the 'salutary truth' but also the *disciplina morum* has the Gospel as its source.

It further clarifies the sense of this term to know that according to the Council of Trent, not everything that is contained in Sacred Scripture would be a matter of Christian faith or practice. This is brought out in Trent's decree on the interpretation of Scripture, which specifies that it is the Church's province to judge the interpretation of Scripture 'in rebus fidei et morum ad aedificationem doctrinae christianae pertinentium' — 'in matters of faith and practice which pertain to the upbuilding of Christian doctrine.'[14] This clearly presumes that not everything found in the Bible falls into this category. A modern confirmation of this idea is found in the encyclical *Divino Afflante Spiritu* of Pope Pius XII, who speaks of the broad areas of Scripture in which Catholic exegetes enjoy complete freedom of research, in view of the fact that 'the norms given by the Church have to do only with matters of faith and morals' (D-S 3831).

128

The important conclusion to be drawn from the consistent description of the proper object of pastoral magisterium as *res fidei et morum*, is that the bishops and the pope cannot claim to speak authoritatively, much less infallibly, unless the matter about which they speak pertains to Christian belief or to the practice of the Christian way of life. In some real way, the *doctrina de fide vel moribus* has to go back to the Gospel as its source.

Now there are two ways in which something can pertain to this object of pastoral magisterium: either directly, as formally contained in the Gospel message; or indirectly, as something in itself not revealed, but necessary for the defence and explanation of Gospel truth.

Matters of Christian belief and practice which are formally revealed constitute what is called the 'deposit of faith'; this is the *primary* object of the magisterium. It embraces everything that God has revealed to us 'for the sake of our salvation' (DV 11).

Other things which are not in themselves formally revealed, but still pertain to the Christian faith and practice insofar as they are required for the defence and explanation of the Gospel, constitute the *secondary* object of the magisterium.

Let us now consider each of these in detail.

The primary object of magisterium: the 'deposit of faith'

We have already spoken of the notion of the deposit of faith in Chapter One. It will be recalled that this deposit cannot be thought of as a series of propositions in which the whole of divine revelation has been or could be expressed. As *Dei Verbum* puts it, 'Sacred tradition and sacred Scripture form one sacred deposit of the word of God, which is committed to the Church.' (DV 10). Now 'sacred tradition' includes all that the apostles 'received from the lips of Christ, from living with Him and from what He did, or what they had learned through the prompting of the Holy Spirit' (DV 7). All of this the apostles handed on 'by their oral preaching, by example, and ordinances,' and so 'the Church, in her teaching, life and worship, perpetuates and hands on to all generations all that she herself is, all that she believes' (DV 8). And 'consequently, it is not from sacred Scripture alone that the Church draws her certainty about everything which has been revealed' (DV 9).

Now this does not mean that we should think of 'sacred tradition' as a certain number of revealed truths which were not written down in the inspired Scriptures, but were transmitted orally by the apostles and then handed on by word of mouth in the Church for generations until they eventually surfaced in some later Christian writings. There is no sound reason to think that there was such a body of revealed truths being explicitly taught and handed on from apostolic times, that would add significantly to what was transmitted in the writings that were eventually collected in the New Testament. Scripture and Tradition are not two distinct and independent bodies of truths; rather it is a question of two ways in which the Gospel — the total Christian message — is preserved and handed on in the Church, namely both in inspired writings, and in the 'teaching, life and worship of the Church'.

The word 'tradition' is used both of what is handed on (the objective sense) and of the process by which this is handed on (the active sense). In current English usage, Tradition (with a capital T) is generally used in the objective sense, to mean the Gospel, the Word of God, precisely as it has been handed on in the Church (*verbum Dei traditum*).

As we have already seen in Chapter One, it has sometimes happened that certain facts of the total Christian mystery have come to be objects of the explicit faith-consciousness of the Church only after centuries of contemplation of this mystery. It is our conviction that insights which are the fruit of such ecclesial contemplation can bring to light truths which are really contained in the total Christ-event, and therefore really contained in the Gospel, even though they are not found explicitly in Scripture or in the early records of explicit Christian belief. We have spoken of the Immaculate Conception and the Assumption as examples of such truths. It is important to see that as Catholics understand the matter, such truths as these are really there in the deposit of faith, even though it took centuries for the Church to come to see them clearly. Such truths as these, which are really, though only implicitly, contained in the Gospel, are still part of the deposit of revelation, and as such belong to the primary object of magisterium. They can be defined as dogmas of faith.

Now there is an important distinction to be made between Tradition, as *verbum Dei traditum*, and traditions, as particular beliefs and practices which have become traditional in the course of the Church's life. The mere fact that a particular belief or practice is traditional does not guarantee that it is really part of the Gospel — or indeed that it is fully in accord with the Gospel. It is possible for unsound practices or super-stitious beliefs to creep into such common usage that they gain a certain respectability as 'traditions'. Of course, on the other hand, there are particular traditions (such, for instance, as the practice of baptising the children of Christian parents) which are vehicles of genuine Tradition. There is need of dis-cernment to determine which traditions reflect the genuine message of the Gospel, and which might need to be reformed or even eliminated.[15] In regard to the question which we are now considering, the important point to note is that not every opinion or practice which has become traditional in the Church is part of the *verbum Dei traditum* which, along with Sacred Scripture, constitutes the deposit of revelation.

To sum up: whatever has been revealed for the sake of our salvation, whether explicitly or implicitly, whether written or handed on, is the primary object of the teaching of the magisterium.

An important conclusion follows from this: that it is only what is in the primary object of magisterium that can be defined as a 'dogma of faith'. A dogma of faith is a proposition which has been definitively declared to be part of the norma-tive faith of the Catholic Church, to be believed on the authority of God who has revealed it. Only what is in itself revealed can be proposed to be believed with such faith.

The secondary object of infallible magisterium

I have said above that the distinction between the primary and secondary objects of infallible magisterium can be found in the sentence of *Lumen gentium* which says that infallibility 'extends as far as extends the deposit of divine revelation, which must be religiously guarded and faithfully expounded'. I have said that the secondary object is intended by the last clause of this sentence. Now it must be admitted that this is not immediately obvious, and some commentators have been misled into taking this text to mean that infallibility is strictly limited to what is in the deposit of revelation: in other words, that Vatican II intends to say that the magisterium can speak infallibly only about what is formally revealed.[16]

131

However, the official explanation of this text given to the Council Fathers makes it quite clear that this was not the intention of the Theological Commission. Their explanation is as follows:

> Obiectum infallibilitatis Ecclesiae, ita explicatae, eandem habet extensionem ac depositum revelatum; ideoque extenditur ad ea omnia, et ad ea tantum, quae vel directe ad ipsum depositum revelatum spectant, vel quae ad idem depositum sancte custodiendum et fideliter exponendum requiruntur . . . (I translate): The object of the infallibility of the Church thus explained, has the same extension as the revealed deposit; hence it extends to all those things, and only to those, which either directly pertain to the revealed deposit itself, or are required in order that the same deposit may be religiously safeguarded and faithfully expounded . . .[17]

That the Theological Commission had in mind the distinction between a primary and a secondary object of infallibility is confirmed by their explanation of an emendation introduced into the sentence that speaks of the infallibility of the dispersed episcopate. The previous draft had said that the bishops could speak infallibly 'in revelata fide tradenda' (in handing on the revealed faith); this was changed to: 'res fidei et morum docentes' (in teaching matters of faith and morals); and the reason given for the change was: 'ne videatur infallibilitas corporis episcopalis coarctari tantum ad ea quae ab eodem ut divinitus revelata credenda proponuntur' (lest the infallibility of the episcopal body seem to be restricted to that only which is proposed to be believed as divinely revealed).[18] Clearly, the intention of this emendation was to avoid using an expression which might have seemed to exclude the secondary object of infallibility.

A third indication of the intention of the Theological Commission lies in the reply given to the complaint of four Council Fathers that nothing was said in the text about the infallibility of the Church with regard to things connected with the deposit of revelation. The Commission replied that this had been equivalently mentioned in the lines of the text which contained the clause: 'which must be religiously guarded and faithfully expounded'.[19]

The term used by these four Council Fathers: 'things connected with the deposit of revelation' is one that occasioned a great deal of difficulty at Vatican I. One of the problems which that council had to face in preparing the definition of papal infallibility was how to define the object about which the pope could speak infallibly. It was commonly admitted that this was not limited to revealed truth, and that there was a secondary object. The question was, how to define this secondary object. Some wished to use the term: 'things connected with the deposit of revelation', but others feared that this was too vague and could be used to justify a claim of infallibility for statements that the pope might make on practically any issue. The commission which drew up the draft of the Constitution on the Church at Vatican I chose a much more restrictive term to describe the secondary object: 'veritates quae necessario requiruntur, ut revelationis depositum integrum custodiatur' (truths which are necessarily required, in order that the deposit of revelation may be preserved intact).[20] As is well known, conciliar discussion on this Constitution had to be left unfinished, and when the Council came to define papal infallibility, it was decided not to try at that time to settle the question how to describe the secondary object. The solution adopted was simply to say that the object of papal infallibility was the same as that of the infallibility of the Church. As Bishop Gasser, spokesman for the *Deputatio de Fide* has explained the matter, since it is a dogma of faith that the Church is infallible concerning the primary object, it will also be a dogma of faith that the pope is infallible when he defines something that is contained in the primary object. On the other hand, it is not a dogma of faith, but is 'theologically certain', that the Church is infallible about the secondary object; hence it will also be theologically certain that the pope is infallible when he defines something in this secondary object.[21] The exact determination of the limits of this secondary object was left to the Constitution on the Church, which of course was never completed.

It was not done at Vatican II either. Since the close of Vatican II there has been one official statement on this issue, in the Declaration of the Sacred Congregation for the Doctrine of the Faith, *Mysterium Ecclesiae* of 24 June 1973. It is as follows:

Secundum doctrinam catholicam, infallibilitas magisterii Ecclesiae non solum ad fidei depositum se extendit, sed etiam ad ea, sine quibus hoc depositum rite nequit custodiri et exponi. Extensio vero illius infallibiltatis ad ipsum fidei depositum, est veritas quam Ecclesia inde ab initiis pro comperto habuit in promissionibus Christi esse revelatam' (According to Catholic doctrine, the infallibility of the magisterium of the Church extends not only to the deposit of faith, but also to those things, without which this deposit cannot be properly safeguarded and explained. However, the extension of this infallibility to the deposit of faith itself, is a truth which the Church has, from the beginning, held for certain to be revealed in the promises made by Christ.)[22]

I would call attention to two points in this statement of the Congregation. First, in describing the secondary object of infallibility, it does not use the broad term 'connected with revelation,' but the more restrictive 'things without which the deposit cannot be properly safeguarded and explained'. This is equivalent to the 'necessario requiruntur' of the schema of Vatican I. Secondly, while the infallibility of the magisterium with regard to its primary object is described as revealed truth, infallibility with regard to the secondary object is merely said to be 'according to Catholic doctrine'. This term is used of doctrines which are commonly held by Catholic theologians to be certain, but are not necessarily revealed truths, and are not dogmas of faith.

While the fact that there is a secondary object of infallibility is held by most Catholic theologians to be certain, there is by no means unanimity with regard to what is contained in this object. I think it would be fair to say that many manuals of ecclesiology prior to Vatican II reflected the broad description of the secondary object as 'truths connected with revelation'. The current trend would be to limit this object to what is strictly required in order that the magisterium might be able to defend and explain the Gospel. Such a limitation is certainly supported by the official documents we have cited.

It might be helpful at this point to mention some of the things which have been thought to come under the heading of the secondary object of infallibility, without attempting to enter into a full discussion here of the reasons for or against including each of them in that category. I shall focus on one issue, however, regarding the natural moral law, since this is crucial to the dispute whether the magisterium has spoken infallibly on the birth-control question.

Some examples of what is in the 'secondary object' of infallibility

1. *The condemnation of propositions contrary to revealed truth.* On this issue the First Vatican Council made the following statement in its *Constitution on the Catholic Faith* (D-S 3018):

> The Church, which along with its apostolic teaching office received the mandate to safeguard the deposit of faith, has the divinely conferred right and duty of condemning what is falsely called knowledge (1 Tim 6:20), lest anyone be led astray by empty deceit (cf. Col 2:8). Therefore all the Christian faithful are not only forbidden to defend as legitimate conclusions of science, such opinions as are recognized to be contrary to the doctrine of the faith, especially if they have been condemned by the Church, but they are moreover strictly obliged to hold them as errors which put on the false appearance of truth.

It is true that Vatican I does not explicitly claim that the Church speaks infallibly when it condemns such propositions, but it would seem that one could defend its capacity to do so, on the grounds that this might be strictly necessary for the defence of revealed truth. This would clearly be the case if the propositions in question were such as would exclude the very possibility of a reasonable act of faith — such, for instance, as that empirical verification is the only reasonable basis for certitude.

2. *Propositions that necessarily follow from revealed truth.* Here it is a question of true propositions which in themselves are not revealed, but which follow with strict necessity as conclusions of a syllogism in which one of the premises is revealed, the other or others naturally certain. Such 'theological conclusions' are said to be virtually revealed. They cannot be defined as dogmas of faith, because strictly speaking they are not part of the deposit of faith. But it is

conceivable that the definition of such a theological conclusion might be necessary in order to elucidate a revealed truth, or to exclude some proposition contrary to it, and this would justify including what is virtually revealed in the secondary object of infallibility.

3. *'Dogmatic facts'.* Certain kinds of historical facts which are not revealed are very closely connected with the exercise of the teaching office of the Church. For instance, the validity of conciliar definitions depends on the ecumenicity of the council. Hence, while the fact that a council was ecumenical is not a revealed truth, it might become necessary for the magisterium to settle the question of its ecumenicity infallibly.

Another kind of dogmatic fact is the compatibility or incompatibility of published opinions with revealed truth. This involves the determination of the objective meaning of what has been published, and the orthodox or heterodox character of this meaning. It is possible that in order to defend the faithful against error, the magisterium might have to issue a peremptory decision about some such published opinion. If the infallibility of such a decision were required for the defence of the faith, the issue could be said to fall within the secondary object of infallibility.

4. *The solemn canonisation of saints.* It has been commonly taught that the pope cannot err when he solemnly canonises a saint, declaring that person to have practised heroic virtue, to enjoy the vision of God, and to be worthy of veneration and imitation by the faithful. It is not clear to me that infallibility on such a question is necessarily required in order for the magisterium to be able to safeguard and explain the deposit of revelation.

Having seen a few examples of what the theological manuals have included in the secondary object of infallibility, let us look more closely now at the question whether the particular determinations of the natural moral law fall within the limits of this object.

The question of infallibility regarding the natural moral law

In discussing this question, I take it for granted that there is such a thing as the natural moral law, that this law is of divine origin, that we do not make this law but have to discover it by reflection on human experience, and that the existence of such a law, our obligation to live according to it, and some of its basic norms, are not only naturally knowable but also revealed.

What then is the role of the magisterium with regard to the natural moral law?

First of all, insofar as the natural moral law is also revealed, it belongs to the primary object of the magisterium. Hence the magisterium could infallibly define propositions of this law if they are clearly confirmed by revelation.

This raises the question: how much of the natural law is also revealed? More specifically: are not only the general principles, but also the particular applications of the natural law to specific kinds of human behaviour, contained in the deposit of revelation?

Some Catholic theologians of the past century asserted that the whole of the natural law is revealed, without making any distinction between the basic principles and more particular norms.[23]

Other more recent theologians, acknowledging the need of distinguishing between basic principles and particular norms, hold that the particular norms are contained at least obscurely, implicitly or virtually in the deposit of revelation, and hence it cannot be asserted that any part or requisite of the natural law is outside the scope of the Church's infallibility.[24]

With regard to this opinion, my first observation is that what is only virtually revealed is not really part of divine revelation, and could pertain only to the secondary object of infallibility: and this only if it were necessary for the magissterium to speak infallibly about it in order to safeguard or adequately explain revealed truth.

My second observation is that the strong trend in current moral thinking is to deny that the particular norms of the natural law are virtually revealed. To say that they are virtually revealed is to claim that they can be somehow deduced from the revealed principles, and most theologians now do not agree that we can arrive at the concrete determinations of the natural law by such a process of deduction from revealed premises.

It is my impression that few, if any, Catholic theologians would now claim that the particular applications of the natural law to the concrete moral issues of modern society, are contained in the deposit of revelation, whether formally or virtually. At the same time, most of them would agree that it is part of the role of the magisterium to speak with authority on such particular moral issues. The question then, is whether, from the authority with which the magisterium teaches particular norms of the natural moral law, the conclusion necessarily follows that it must be able to speak infallibly on these issues.

Some would say: if the magisterium can speak authoritatively, it must also be able to speak infallibly on these issues.

Others, and I believe the majority today, would say that from the fact that the magisterium can speak with pastoral authority on particular applications of the natural moral law, it does not follow that it can speak infallibly about them.

Let us now look more closely at what is involved in this discussion. The first point is the generally accepted premise that the magisterium has the right and duty to speak with authority on particular issues of the natural moral law.

The authority of the magisterium on questions of natural moral law

Vatican II deals with this question in two places. In *Gaudium et Spes*, apropos of the judgments which parents have to make about bringing more children into the world, the Council says:

> The parents themselves should ultimately make this judgment, in the sight of God. But in their manner of acting, spouses should be aware that they cannot proceed arbitrarily. They must always be governed according to a conscience dutifully conformed to the divine law itself, and should be submissive toward the Church's teaching office, which authentically interprets that law in the light of the gospel.[25]

There is every reason to believe that when the Council speaks of the 'divine law' in this context, it means the natural law, which of course is divine in its origin.

The other text of Vatican II on this issue is found in the Declaration on Religious Freedom, *Dignitatis Humanae*:

> In the formation of their consciences, the Christian faithful ought carefully to attend to the sacred and certain

doctrine of the Church. The Church is, by the will of Christ, the teacher of the truth. It is her duty to give utterance to, and authoritatively to teach, that Truth which is Christ Himself, and also to declare and confirm by her authority those principles of the moral order which have their origin in human nature itself.[26]

In view of this clear teaching of Vatican II, it does not seem necessary to multiply citations from the many papal encyclicals which have affirmed and exercised such teaching authority on concrete moral issues. One brief citation, however, will be given which suggests the reasoning on which the claim to teaching authority in these matters is based. It is a statement of Pope Pius XII:

The power of the Church is not bound by the limits of 'matters strictly religious,' as they say, but the whole matter of the natural law, its foundation, its interpretation, its application, so far as their moral aspect extends, are within the Church's power. For the keeping of the natural law, by God's appointment, has reference to the road by which man has to approach his supernatural end. But on this road the Church is man's guide and guardian in what concerns his supreme end. The apostles observed this in times past, and afterward from the earliest centuries the Church has kept to this manner of acting, and keeps to it today, not indeed like some private guide or adviser, but by virtue of the Lord's command and authority.[27]

I realise that this claim of the magisterium to teach with authority on questions of the natural moral law raises a number of questions, concerning, for instance, the obligation on the part of the faithful to form their consciences in conformity with such teaching, and the possibility, conditions and consequences of legitimate dissent from such teaching. I intend to consider such questions in a later chapter. For now it suffices to know that most Catholic theologians agree that the magisterium does have the right to speak with authority on such issues. They differ on whether one can rightly argue from its authority to its authority on this kind of question. Let us now look at the reasons given by those who argue for infallibility.

Arguments for the infallibility of the magisterium on questions of natural law

I shall begin with an argument that is rather simplistic, but is still sometimes heard: namely, that the magisterium is infallible in matters of faith and morals: but particular norms of the natural law are matters of morals; therefore the magisterium can speak infallibly about them.

The weakness of this argument is that it ignores the difference between what is revealed and what is not revealed with regard to morals. It presumes that the term 'matters of faith and morals' is rightly understood to include all moral issues, regardless of their relationship to the deposit of revelation. But this is certainly not the case. An illuminating proof of this is found in a response made by Bishop Gasser, the spokesman for the *Deputatio de Fide* of Vatican I, to a proposal to substitute the term 'principles of morals' for the more usual term: *res morum*. One of the reasons this proposal was rejected was given by Gasser as follows: 'Insuper principia morum possunt esse alia mere philosophica naturalis honestatis, quae non sub omni respectu pertinent ad depositum fidei.'[28] I translate: 'Moreover, principles of morals can be other merely philosophical principles of natural morality, which do not in every respect pertain to the deposit of faith.' This is striking evidence that the term *res fidei et morum* was not understood at Vatican I to embrace all possible questions of natural morality.

The second argument I shall consider is taken from the draft of the Constitution on the Church which was drawn up by the Preparatory Theological Commission and submitted to the first session of Vatican II in 1962. As is well known, this *schema* was found so unsatisfactory that it was withdrawn without ever being put to a vote. In Chapter 7, n. 29, this *schema* contained the following statement:

Cum vero idem magisterium sit ministerium salutis, quo homines docentur quam viam sequi debeant ut ad aeternam vitam valeant pervenire, ideo munus et ius illi competunt non modo revelatam sed et naturalem legem interpretandi et infallibiliter declarandi, et de obiectiva conformitate omnium actionum humanarum cum evangelica doctrina et divina lege iudicandi.[29] (I translate): Since this same magisterium is the ministry of salvation by which men are taught the way they must follow in order to be able to attain to eternal life, it therefore has the office and the right of interpreting and of infallibly declaring not only the revealed law but also the natural law, and of making judgments about the objective conformity of all human actions with the teaching of the Gospel and the divine law.

There is no officially promulgated document of the magisterium which makes such an explicit claim to infallibility in interpreting the natural law. It must surely be seen as significant that this claim was not retained in the new draft of the Constitution on the Church which was substituted for that of the Preparatory Commission, nor was any such claim subsequently introduced in any document of Vatican II.

What is the force of the argument offered for this claim in the statement we have quoted? It seems to suppose that the magisterium could not fulfil its ministry of teaching men the way to salvation unless it could interpret and declare the requirements of the natural law not only with pastoral authority but also with infallibility. But this is what needs to be proven. The omission of this claim to infallibility regarding the natural law, in the treatment of the magisterium in *Lumen gentium*, suggests that the bishops were not convinced of this argument.

The third argument for infallibility is the one suggested in the report of the minority of the commission of experts appointed by Pope Paul VI to study the question of birth control, prior to the encyclical *Humanae vitae*. The argument is based on the grave consequences of erroneous moral teaching by the Church. Speaking of the Church's teaching on the sinfulness of contraception, this report declares:

> ... there is no possibility that the teaching itself is other than substantially true. It is true because the Catholic Church, instituted by Christ to show men the sure road to eternal life, could not err so atrociously through all the centuries of its history. The Church cannot substantially err in teaching a very serious doctrine of faith or morals through all the centuries — even through one century — a doctrine constantly and insistently proposed as one necessarily to be followed in order to attain eternal salvation. The Church could not substantially err through so many

centuries — even through one century — in imposing very heavy burdens under grave obligation in the name of Jesus Christ as it would have erred if Jesus Christ does not in fact impose these burdens. The Catholic Church could not in the name of Jesus Christ offer to the vast multitude of the faithful, everywhere in the world, for so many centuries an occasion of formal sin and spiritual ruin on account of a false doctrine promulgated in the name of Jesus Christ.[30]

What is to be said of such an argument? It draws its conclusion, that the Church cannot err in its moral teaching, from two assertions: 1) that error in the Church's moral teaching would be the occasion of formal sin and spiritual ruin of the faithful; and 2) that it is impossible that the Church should be the cause or occasion of such harmful consequences.

One problem with this argument is that if it were valid, and its conclusion were true, it would also have to be true that the Church has never erred when it has taught something to be gravely sinful. The argument would have to be able to stand up to the test of history. As I am not a historian of moral theology, I leave this question to those who are competent in the field.

Another problem is that this argument seems to suppose that we know how much spiritual harm God is prepared to allow the leaders of the Church to be the occasion of. How can it be shown that erroneous moral teaching would cause more spiritual harm than has been caused by the scandalous conduct of which Church leaders have certainly been guilty? If God has permitted the latter, why could He not permit the former as well?

Now we come to the arguments which John C. Ford and Germain Grisez have proposed in a recent article, the whole burden of which is to prove that all the conditions required for the infallibility of the ordinary universal magisterium have been fulfilled in the case of the Church's teaching on the sinfulness of contraception.[31] Essentially, what they wish to prove is that this moral norm falls within at least the secondary object of infallibility, and that it has actually been infallibly taught, because it has been taught for a long time by the whole Catholic episcopate as a norm definitely to be held.

The arguments of Ford and Grisez for the infallibility of the Church's teaching on contraception

My purpose in this discussion, as I have said at the beginning of this chapter, is to illustrate the ecclesiological principles regarding the infallibility of the ordinary universal magisterium by applying them to the controverted question whether the sinfulness of contraception has been infallibly taught. Hence I shall be looking especially at the premises on which Ford and Grisez have based their arguments.

Let us look first at the premises on which they base their contention that the morality of contraception falls within at least the secondary object of infallible teaching. They present their position as follows:

> We do not assert that the norm is divinely revealed. This question is one from which we have prescinded. Our position rather is this: if the norm is not contained in revelation, it is at least connected with it as a truth required to guard the deposit as inviolable and to expound it with fidelity. . . . Admittedly, it does not seem there is any way to establish *conclusively* that this teaching either pertains to revelation or is connected with it apart from the fact that the ordinary magisterium has proposed the teaching in the manner in which it has, and the faithful as a whole until recently have accepted the norm as binding. But a similar state of affairs has been used as a basis for solemnly defining at least one dogma: that of the Assumption of the Blessed Virgin Mary.[32]

Let us now analyse this statement. The clause that begins 'apart from' clearly implies that there is one way to establish conclusively that the morality of contraception falls within at least the secondary object of infallibility: namely from the way the magisterium has proposed this teaching, and the way the faithful have accepted it. If I understand this correctly, what it means is that we can know for certain that this is a proper object for infallible teaching from the fact that the magisterium has taught it infallibly. And, as we shall see, the fact that the magisterium has taught it infallibly is seen in the fact that the magisterium has consistently taught it as an obligatory norm, binding under grave sin, and that the faithful have accepted it as such.

In support of this argument, Ford and Grisez appeal to what they see as a parallel, in the case of the definition of the dogma of the Assumption. In a footnote they point out where they see the analogy: 'In defining the dogma of the Assumption, Pius XII argues . . . from the universality of the acceptance of the doctrine as a matter of faith to its objective status as a truth pertaining to divine revelation.'[33]

Now it seems to me that the differences between these two issues are so great as to rule out the conclusion that Ford and Grisez wish to draw from the analogy between them. What justified the conclusion that the doctrine of the Assumption must be a revealed truth was the fact that for centuries it had been a matter of universal Christian *faith*. The major premise there was the infallibility of the whole People of God in its faith.

On the other hand, the fact that the faithful accepted the Church's teaching on contraception as binding does not prove that they accepted it as revealed or even as necessarily connected with revealed truth. Indeed, it seems likely that many of them accepted it simply as a binding law of the Church, which they had to observe whether they were convinced of its truth or not. So I do not see the parallel with the dogma of the Assumption as convincing.

My major difficulty with the argument that Ford and Grisez have proposed as the one that in their opinion would conclusively establish their case, is that it would eliminate the possibility of challenging any magisterial act that was claimed to be infallible by questioning whether the subject-matter of that act fell within the limits of the proper object of infallibility. In other words, the supposition of their argument seems to be: if the magisterium speaks in a definitive way about something, it must necessarily be the case that what they speak about is a proper object of infallible teaching. The question of the object would no longer be an independent criterion by which it could conceivably be judged that the magisterium had not really spoken infallibly, on the grounds that the matter on which it spoke was not a proper object of infallible teaching.

Against such a view I would argue that if it were true, there would be no point at all in the insistence of Vatican I and Vatican II that the magisterium can speak infallibly only on matters of faith and morals. It would have been necessary to say only this: whenever the magisterium speaks in a definitive way it must be speaking infallibly, because the very fact that it speaks in a definitive way would guarantee that what it speaks about would be a proper matter for infallible teaching. What then would have been the point of mentioning the limits of the matter about which the Church can teach infallibly? It seems to me that the supposition underlying the argument of Ford and Grisez would open the door to absolutism in the exercise of magisterium.

With regard to the other arguments which they offer in support of their view that the question of the morality of contraception falls within at least the secondary object of infallibility, I will say only that I believe that at most they would suffice to show that this moral teaching is connected with revelation; however, I do not think they show that it is so necessarily connected with revelation that the magisterium could not safeguard and expound revelation if it could not teach this particular norm with infallibility.

As we have just seen, the only argument which Ford and Grisez think would conclusively prove that the morality of contraception is a proper matter for infallible teaching is based on their contention that it has actually been infallibly taught. And their case that it has been infallibly taught is based on their contention that for many centuries it was taught by the universal Catholic episcopate as a moral norm *to be held definitively*. This brings us to the crucial question: how do they understand what it means to teach something as to be held definitively?

Before discussing the answer which Ford and Grisez give to this question, I remind the reader that I have already treated it earlier in this chapter, where I expressed my agreement with the view of Salaverri and Rahner that to propose a teaching to be held definitively means to oblige the faithful to give it their irrevocable assent. This is quite different from the way that Ford and Grisez explain what it means to teach something as to be held definitively. They say:

> A point of teaching surely is proposed as one to be held definitively if a bishop proposes it in the following way: not at his option but as part of his duty to hand on the teaching he has received; not as doubtful or even as very

145

probable but as certainly true; and not as one which the faithful are free to accept or to reject but as one which every Catholic must accept.[34]

Now it seems to me that there is a very real difference between authoritative teaching which calls upon the faithful to give their assent to it as certainly true, and the kind of teaching which proposes a doctrine as irreformably true and calls for an irrevocable assent.

The question, then, is: which of these is the correct interpretation of what it means to teach something as definitively to be held? Is this the same thing as to teach something as certainly true? I find the following remarks of John Reed helpful in answering this question:

Besides infallible teachings of the magisterium, however, whether in solemn definition or in constant and universal ordinary teaching, there is that exercise of its authority which, while not infallible, is still authentic and binding. This is perhaps even more important in matters of natural law than in other areas of Catholic doctrine. In this connection it is important to distinguish the notions of infallibility and certainty. In matters of conduct, a doctrine which is not taught with the plenitude of infallibility may still be taught with certainty, in the sense of moral, practical, certitude, so as to exclude any solidly probable opinion to the contrary here and now, i.e. with the effect that at a given time a particular mode of conduct is certainly licit or certainly illicit, without the abstract question of its relation to right order being definitively closed. Infallibility excludes the absolute possibility of error. Certitude, in the sense of moral, or practical, certitude, excludes the prudent, proximate fear of error. While such a teaching does not altogether close the question from a speculative point of view, it does normally preclude the possibility of acting in contradiction of the doctrine, relying on the principle of probabilism.[35]

This explanation by Reed of how a mode of conduct can be taught as certainly illicit without the question of its relation to right order being definitively closed also brings out the weakness of the principal argument which Ford and Grisez have advanced to show that the sinfulness of contraception was being taught as a moral doctrine to be held definitively.

146

They base this claim primarily on the fact that the magisterium condemned contraceptive behaviour as gravely sinful. And, in their view, 'to propose a norm excluding some kind of act as mortally sinful is to propose a teaching to be held definitively'.[36] Now, when Reed speaks of teaching that an act is 'certainly illicit', I think it safe to assume that he would include 'gravely illicit'. And yet he insists that such teaching does not necessarily mean that the speculative question is definitively closed.

Karl Rahner takes the same position in his reply to Hans Küng, who argued, as Ford and Grisez do, from the fact that the bishops taught that contraception was gravely sinful, to the conclusion that they must have been teaching this as a doctrine to be held definitively.[37] Rahner replied:

> The only question is whether the teaching of Pius XI and *Humanae vitae* is proclaimed as a teaching that must be 'definitively' affirmed ... Küng has not at all proven that such an absolute assent was demanded – which is something completely different from a very urgent claim on an assent which is not qualified as absolutely definitive (even over a long period of time and under the appeal to Church teaching authority.) It is also something completely different from the assertion that such a theoretical teaching implies a serious moral obligation before God.[38]

In other words, it is one thing to teach that something involves a serious moral obligation; it is quite another to claim that this teaching is now absolutely definitive, and demands an irrevocable assent. But if the argument proposed by Ford, Grisez and Küng were valid, it would mean that the Church could not declare any mode of conduct gravely wrong unless it were prepared to make an irreversible judgment on the matter. This would practically rule out any ordinary, non-infallible exercise of the Church's teaching authority on moral issues.

The other argument which Ford and Grisez use to show that the doctrine on contraception was being taught as to be held definitively is that it was often proposed as a divinely revealed moral norm. They argue from this in the following way:

> The teaching on the morality of contraception often was

proposed as a moral norm divinely revealed. Since it was proposed as revealed, a fortiori it was proposed as a teaching *to be held definitively*. We prescind from the question whether the evidence alleged to show that the condemnation of contraception is divinely revealed does or does not show this. The point we wish to make is simply this: when one who is proposing a teaching appeals to divine revelation to confirm the truth of what he proposes, he implicitly calls for an assent of divine faith, and thus proposes the teaching as one to be held definitively.[39] . . .
If one considers the explicit appeals made to Gen 38: 9-10 together with the implicit appeals made to the same passage, to Rom 1:26-27, and to the Ten Commandments, one realizes that most who handed on the Catholic teaching on contraception claimed the authority of Scripture, which they believed to be the authority of divine revelation, in support of this teaching. Whether one thinks this claim was valid or not — a question we are not considering here — no one can deny that those who made it proposed the teaching on behalf of which they made it as a moral norm *to be held definitively*.[40]

Now it seems to me that if this argument were valid, it would eliminate practically all ordinary, non-definitive teaching by the magisterium. For, whenever any appeal was made to Scripture in support of what was being taught, this would automatically become definitive teaching. Are we to conclude that the popes, who regularly appeal to Scripture in their encyclicals, have in all such cases been proposing their doctrine as definitively to be held?

The more common opinion: particular norms of natural law are not object of infallible teaching
Having spent perhaps too much time examining the arguments of those who claim that the magisterium can infallibly determine the concrete norms of the natural moral law, I shall conclude this chapter with a brief consideration of the views of those who reject this claim.
First a word about the opinion of the Catholic moralist, Daniel Maguire, who seems to rule out the possibility that the magisterium could speak with infallibility on any moral issue whatever, when he says flatly that the term 'infallible' does

not in fact aptly describe the nature or function of the moral magisterium.[41] However, it seems that what he has in mind as the 'function of the moral magisterium' is 'to apply the moral vision of the Gospel to complex natural law questions such as are presented by medical ethics, genetics, business ethics, international law, social reconstruction, and war and peace.'[42] In this case, his position, while more radically stated, would not differ substantially from the more common view, which distinguishes between the more general principles of the natural law, and the determination of the requirements of the natural law when it is applied to the concrete moral problems that face people in the modern world.

I believe that the majority of Catholic moral theologians today would subscribe to the following propositions concerning the 'moral magisterium'.

1. At least some of the basic principles of the natural law are also formally revealed, and as such, belong to the primary object of infallible magisterium. It does not seem that any such moral principle has ever been solemnly defined, but since Vatican I declared that the pope has the same infallibility which the Church has in defining 'doctrine of faith and morals', it seems necessary to conclude that at least some doctrines regarding morals could be infallibly defined. Catholic moralists generally agree that those basic norms of the natural law which have also been revealed to us 'for the sake of our salvation' could be infallibly taught, either by solemn definition or by the universal ordinary magisterium.

2. The magisterium is competent to exercise its ordinary teaching authority by applying the natural law, in the light of the Gospel, to the particular and concrete moral issues facing individuals and society today. It is true that at least one Catholic moralist, Jakob David, invokes a distinction between 'magisterial' and 'pastoral' authority, and denies that the competence of the hierarchy regarding concrete issues of natural law can be called 'magisterial' authority.[43] But it seems to me that he is identifying magisterial authority with the capacity to teach infallibly. He explains 'pastoral authority' regarding the natural law as the competence of the bishops and pope to guide the faithful in the formation of their consciences. Following St Thomas, who speaks of the *magisterium cathedrae pastoralis* of the bishops, I see no reason not to

speak of the teaching function of the bishops, especially in its ordinary exercise, as 'pastoral magisterium'. It is this magisterium which they exercise when they help the faithful to form their consciences on concrete problems of the natural law.

3. The concrete determinations of the natural law with regard to the complex problems facing people today are neither formally nor virtually revealed. That is to say, they are not among the truths which God has revealed to us for the sake of our salvation, nor can they be strictly deduced from any such truths. It is now generally agreed that the process by which we arrive at the knowledge of the concrete norms of the natural law is through shared reflection on human experience; it is rather an inductive process than a deductive one. Christians seek the answers to concrete moral problems in the light of the Gospel, but these answers are not conclusions that follow with metaphysical certitude from revealed premises.

4. Nor can it be shown that the magisterium would not be able to defend and explain the moral principles and values of the Gospel unless it could infallibly determine the correct application of the natural law to the concrete and complex problems of modern man. No doubt these are moral issues, and they are connected with the moral values of Christian revelation. But, as we have seen, in order for something which is neither formally nor virtually revealed to fall within the 'secondary object' of infallibility, it has to be so necessarily connected with revealed truth that the magisterium would be unable to defend or explain revelation itself if it could not speak infallibly about this also. Since 'nothing is to be considered infallibly defined or declared unless this is manifestly the case',[44] the burden of proof is on those who would claim that the magisterium could not defend or explain some revealed truth unless it could infallibly determine some particular application of the natural law.

5. Finally, to say that a proposition has been infallibly taught is to say that it must be irreversibly true. From this it follows that for a moral norm to be the proper object of infallible teaching, it must be a norm which, at some point in history, can be so irreversibly determined that no future development could possibly call for the substantial revision

150

of this determination of what the natural law requires. It is the more common opinion of Catholic moralists today that the concrete norms of the natural law simply do not admit of such irreversible determination.

This judgment is based on an understanding of the very process by which we arrive at our knowledge of the natural law as it applies to concrete moral issues. This understanding involves the following elements: (a) the moral problems facing mankind today tend to be particularly complex; (b) while the Gospel sheds light on these problems, it does not provide their solution; (c) an indispensable role in the process of finding answers to concrete moral problems is played by human intelligence, reflecting on human experience; (d) Christians share this arduous search along with all other men of good will.

Several passages of *Gaudium et Spes* suggest that this was the approach of Vatican II to this issue. For instance:

> Through loyalty to conscience Christians are joined to other men in the search for truth and for the right solution to so many moral problems which arise both in the life of individuals and from social relationships (GS 16).

> The Church is guardian of the heritage of the divine Word and draws religious and moral principles from it, but she does not always have a ready answer to every question. Still, she is eager to associate the light of revelation with the experience of mankind in trying to clarify the course upon which mankind has just entered (GS 33).

> Having set forth the dignity of the human person and his individual and social role in the universe, the Council now draws the attention of men to the consideration, in the light of the Gospel and of human experience, of some more urgent problems deeply affecting the human race at the present day (GS 46).

Now if the process by which we have to arrive at our knowledge of the concrete norms of the natural law is by the exercise of human intelligence, reflecting on human experience, it must be admitted that there are elements in this process which militate against the possibility of reaching an absolutely irreversible determination of a concrete norm of the natural law. One is the fact that human experience is an

151

on-going, open-ended reality. We can never exclude the possibility that future experience, hitherto unimagined, might put a moral problem into a new frame of reference which would call for a revision of a norm that, when formulated, could not have taken such new experience into account.

Another factor is that human nature itself is not a static, closed reality, but a dynamic, evolving one. As Karl Rahner explains it, the immediate norm of natural morality is man himself in his concrete nature. But this concrete nature of man in all its dimensions (biological, social, etc.) is itself precisely subject to a most far-reaching process of change. While some universal moral norms may be said to flow from the metaphysical nature of man, the particular norms are based on human nature as it exists in history, as subject to change. Such norms cannot lay claim to any absolute or permanent validity.[45]

It is the consideration of such factors as these in the process by which we come to know the particular norms of the natural law, which has led most of the Catholic theologians who have written on this question in recent years, to the conclusion that such norms are not proper matter for irreformable teaching.[46] This judgment rules out not only the possibility of the infallible definition of such a norm, but also the claim that such a norm has ever been, or could be, infallibly taught by the ordinary universal magisterium.

However, this judgment would not at all rule out the exercise of that ordinary, non-infallible magisterium by which the pastors of the Church offer their authoritative guidance to the faithful for the formation of their conscience on complex moral issues. It is to this ordinary magisterium that we must now turn our attention.

7.

The Non-Definitive Exercise of Papal and Conciliar Teaching Authority

In his opening speech on the first day of the Second Vatican Council (11 October 1962), Pope John XXIII called upon this council to exercise a teaching authority that would be predominantly pastoral in character.[1] In response to this papal invitation, the council chose not to exercise its authority to condemn any propositions as heretical or to define any new dogmas of faith. In other words, it chose not to pronounce any solemn judgments that would set new, more precise limits to the communion of Catholic faith, and exclude from this communion those who refused to accept such solemn decrees.

At the same time, as I have already had occasion to mention, the Secretary General of the Council officially promulgated a statement of the Theological Commission concerning the obligatory force of the non-definitive teaching of Vatican II. According to this statement, the teaching of this Council, even though not defined, is still 'doctrine of the supreme teaching authority of the Church', which 'each and every member of the faithful is obliged to accept and embrace according to the mind of the Sacred Synod'.[2]

What the Theological Commission said about the teaching of the Council, the Council itself said about the non-definitive teaching of the pope. I shall first quote the official Latin text, because it will be necessary to discuss the translation of some of the terms used:

> Hoc vero religiosum voluntatis et intellectus obsequium singulari ratione praestandum est Romani Pontificis authentico magisterio etiam cum non ex cathedra loquitur; ita nempe ut magisterium eius supremum reverenter agnos-

catur, et sententiis ab eo prolatis sincere adhaereatur, iuxta mentem et voluntatem ipsius, quae se prodit praecipue sive indole documentorum, sive ex frequenti propositione eiusdem doctrinae, sive ex dicendi ratione.[3]

This religious submission of will and of mind must be shown in a special way to the authentic teaching authority of the Roman Pontiff, even when he is not speaking *ex cathedra*. That is, it must be shown in such a way that his supreme magisterium is acknowledged with reverence, the judgments made by him are sincerely adhered to, according to his manifest mind and will. His mind and will in the matter may be known chiefly either from the character of the documents, from his frequent repetition of the same doctrine, or from his manner of speaking.

A comparison of these two statements shows that they are practically identical. Each of them speaks of the teaching authority involved (whether of the council or the pope) as 'supreme', and each insists on the obligation on the part of the faithful to 'accept and embrace' or to 'adhere to' what is taught, 'according to the mind' of pope or council.

It is obvious that the focus of both of these statements is on the obligatory force of this non-definitive exercise of the magisterium. And it has to be admitted that this is a one-dimensional treatment of the question. Our discussion, then, while it has to include the exegesis of the conciliar text, must embrace other aspects of this 'ordinary' magisterium which are left unmentioned in the conciliar documents.

Since the most familiar examples of the non-definitive exercise of papal teaching authority are the papal encyclicals, let us begin with a few remarks about them.

Papal encyclicals

Pope Gregory XVI is generally credited with being the first pope to use an encyclical letter as the vehicle of his pastoral teaching authority; the first such encyclical was his *Mirari Vos* of 15 August 1832. Successive popes, especially Pius IX, Leo XIII, Pius XI and Pius XII used this teaching instrument with increasing frequency and with an increasing emphasis on its obligatory force. Especially during the pontificate of Pius XII, there was a tendency in some circles of Catholic theology to attribute infallibility to the ordinary magisterium of the pope, and to require a response to it that hardly differed from the response required by a solemn dogmatic definition.[4]

While no pope went so far as to claim infallibility for his ordinary teaching, the high point in official papal statements regarding the obligatory character of such teaching is found in the encyclical *Humani generis* of Pius XII (August 12 1950).[5] This is my translation of the text:

Nor is it to be thought that what is set forth in Encyclical Letters does not of itself demand assent, on the grounds that in them the Pontiffs do not exercise the supreme power of their magisterium. For these things are taught with their ordinary teaching authority, of which the saying also holds: 'He who hears you, hears me' (Lk 10:16). And for the most part what is set forth and inculcated in Encyclical Letters already belongs to Catholic doctrine on other accounts. And if the Supreme Pontiffs, in their official documents, deliberately pass judgment on a matter hitherto controverted, it is evident to all that, in accordance with the mind and intention of the same Pontiffs, that question can no longer be considered a subject for free debate among theologians.

The draft of the Constitution on the Church prepared for Vatican II by the Preparatory Commission echoed this statement of Pope Pius XII, with one modification: in the final sentence it substituted 'public debate' for 'free debate', perhaps with the intention of recognising the liceity of some discussion among theologians, provided it was not 'public'.[6]

It can hardly be without some significance that this idea of the exclusion of debate among theologians, whether 'free' or 'public', concerning what had been taught in papal encyclicals, does not appear in the final Constitution on the Church ratified by Vatican II.

In the aftermath of the promulgation of the encyclical *Humanae Vitae* by Pope Paul VI, there has been a lively, and often vehement, discussion not only about the doctrine of that encyclical, but about the obligatory force of such teaching, the nature of the response it calls for, the possibility and the conditions for legitimate dissent, and the consequences thereof, especially regarding the liceity of following one's own judgment in moral matters if it differs from that of the pope. While in some respects this public debate has been painful, it has also served to bring out some important truths about this kind of teaching which were surely not unknown to the framers of *Lumen gentium*, but which they chose not to mention in the conciliar text.

One of the most significant contributions to the post-conciliar discussion of the ordinary papal magisterium has been made by the German bishops in their letter of 22 September 1967.[7] The following passages of that letter seem particularly worth quoting at some length here:

> At this point a difficult problem arises, calling for realistic discussion. It is one which today more than formerly threatens either the faith of many Catholics or their attitude of free and unreserved trust towards the teaching authorities of the Church. We refer to the fact that in the exercise of its official function this teaching authority of the Church can, and on occasion actually does, fall into errors. The fact that such a thing is possible is something of which the Church has always been aware and which she has actually expressed in her theology. Moreover she has evolved rules of conduct to cater for the kind of situations which arise from this. . . .
>
> Now let us consider the possibility or the fact of error in non-defined statements of doctrine on the part of the Church, recognising that these themselves may differ very widely among themselves in their degree of binding force. The first point to be recognised resolutely and realistically is that human life, even at a wholly general level, must always be lived 'by doing one's best according to one's lights' and by recognised principles which, while at the theoretical level they cannot be recognised as absolutely certain, nevertheless command our respect in the 'here and now' as valid norms of thinking and acting because in the existing circumstances they are the best that can be found. This is something that everyone recognises from the concrete experience of his own life. Every doctor in his diagnoses, every statesman in the political judgments he arrives at on particular situations and the decisions he bases on these, is aware of this fact. The Church too in her doctrine and practice cannot always and in every case allow herself to be caught in the dilemma of either arriving at a doc-

trinal decision which is ultimately binding or simply being silent and leaving everything to the free opinion of the individual. In order to maintain the true and ultimate substance of faith she must, even at the risk of error in points of detail, give expression to doctrinal directives which have a certain degree of binding force, and yet, since they are not *de fide* definitions, involve a certain element of the provisional even to the point of being capable of including error. Otherwise it would be quite impossible for her to preach or interpret her faith as a decisive force in real life or to apply it to each new situation in human life as it arises. In such a case the position of the individual Christian in regard to the Church is analogous to that of a man who knows that he is bound to accept the decision of a specialist even while recognising that it is not infallible.[8]

The 'reformable' character of non-definitive teaching

It seems impossible to fault the reasoning of the German bishops: if the non-definitive teaching of the magisterium is not infallible, it can be erroneous; if it is not irreformable, it can stand in need of correction. Indeed, they honestly recognise that such non-infallible teaching not only can be erroneous, but actually has been so; not only can need correction, but historically has been corrected.

In this respect, it is more fruitful to consider what the Second Vatican Council did than what it said. While in its treatment of the ordinary papal magisterium it spoke only of its obligatory force and said nothing about the possibility of its needing to be corrected, on several important issues the council clearly departed from previous papal teaching. One has only to compare the Decree on Ecumenism with such an encyclical as *Mortalium animos* of Pope Pius XI, or the Declaration on Religious Freedom with the teaching of Leo XIII and other popes on the obligation binding on the Catholic rulers of Catholic nations to suppress Protestant evangelism, to see with what freedom the Second Vatican Council reformed papal teaching. I think it would be true to say that the deepest divisions at Vatican II were between those bishops who saw the council as bound to affirm what had already been taught by the popes, and those who recognised the need for the Council to improve upon, and in some cases, to correct such teaching.

But the question remains: can teaching which does not claim to be infallible, and may be in fact erroneous, still be authoritative? And if so, on what grounds?

'Provisional', 'reformable', and still authoritative?

Again, I believe that the German bishops have given a sound reply to this question. As they point out, it is part of the role of the magisterium to interpret the faith as a decisive force in real life and to apply it to new human situations as they arise. It is incumbent on the magisterium to give directives to the faithful in matters of faith and morals, and the concrete situation can call for the issuing of such directives even when it is not yet possible to arrive at an irreformable decision. As the bishops insist, the Church cannot in such a case allow herself to be caught in the dilemma of either defining the issue or saying nothing at all. When there is confusion or doubt concerning matters pertaining to Christian belief or practice, it is up to the bearers of the pastoral magisterium to provide the authoritative guidance that is needed at the time. Obviously they can only provide the answer which they are convinced is true, and they are obliged to make every effort to be sure that what they will say is true. But it will not always be possible to provide an answer that could not possibly be seen eventually to need correction.

As a matter of fact, if we accept the opinion which is now more common among Catholic theologians to the effect that the concrete norms of the natural law are not a proper object for infallible teaching, it follows that this is a whole area wherein the magisterium, on the one hand, cannot make irreformable decisions, and on the other hand, has the duty to give authoritative guidance to the faithful for the formation of their moral judgments. As we have already seen in the previous chapter, Catholic theologians agree that the magisterium speaks with pastoral authority when it determines particular norms of the natural law, even though it does not, and, as most would say, cannot make irreformable pronouncements on matters of this kind.

The response called for by non-definitive papal and conciliar teaching

1. *The meaning of what Vatican II says about this.* In a

recent article, Bishop B.C. Butler has raised some questions concerning the interpretation of what Vatican II has said about the response called for by ordinary papal teaching, so I shall begin this section by looking at his suggestions as to how the pertinent passage of *Lumen gentium* should be understood.[9]

His first question has to do with the meaning of the *obsequium* which the text says is required by non-infallible papal teaching. The English translations edited by Abbott and by Flannery render *obsequium* by 'submission', but Bishop Butler finds this too strong a term. He notes that *obsequium* is used three times in *Lumen gentium* 25: first of the response due to the teaching of one's own bishop, then of the response due to the teaching of the Roman Pontiff, and finally of the *obsequium fidei* to be given to the dogmatic definitions of an ecumenical council. Obviously, different degrees of *obsequium* are called for by these three levels of teaching authority. Butler insists on the 'variable' sense of the term as used here, and concludes that when it is used of the response due to papal teaching, *obsequium* means no more than 'due respect'.[10]

With all due respect for the opinion of the Bishop, I must say that I believe that the published English translations are correct in using the word 'submission' when they render the phrase: 'religiosum voluntatis et intellectus obsequium'. First of all, according to the authoritative Latin Dictionary of Lewis and Short, the word *obsequium*, from *obsequi*, 'to follow' or 'to yield to', means 'compliance, yielding, consent, obedience, allegiance', and not mere 'respect'. Secondly, it is really difficult to see what would be meant by 'religious respect of will and mind'; whereas this phrase makes good sense when *obsequium* is translated by 'submission'. Thirdly, while there are certainly different degrees of *obsequium* required by the three kinds of magisterium that are mentioned in *Lumen gentium* 25, they can all be understood as degrees of 'submission', but 'due respect' is certainly not the meaning of *obsequium* in the term *obsequium fidei*.

The second question that Bishop Butler raises has to do with the meaning of the verb *adhaerere*. This verb is also used three times: of the response due to the teaching of the local bishop, the non-definitive teaching of the pope, and the

159

definitions of ecumenical councils. In each case the text speaks of an obligation to 'adhere' to the judgments made. It is Butler's view that the phrase: 'et sententiis ab eo prolatis sincere adhaereatur', which refers to the response due to the ordinary magisterium of the pope, is incorrectly translated in the Flannery edition of the documents by: 'and sincere assent be given to decisions made by him'. His objection is to the use of the English word 'assent', and is based on Newman's idea that assent must always be unconditional. Arguing that only infallible teaching can command unconditional assent, Butler concludes that 'non-infallible teaching cannot, taken by itself, generate assent.'[11]

Again, with all due respect, I must express my disagreement with his criticism of the published translations of this text.

First, I do not know what the phrase: 'sententiis sincere adhaerere' can mean if it does not mean to give one's sincere assent. What other translation would do justice to the Latin words used here? Secondly, the Theological Commission also spoke of the response called for by the non-definitive teaching of the council itself. The terms used in that instance were: 'doctrinam excipere et amplecti',[12] which can hardly be understood except as meaning 'to give one's assent to the doctrine.'

Thirdly: while it is true that according to Newman, genuine assent is always unconditional, it seems quite alien to Newman's thought to interpret him to mean that one can give one's assent to a proposition only if it has been infallibly arrived at. Does he not rather insist, in his *Essay in Aid of a Grammar of Assent*, that one can rightly give an 'unconditional' assent to a proposition, even though the process by which one arrived at that proposition could not be described as 'infallible'?[13]

The question, then, is: what does Newman mean when he says that assent must be 'unconditional'? His own reply to this question is that 'assent is an adhesion without reserve or doubt to the proposition to which it is given.'[14] For Newman, the word 'assent' 'stands for an undoubting and unhesitating act of the mind.'[15] In other words, what Newman excludes from assent is any present *doubt* about the truth of what one affirms.

Now, as I see it, an assent which excludes present doubt about the truth of what one affirms, does not necessarily exclude the recognition of the *possibility* that one might be in error. All that is required to justify undoubting assent is that one sees no *probability* that the proposition is erroneous: no grounds for prudent *fear* that one is making a mistake in affirming it. I conclude that Newman's 'unconditional assent' can coexist with the recognition that one is not *infallible* in judging this proposition to be true.

For these reasons, I maintain that the Latin: 'et sententiis ab eo prolatis sincere adhaereatur' is correctly translated: 'and sincere assent be given to decisions made by him', understanding that while the assent given to non-infallible teaching does not exclude the possibility that the proposition which one affirms might be erroneous, it can still be 'unconditional' in the sense that it is given without present doubt as to the truth of what is affirmed.

If such an assent should not be described as 'conditional', how should it be named, so as to distinguish it from the kind of assent that is given to what is infallibly taught? I suggest that it could be called a 'morally certain assent', since 'moral certitude' excludes the prudent fear of being in error, but not the recognition of the possibility that one might be in error.

An important conclusion to be drawn from this discussion is that I cannot really give my assent to a proposition while retaining serious doubt in my mind as to whether or not it is true. This will have to be kept in mind when we come to discuss the question of dissent from authoritative teaching.

Before coming to that, however, we must take up a question that is often raised about our subject: namely, how can authority, and submission of will, enter into the giving of the assent of one's mind to truth?

2. *What have authority and submission of will to do with assent?* I have argued that the translators of *Lumen gentium* were correct when they said that the Council calls for 'religious submission of will and mind' and 'sincere assent' to the ordinary magisterium of the Roman pontiff. In the same context, this non-infallible teaching is described as *authenticum*: a word which, as I have already suggested, should be rendered 'authoritative', rather than 'authentic'. So we must now consider in what way 'authority', and 'submission of will' can

enter into what, if it can rightly be called 'assent', must ultimately be an act of the mind judging a proposition to be true.

First, perhaps, it would be useful to point out the difference between the response called for by legislation, and the response called for by a decision of the magisterium. Legislative acts call for obedience, which simply means doing what is prescribed or refraining from doing what is forbidden. Obedience to law does not require an act of the mind approving the law as wise or appropriate. It suffices that it sees no conflict between this and some higher obligation. On the other hand, the authoritative exercise of the magisterium calls for religious submission of the mind as well as of the will; it calls for sincere assent, which is an act of the judgment.

Let us apply this distinction to the specific case of the encyclical *Humanae vitae*. If this were an example of Church law, the only persons called upon to obey it would be those who engage in marital intercourse, and their obedience would consist simply in refraining from the forbidden methods of birth control. But the fact is that *Humanae vitae* is not Church law; it is an exercise of papal teaching authority, which calls upon all Catholics (married or not) to conform their judgment about the morality of contraception to the judgment expressed by the Pope. Obedience in this case means not merely not doing what is forbidden; it means bringing one's thinking about birth control into line with the teaching of Pope Paul VI on this question. What this means is that the response called for by the authoritative magisterium is not the relatively simple obedience of the will, but the complicated business of 'obedience of the judgment'.

'Obedience of the judgment'

The notion of obedience of the judgment is based on the fact of experience that the attitude of our free will can have considerable influence on the formation of our judgment about a question, when our minds are not compelled to embrace some particular judgment because its truth is evident to us. Our minds are not free to deny what is evidently true; truth is the proper object of the mind, and truth that is evident to us has compelling force upon our assent.

162

However, there are a great many matters in the natural order, and even more in the area of revealed religion, concerning which few, if any people, have the kind of knowledge that makes the truth of particular propositions so evident to them that their minds are compelled to embrace them. It is in such areas as these that the free choice of our will can have a strong, even decisive, influence on the formation of our judgment.

Indeed, this is fundamental to the notion that our act of faith is meritorious for salvation, which it could not be if it did not depend on the free choice of our will. The act of faith is an assent of our mind, and therefore it has to be a reasonable act, befitting a person endowed with a mind focused on truth. But since the intrinsic truth of what God has revealed to us is in most cases not so evident as to be compelling to our mind, our free will, responding to God as to our ultimate Good, brings its influence to bear upon our judgment in such a way that we can speak of the act of faith itself as free. This does not mean, of course, that the act of faith is purely and simply an act of our will. It is an intellectual assent, and our mind has to be satisfied that what it assents to is true. But it can rightly be called a free act, because of the influence which our will has brought to bear on our mind to induce it to make this assent.

When we talk about 'obedience of the judgment', then, the first point to be kept in mind is that we are talking about situations in which our free will can actually bring its influence to bear on our judgment, so that our assent to authoritative teaching, while an intellectual assent, is also in some real sense free. Now this requires that what is taught not impress our mind as so evidently false that our mind is compelled to reject the teaching. I think this would be a rare case.

What is more likely to be the case, — one that no doubt was verified for many Catholics when the encyclical *Humanae vitae* was published — is that I have already formed my opinion in a certain way, and find that I am now called upon to embrace the contrary view, as proposed to me by the ordinary papal magisterium.

What can my free will do in such a case? What is it called upon to do, by the authority with which the pope proposes his teaching to me?

It seems to me that one could sum up what the free will is called upon to do, by saying that I am obliged to renounce any attitude of *obstinacy* in my own opinion, and to adopt an attitude of *docility* toward the teaching of the pope. Now it is crucial to recognise that both of these are attitudes of my will, which can have a powerful influence on the forming and maintaining of my opinions.

What is involved in the renunciation of an attitude of obstinacy? My free will can oblige me to look honestly at my own opinion, to see whether it really is a case of the truth being so evident to me that I have no choice but assent to it, or rather a case where my preferences have inclined me to embrace an opinion whose truth is really not evident to me. Renouncing obstinacy would mean rejecting a tendency to close my mind to the official teaching, to refuse even to give it a fair hearing, to adopt the attitude: 'I've already made my mind up; don't bother me.'

Positively, what would an attitude of docility involve? Docility is a willingness to be taught, a willingness to prefer another's judgment to one's own when it is reasonable to do so. Docility calls for an open attitude toward the official teaching, giving it a fair hearing, doing one's best to appreciate the reasons in its favour, so as to convince oneself of its truth, and thus facilitate one's intellectual assent to it.

The effort involved in working to renounce an attitude of obstinacy and to adopt one of docility towards the teaching of the magisterium is the response of one's free will that justifies speaking of this as 'obedience of the judgment', or to use the term used by the Council, *obsequium religiosum*. It is 'religious' submission, because it is an exercise of virtue whose motive is ultimately directed to Christ, from whom the pastors of the Church have received their authority and in whose name they teach.

As I understand it, then, to give the required *obsequium religiosum* to the teaching of the ordinary magisterium means to make an honest and sustained effort to overcome any contrary opinion I might have, and to achieve a sincere assent of my mind to this teaching. But here a crucial question arises: can people who have made such an honest and sustained effort, still find themselves unable to give their sincere assent to some particular teaching of the magisterium? It must be

164

said that this can happen. Let us look at some reasons why this is so.

The first point to note is that interior assent to a proposition is not an act of the free will but a judgment of the mind. And the proper object of the mind is truth. The mind cannot assent to a proposition unless it can accept it as true. This does not mean that it must necessarily grasp the intrinsic reasons why the proposition is true; on a great many matters we have to take things to be true on the authority of others. But in any case, it must be reasonable to judge the proposition to be true. And authority cannot *make* a proposition to be true.

Since assent is an act of judgment, it follows that the magisterium cannot be content to appeal to the will of the faithful, it must also appeal to their mind, by presenting its teaching with reasons that are clear and convincing. Perhaps an appeal to formal authority will be enough for those who have no opinion of their own on the question, or who feel themselves incompetent to judge the reasons involved. But it is quite a different matter when the magisterium pronounces its judgment on an issue like birth control, about which a great many people already had formed their opinion, and many were competent to judge the question on its merits.

Indeed it would be inconsistent for the magisterium to propose a moral norm as a requirement of the natural law (i.e. law which has to be discovered by human intelligence reflecting on experience) and not offer convincing reasons that would appeal to the intelligence of those to whom this teaching is directed. When the norm itself is said to be discoverable by human reasoning, it would be a mistake to rely too heavily on merely formal authority in proposing it for acceptance by thinking people. In such a case it would surely not be surprising if for many of the faithful the formal authority of the magisterium did not suffice to overcome the doubt that remained in their minds concerning the truth of the official teaching. And, as we have seen, it is simply impossible to assent to a proposition while retaining serious doubt in one's mind whether it is true.

On the other hand, I do not mean to say that the teaching of the magisterium has no more claim on our assent than the strength of its arguments would warrant. If that were true, papal teaching would have no more claim on the assent of Catholics than it does on the assent of anyone else who might happen to read an encyclical. In that case, I do not see how the notion of *obsequium religiosum* would have any meaning whatsoever. But what I am saying is that if the magisterium fails to offer convincing arguments for its teaching, and relies too heavily on merely formal authority, it will not be offering to the faithful the help that many of them will need to rid themselves of their doubts about the truth of the official teaching, and achieve a sincere assent to it.

The second conclusion I would draw is that if, in a particular instance, Catholics have offered their 'religious submission of mind and will' to the authority of the magisterium, by making an honest and sustained effort to achieve internal assent to its teaching, and still find that doubts about its truth remain so strong in their minds that they cannot actually give their sincere intellectual assent to it, I do not see how one could judge such non-assent, or internal dissent, to involve any lack of obedience to the magisterium. Having done all that they were capable of doing towards achieving assent, they actually fulfilled their obligation of obedience, whether they achieved internal assent or not.

Official recognition of the possibility of legitimate dissent

While the text of *Lumen gentium* makes no mention of this possibility, the Theological Commission of Vatican II, in its reply to an emendation proposed by three bishops, made a remark that clearly indicates that the members of this commission were aware of the possibility of legitimate dissent from ordinary papal teaching. The proposed emendation and the reply of the commission are as follows:

> Tres Patres invocant casum particularem, saltem theoretice possibilem, in quo eruditus quidam, coram doctrina non infallibiliter proposita, ob fundatas rationes, *interne* assentire non potest.
> R. De hoc casu consuli debent probatae expositiones theologicae.[16]
> Three Fathers invoke a particular case, which is at least theoretically possible, in which a certain learned person, in the face of a doctrine that has not been infallibly proposed, cannot, for well-founded reasons, give his internal assent.

Resp. On this case the approved theological treatises should be consulted.

It is obvious from this response that the members of the Theological Commission knew that the manuals of theology in use in Catholic seminaries treated the question of dissent from the non-infallible teaching of the magisterium. As a typical example of such an 'approved treatise', I shall quote the widely-used manual of Lercher:

Si Romanus Pontifex auctoritative, sed non summo gradu, omnes obligat ad assensum in rem ut veram (revelatam, vel cum revelatis cohaerentem), non videtur de jure infallibilis, neque necesse est dicere: Spiritus Sanctus numquam permittet, ut tale decretum erroneum edatur. Certe Spiritus Sanctus numquam permittet, ut per tale decretum ecclesia in errorem inducatur. Modus, quo error excluditur, probabilius consistit in assistentia Spiritus Sancti capiti ecclesiae praestita, qua impeditur tale decretum erroneum. Attamen, non absolute repugnat, ut error per Spiritum Sanctum excludator, eo, quod subditi detegant errorem et desinant, interne assentiri decreto.[17]

(I translate): If the Roman Pontiff, using his authority but not to its highest degree, obliges all to give their assent to something as true (whether as revealed or as connected with revelation), it does not seem that in principle he is infallible, nor must we say that the Holy Spirit will never permit him to issue an erroneous decree. Certainly, the Holy Spirit will never permit it to happen that by such a decree the Church would be led into error. The way in which the error would be excluded more probably consists in the assistance of the Holy Spirit given to the head of the Church, by which such an erroneous decree would be prevented. However, it is not unthinkable that the error (on the part of the Church) should be excluded by the Holy Spirit in this way: that the subjects recognize the decree to be erroneous and cease to give their assent to it.

Now, while the question raised by the three bishops at Vatican II spoke of the case in which a 'learned person' would find himself unable to assent to some ordinary papal teaching 'for well-founded reasons', Lercher does not restrict the possibility of such dissent to the learned, but speaks simply of the 'subjects' withholding their assent to doctrine which they recognise to be erroneous, and being led to do this by the Holy Spirit! Perhaps in such a case one should attribute their dissent to the 'supernatural sense of the faith' by which the faithful are inclined in an almost instinctive way towards what is consonant with their faith, and away from what does not resonate with it.

The 'reception' of non-infallible teaching

The way Lercher treats this issue suggests the importance of the reception of the teaching of the magisterium on the part of the faithful. He recognises the possibility that dissent of the faithful to non-infallible teaching could be a sign that the teaching is erroneous. But this raises some difficult questions. How general would such dissent have to be to justify drawing the conclusion that the teaching is in error? If, as seems likely to be the case, the faithful are divided, some accepting and some rejecting the teaching, how can one be sure that the Holy Spirit is on the side of the dissenters? And would not one have to take into account the quality of faith and practice that is otherwise manifested by those who dissent from this teaching?

Several considerations occur to me at this point. First: history shows that it has sometimes taken a rather long time for even the decrees of an ecumenical council to obtain universal reception. Therefore it would be risky to base a judgment on the phenomenon of dissent until a sufficient period of time had elapsed to show whether the teaching was going eventually to obtain more general assent.

Secondly: besides actual dissent, there is also the possibility that the teaching of the magisterium may meet with an attitude of indifference or apathy. In my opinion, this could be an even more serious matter than dissent.

Thirdly: both dissent and indifference, if they are at all widespread, deserve to be studied with careful attention, to see what might be their cause. It is possible that it is not the doctrine itself, but the way the decision was reached, or the unconvincing arguments with which it was proposed, that are largely responsible for the negative reaction to the decree.

Fourthly: since I maintain that Catholics have to have made a serious effort to achieve assent to the teaching of the magisterium, renouncing obstinacy and practising the virtue of docility in its regard, and to have found themselves really unable to give their sincere assent, before their dissent can be called justified, I am far from thinking that all dissent, and every way of expressing it, is objectively without blame. It is quite possible that an attitude of dissent may be adopted and expressed in ways that manifest a lack of the *obsequium religiosum* which the teaching of the magisterium has a right to expect.

Fifthly: on the other hand, I think it is unjust to treat all dissent from the teaching of the ordinary magisterium as disobedience, or to turn agreement with this non-infallible teaching into a test of loyalty to the Holy See. No doubt there are Catholics whose respect for the teaching authority of the pope is so great that the simple appeal to his formal authority is enough to convince them that his teaching must be true, so that no reasons that present themselves to the contrary would have any effect on their ability to give their assent. But such persons should resist the temptation to think 'disloyal' other Catholics in whose minds the reasons against the teaching make so strong an impression that the formal authority of the magisterium is not enough to overcome their doubts and make it possible for them to give their internal assent.

Dissent from the moral teaching of the magisterium

Dissent from the moral teaching of the Church raises some special questions, because of the direction which the faithful are expected to receive from the magisterium for the formation of their conscience, or moral judgments.

I have already had occasion to quote the statement of Vatican II in its Declaration on Religious Freedom: 'In the formation of their consciences, the Christian faithful ought carefully to attend to the sacred and certain doctrine of the Church.'[18] During the council debate on this document, an emendation of the text was proposed, according to which, instead of saying: 'ought carefully to attend to', the text should say: 'ought to form their consciences according to'. The response of the Theological Commission in charge of this text was: 'The proposed formula seems excessively restrictive. The obligation binding on the faithful is sufficiently expressed in the text as it stands.'[19]

169

As far as I know, there was no outcry raised at the Council against the view of the Commission that it would be 'excessively restrictive' to say that the faithful are obliged to form their consciences *according to* the moral teaching of the magisterium. In any case, the Council approved the text which simply calls on them, in the formation of their consciences, *carefully to attend* to this teaching. It seems to me that this way of expressing the obligation of the faithful in the face of the moral teaching of the magisterium leaves a certain amount of room for them to exercise their personal judgment in the formation of their consciences. This, I take it, is an expression of respect for the moral sense of the faithful.

No mention is made in the conciliar text of the possibility that this moral sense might lead someone to dissent from the official teaching. But this must surely be reckoned with as a possibility.

Dissent from the moral teaching of the magisterium has special consequences, since it means that Catholics are forming their consciences: i.e. their personal judgment as to the moral rightness or wrongness of particular kinds of conduct, in a way that conflicts with the judgment of the teaching authority of their Church. In the hypothesis that they have 'carefully attended to the official teaching', but have really been unable to 'form their consciences according to it', despite serious and sustained effort to do so, I do not see how one could accuse them of moral fault in the way that they have formed their consciences. At least they cannot be accused of a lack of religious submission to the teaching authority of the Church, because they have actually exercised the virtue of docility in its regard, without being able to rid themselves of serious doubt as to the correctness of a particular doctrine and achieve internal assent to it.

Now the question inevitably arises: can they in practice follow their own judgment in this matter without moral fault? Or would it be imprudent for Catholics to decide to follow their own judgment about the morality of a way of acting, when they know that their judgment conflicts with the official teaching of their Church?

Now this is a problem for the moral theologian, not the ecclesiologist, to solve, so the prudent thing for me to do is to refer the reader to the approved treatises of moral theology. But I shall venture one observation: that the question of the prudence or imprudence of following one's own judgment would certainly have to take account of the degree to which one's opinion was shared by other Catholics, especially by those whose opinion deserved special consideration, by reason of their exemplary Christian lives, or their theological expertise. I shall conclude this question by quoting another section of the pastoral letter of the German bishops on the response due to the ordinary, non-infallible magisterium:

> The Christian who believes he has a right to his private opinion, that he already knows what the Church will only come to grasp later, must ask himself in sober self-criticism before God and his conscience, whether he has the necessary depth and breadth of theological expertise to allow his private theory and practice to depart from the present doctrine of the ecclesiastical authorities. The case is in principle admissible. But conceit and presumption will have to answer for their wilfulness before the judgment-seat of God.[20]

Conclusion

I realise that I have spent a considerable portion of this chapter discussing the possibility and the conditions of legitimate dissent from the ordinary teaching of the magisterium. I think that this was necessary, especially because the text of *Lumen gentium* speaks only of the obligation to give 'religious submission' to this kind of teaching, with no mention of the possibility that it could be erroneous, or that dissent from it could be justified. I am convinced that it is important for Catholics to be aware of the difference between infallible and non-infallible teaching by the magisterium, and of the corresponding difference between the kinds of assent that each of them calls for.

Ignorance of these differences can have several unhappy consequences. One is that Catholics who have actually fulfilled their obligation to practice docility regarding such teaching, and have been really unable to give their interior assent to it, may still feel themselves guilty of disobedience to the pope because they do not follow his teaching on a

171

particular point. Another is that Catholics who do accept such teaching may judge all others who do not, to be disobedient or disloyal, and may be scandalised to know that even some priests or theologians have reservations about certain points of ordinary papal teaching.

The tendency to obscure the difference between the infallible and the non-infallible exercise of magisterium, by treating papal encyclicals as though they were practically infallible, has, I believe, been largely responsible for the fact that many people, when they learn that encyclicals are not infallible after all, jump to the conclusion that one need pay no attention to them. If people have been led to think of the infallibility of the pope as the basic motive for giving their assent to his teaching, it is not surprising that when this motive is no longer available, their assent will fail as well.

The 'inflation' of the notion of magisterial infallibility that took place after the First Vatican Council, tended to foster the idea that the infallibility of the pope was a primary truth, on which the certitude of our Catholic faith somehow depends. The truth of the matter, of course, is that our belief in the infallibility of the pope depends on our much more basic faith in the guidance of the Church by the Holy Spirit.

What is needed is a deeper realisation of the fact that our faith in the guidance of the Church by the Holy Spirit justifies our confidence in the general reliability of the ordinary teaching of the magisterium, even when this guidance does not actually guarantee the infallibility of such teaching, so as to exclude the possibility that on some particular points it might eventually be seen to need correction. As the German bishops have pointed out, there are a great many instances in the course of human life when it is obviously reasonable, and indeed necessary, to base important decisions on judgments made by 'authorities' whom one has reason to respect as reliable, even though one knows they are not infallible.

Now that so many Catholics have come to realise that ordinary papal teaching is not infallible, it is all the more important that they should understand the reasons which they have to respect this kind of teaching as generally reliable, as enjoying the presumption of truth, as deserving their attitude of docility, and their sincere effort to give it their intellectual assent.

There are a great many problems facing human society today about which it is hardly possible to make absolutely certain, irreformable, judgments, and yet about which Catholics, and indeed many other thinking people, look to the pope and the Catholic bishops as reliable spokesmen of a Christian point of view. Indeed, these spokesmen come in for severe criticism and are accused of grave dereliction of their duty when they fail to speak out on pressing moral issues (such, for instance, as the treatment of the Jewish people of Europe by Nazi Germany). On the other hand, many thinking people, whether Christian or not, have paid close attention to papal teaching, especially on issues of peace, social justice, the rights of minorities, etc., and have seen such teaching as a precious contribution to the progress of mankind towards a more just and humane society.

The bishop of Rome and the other Catholic bishops are called upon to exercise a prophetic role in the world today, as spokesmen of a well-informed Christian conscience. If even non-believers listen with respect to their voice, there is all the more reason for Catholics to do so, even without the mistaken belief that every pronouncement they make must be infallible.

8.

The Magisterium and the Role of Theologians in the Church

It seems inevitable that on the question which I propose to treat in this final chapter, statements by members of the hierarchy will tend to stress the authority of the magisterium and the obligation on the part of theologians to follow its directives, while statements by theologians will tend to stress the freedom of theological research and publication, and the critical role of theology even with regard to documents of the magisterium. It is not easy to handle this question in such a way as to satisfy the legitimate preoccupations of both sides.

That is why I feel that I am fortunate in being able to base this chapter on the *Theses on the relationship between the ecclesiastical magisterium and theology* which were published by the International Theological Commission as the fruit of the symposium which it devoted to this question in its plenary session held in Rome, 25 Sept.-1 Oct. 1975.[1]

While on the one hand there is reason to believe that these 'theses' would reflect a fairly broad consensus in the Catholic theological community, on the other hand there is also reason to believe that they were acceptable to the official organ of the papal magisterium, namely, the Congregation for the Doctrine of the Faith. These reasons are based on the very make-up of the International Theological Commission (ITC), and on its relationship with the Congregation for the Doctrine of the Faith (CDF). So a few words about the ITC are in order before we examine its theses on the relationship between the ecclesiastical magisterium and theology.

The International Theological Commission
The proposal to establish a commission made up of eminent

174

theologians of various schools living in various parts of the world, 'for the purpose of offering effective assistance to the Holy See, and in particular to the Congregation for the Doctrine of the Faith, especially in doctrinal questions of greater moment', was presented to Pope Paul VI by the First Synod of Bishops on 27 October 1967.[2] There can hardly be any doubt that the motive for this proposal was the feeling among the bishops that there was need for the consultation of a wider spectrum of Catholic theological opinion on the part of the CDF, whose regular consultors were necessarily resident in Rome, and tended to represent a distinctively 'Roman' point of view.[3]

The same Synod likewise approved the proposal that the Episcopal Conferences suggest to the Pope the names of theologians for such a commission, and that they consult the universities and theological faculties of their respective regions, in order to be sure of presenting truly competent men.[4]

After a delay of about a year and a half, Paul VI, having approved the provisional statutes drawn up for the ITC by the CDF,[5] announced its establishment in his address to the Consistory on 28 April 1969.[6] The first plenary session of the ITC was held in October 1969, and it has had a session each year but one since then. Pope John Paul II promulgated definitive statutes for the ITC in his *motu proprio* of 6 August 1982.[7]

While it is true that the intention of the Synod was that the ITC be a consultative body for the Holy See, and in particular for the CDF, one may wonder whether the Synod envisioned quite so thorough-going a subordination of the ITC to the CDF as is laid down in these definitive statutes. The president of the ITC is the Cardinal-Prefect of the CDF, and it is he who suggests to the pope the names of theologians for the commission, after consulting the episcopal conferences. (There is no mention of the consultation of universities or faculties of theology). The three qualifications mentioned by the Synod for the choice of members of the ITC were: 'profound wisdom, distinguished repute, and outstanding scientific formation'; in the statutes the qualities required are 'eminent knowledge, prudence and fidelity toward the magisterium of the Church'. The documents which are approved by the majority of the ITC are submitted to the Pope, and they can be published only if there are no difficulties on the part of the Holy See. The members of the ITC are expected to observe the norms of 'professional secrecy' regarding the matters treated, and where special collaboration with the CDF is concerned, they are bound to observe the 'pontifical secrecy' proper to the work of this congregation.

If one asks whether the ITC has actually been functioning as the Synod of 1967 intended it should, I think the most important question is whether this international body of theologians has been consulted, and has played any significant role, in the preparation of the important doctrinal statements that have been issued by the CDF in the years since the ITC was established. I have in mind such documents as 'Declaration in defence of the Catholic doctrine of the Church against certain errors of the present day' (*Mysterium Ecclesiae*, 1973); 'Declaration on certain questions concerning sexual ethics' (*Persona humana*, 1975); and 'Declaration about the question of the admission of women to priestly ministry' (*Inter insigniores*, 1977).[8]

But to explore the question as to how the ITC might more adequately perform the service which I believe the Synod of Bishops intended it to have would be a digression; let us return to the point at issue, which is:

The theses of the ITC on the relationship between the magisterium and theology

I have expressed the opinion that these theses would reflect a fairly broad consensus of Catholic theological thought. But at the same time I would agree with Karl Rahner when he says that a commission that is chosen and operates according to the statutes laid down for the ITC can only be seen as an instrument of the CDF, and cannot be taken as representative of all Catholic theologians throughout the world.[9] However, it is in fact an international body of Catholic theologians with very respectable academic credentials, and I am not aware of any complaints from the Catholic theological community about the quality of the men (so far no women!) who have been appointed to it.[10] For this reason I feel confident that I can take the theses that were approved by 'the great majority' of this commission, after serious discussion, as representing a point of view that would be shared by a good number — perhaps a majority — of Catholic theologians today.

At the same time, the very fact that these theses have been published is a clear sign that they were also acceptable to the CDF and to the pope, and thus represent the point of view of the ecclesiastical magisterium.

Obviously there is no question of taking these theses as the last word on the subject; indeed, the General Secretary of the ITC, P. Delhaye, in his presentation of the theses, makes it clear that the Commission did not intend them as such. [11] They are a working document, open to criticism and improvement, and I shall express my reservations where I feel they are justified. However, I cannot think of any better starting point than the one they offer for a discussion of the magisterium and the role of theologians in the Church today.

My plan in this chapter is to quote the full text of each thesis, and after each one to comment on those points which I think deserve fuller treatment, or on which I would have some criticism to offer. This method will have the advantage of presenting the full text of the theses to the reader, and spare me the need of saying again what is already well said by the ITC. Rather than quote the English translation of the USCC publication, I prefer to offer my own translation, which I have checked against the German translation made by O. Semmelroth, and against the French version that was approved by the Secretariat of the ITC. [12]

After a brief introduction, and a first thesis which defines the terms, the theses are divided into three parts: 1) common elements; 2) differences; 3) practical methods of collaboration.

Introduction. 'The relations between the Magisterium and Theology not only are extremely important, but they must be seen as matters of very great relevance today.' The theses which follow are an attempt to clarify the relationship between the 'mandate laid upon the ecclesiastical Magisterium to safeguard divine revelation, and the task entrusted to theology, to understand and explain the doctrine of the faith.'

The ITC introduces its theses with two brief quotations from the address of Pope Paul VI to the International Congress on the Theology of Vatican II, which was held in Rome from 26 September to 1 October 1966. [13] The principal theme of that address was the same one which the ITC was discussing, and, as we shall see, several of the ideas developed by Paul VI have been incorporated into these theses.

The only comment I would make on the introduction is to call attention to the terms which Paul VI used to describe the respective functions of the magisterium and of theology: that of the former is to *safeguard* (*tutandi*) revelation; that of the latter is to *understand and explain* it (*cognoscendi et explicandi*).

Thesis 1. By 'ecclesiastical magisterium' is meant the office of teaching which, by Christ's institution, is proper to the college of bishops or to individual bishops joined in hierarchical communion with the Supreme Pontiff. By 'theologians' are meant those members of the Church who, by their studies and their life in the community of the Church's faith, are qualified to serve the Word of God by seeking a deeper understanding of it, in the scientific manner proper to theology, and also, by virtue of a canonical mission, to serve the Word of God by their teaching. The New Testament and subsequent tradition speak about the magisterium of pastors, and about theologians or teachers, in an analogous way, that is, as both similar and dissimilar; there is continuity, but there are also rather profound changes. The concrete ways in which they have been related to one another and coordinated have been varied in the course of history.

A note on the use of the term 'magisterium' in these theses

In Chapter 2 we saw that while in the time of St Thomas 'magisterium' was used of the teaching function both of bishops and of theologians, in more recent times this term has come to be identified with what this first thesis calls 'ecclesiastical magisterium', or the 'magisterium of pastors'. In these two instances, the term refers to the office or function which is proper to the bishops. There is no instance, in any of these theses, where the term 'magisterium' is used of the teaching function of theologians (although the USCC translation mistakenly gives this impression with the phrase 'the magisterium of pastors, theologians or teachers'). When 'magisterium' is used of the teaching function proper to bishops, its correlative is 'theology' (as in the title: 'Theses

178

on the relationship between the ecclesiastical magisterium and theology').

In fact, however, after this first thesis, the term 'the magisterium' almost always refers not to the teaching office as such, but to the men who have it; in this sense, 'the magisterium' is correlative to 'theologians'. As Congar has pointed out, the use of the term 'the magisterium' as a synonym for 'the hierarchy' is a very recent development. The fact that this is the way the term is most often used in these theses is a good indication of how common this usage has come to be.

The qualifications of theologians

Two questions arise here: (1) why 'life in the community of faith' is a requirement; and (2) whether one can be a theologian without a 'canonical mission'.

The first of these questions is touched on again in thesis 6, which describes theology as 'the science of the faith', which 'cannot be pursued without a living experience and practice of the faith.' This requirement is based on the classical (Anselmian) definition of theology as 'faith seeking understanding'. As Juan Alfaro puts it, 'The first word, *fides*, indicates that theology starts with faith, presupposes it, and is required by it. The fact that the theologian believes (is a Christian) cannot be merely accidental in relation to his theology; rather it belongs to the very essence of his theology.'[14] As Alfaro further goes on to show, the reason for this is that the faith which seeks understanding in theology cannot be identified with the purely objective data of the doctrine and practice of the Christian religion in the sense that these are phenomena to be studied by the method of the history or philosophy of religion. The faith which seeks understanding in theology is both the *fides quae* (what is believed) and the *fides qua* (the attitude of faith). Genuine faith is a total response of the human person to God's saving revelation of himself in Christ, involving not only cognitive assent, but also a self-surrender to God in hope and love. This means that one cannot really do Christian theology as an uncommitted observer of the phenomena of the Christian religion.

Avery Dulles has also addressed the question why 'life in the community of faith' is a necessary qualification of a theologian. Like Alfaro, he bases his answer on a consideration of the nature of the faith which theology seeks to understand.

Christian faith is a participatory form of knowledge available within the Church through a lived sharing in the meaning of the Christian symbols. The Christian is one who adheres to Christ and the Church as signs of salvation, or rather, more correctly, to Christ in the Church as a single and all-embracing sign of salvation. Since the sign is a symbol or sacrament, its meaning can never be fully spelled out in explicit language. . . . The task of theology is to conduct a methodic or systematic reflection on faith. As an ecclesial discipline, theology is done within the believing community. It endeavours to give a coherent systematization of Christian faith, guided by the symbols and by past formulations, especially those which have normative value in the Church. According to the sacramental understanding, these formulations refer back to the experience of conversion, which continually goes on within the Church. They express certain aspects of a commitment that necessarily remains, in great part, tacit or implicit. . . . To be a true theologian one must dwell in spirit within the community of faith; one must participate in the Christian symbols and in their meaning for the community. This kind of participatory knowledge will make it possible to see the formulas in relation to the unexplicit meaning which they carry to those who share in the tradition. . . . Through the experience of living in the community, and especially through sharing in its life of worship, the believing theologian has a certain familiarity with the meaning of the symbols not accessible to the outsider.[15]

Avery Dulles has likewise touched on the second question I have raised concerning the first thesis of the ITC, namely, whether one needs a 'canonical mission' in order to be a Catholic theologian.[16] He expresses concern that what is said here could give that impression. However, it is quite clear from what is said later, in thesis 7, that the ITC did not intend to say that one could not *be* a theologian, or *do* theology, without such a canonical mission. It is another question, however, whether one needs a canonical mission in order to be qualified to *teach* theology. I shall postpone discussion of this question until we get to thesis 7.

The history of the relationship between the magisterium and theologians

The last two sentences of thesis 1 refer to the topics which Yves Congar treated in his two contributions to the symposium of the ITC, namely, the history of the term 'magisterium', and the forms which the relationship between magisterium and theology has taken in the course of history.[17]

I have already made use of the first of these two studies in my treatment of the term 'magisterium' in Chapter 2. Obviously there is no question here of going into the detail that Congar provided in his typically well-documented study of the history of the relationship between magisterium and theology, but it seems important at least to mention some key points which he has brought to light. Another way of treating this same question would be to describe various 'models' of this relationship in the course of history. This is the approach which H. Jedin and M. Seckler have taken, and I have also found their studies helpful.[18] Another valuable contribution to this discussion was made by the Summer 1978 issue of *Chicago Studies*, with a series of articles on the topic: 'Magisterium and Theologians: Historical Perspectives'.[19]

The development of theology as 'faith seeking understanding' in the critical, methodical and systematic way that justifies speaking of it as a science, is contemporaneous with the rise of the universities, with their faculties of theology, in the early part of the second millennium. It was only at this time that there appeared a clear distinction between the *magisterium cathedrae pastoralis* of pope and bishops, and the *magisterium cathedrae magistralis* of the *doctores*, i.e. the university professors of theology. During the greater part of the first millennium, most theologians were also bishops, and many of the more influential bishops were theologians. Seckler suggests that the kind of theology which was done by bishops, and then in the monastic schools, should be described as a kind of 'intellectual contemplation', rather than as scientific theology in the medieval and modern sense of the term.[20] He speaks of the relationship between magisterium and theology, or between bishops and theologians, during the first half of the Church's history, as a *perichoresis*, a 'mutual indwelling'.[21]

The Middle Ages show quite a different picture, where

very few theologians (like Anselm of Canterbury and Peter Lombard) were bishops, and scholastic theology reigned as 'queen of the sciences' in the universities, where the doctors of theology achieved great prestige, and their faculties became arbiters of orthodoxy, instituting proceedings against the proponents of questionable doctrines, and passing sentences with grave consequences for those judged guilty of heresy.

In the Late Middle Ages, and especially during the heyday of conciliarism, the encroachment of the *doctores* on the magisterial role of bishops reached its apogee. The Councils of Constance and Basel were dominated by the university faculties of theology. Anyone with a doctorate in theology or canon law was given full voting rights, with the astonishing result that at the thirty-fourth session of the Council of Basel (25 June 1439) there were three hundred *doctores* with voting rights, and only seven bishops! This, of course, was an aberration, and the council ended in a fiasco. The inevitable reaction to the excesses of Basel led to a strong assertion of the hierarchical magisterium: not so much that of the bishops, however, as that of the papacy, since many bishops, especially in Northern Europe, were too much involved in secular business to be qualified to judge doctrine, and the popes enlisted competent theologians to help them in their magisterial task. At the same time, the university faculties retained their role as arbiters of orthodoxy, and it was they that first sat in judgment on the theses of Luther. The papal bull 'Exsurge Domine' was largely based on the critique of Luther's theses by scholastic theologians. In Jedin's judgment, this accounts for the fact that some of Luther's theses were condemned rather because they rejected accepted positions of scholastic theology than because they were incompatible with the Christian faith.[22] Congar is likewise critical of the extent to which magisterial pronouncements of the Late Middle Ages introduced theological concepts and terms into dogma.[23]

When we come to the Council of Trent, however, the authors whom I am following agree that the success of this council was in large part due to the fact that it achieved a fruitful collaboration between bishops and theologians, maintaining a clear distinction between their respective roles.

Before a question was put before the bishops it was discussed in 'congregations of theologians', whose conclusions were then presented to the bishops by one of the leading theologians. Jedin insists that in no case did the bishops, some of whom were also good theologians, simply say 'amen' to what the theologians told them. While the theologians made an important contribution to the council as *periti*, there was no question of their encroaching on the role of the bishops, who exercised their rightful magisterium and had the decisive voice.[24]

The period since the French revolution has been marked by an increasing emphasis on the formal authority of the hierarchy, and especially on that of the papal magisterium. After the suppression of most of the Catholic faculties of theology in Northern Europe, the Roman faculties assumed a leading role, and theologians teaching in or trained in Rome were the leading *periti* at Vatican I, which defined the supremacy and infallibility of the papal magisterium. It was the pope of this Council, Pius IX, who declared that it was the most noble task of theology to show how the doctrine defined by the Church was contained in the sources of revelation, in that very sense in which it had been defined.[25]

This statement of Pius IX, which was quoted with approval by Pope Pius XII in his encyclical *Humani generis* (D-S 3886), has been severely criticised by Joseph Ratzinger in his authoritative commentary on *Dei Verbum*.

> The risk of a false orientation cannot be dismissed when *Humani generis* (which incidentally quotes Pius IX on the point) declares that it is obviously wrong to seek to clarify what is clear by the help of what is obscure — which means in the context that it is not the teaching office that can be clarified by Scripture, but only, on the contrary, Scripture by the teaching office. This is then developed to the point at which the task of theology is described as that of showing how what the teaching office has established is contained in the sources — 'and that precisely in the sense in which it has been defined.' One can hardly deny that the point of view which sees only Scripture as what is unclear, but the teaching office as what is clear, is a very limited one and that to reduce the task of theology to the proof of the presence of the statements of the teaching office in the

sources is to threaten the primacy of the sources which, (were one to continue logically in this direction) would ultimately destroy the serving character of the teaching office.[26]

All of the authors whom I am following in this survey are critical of the theory and practice of the relationship between the magisterium and theology which characterised the pontificate of Pius XII. Congar, for instance, agreeing with Seckler that Pius XII saw the theologian teaching only by delegation from the magisterium, and working strictly in its service and under its control, asks: 'Is this consonant with what nineteen centuries of the Church's life tell us about the function of the *didaskalos* or *doctor*? No, not exactly.'[27] A little later he expresses himself more strongly, saying: 'We cannot fail to take into account the critical historical study of the magisterium in modern times. Its pretensions seem excessive and unreal.'[28]

From his study of the various historical models of the relationship between ecclesiastical magisterium and theology, Jedin draws the conclusion that there have always been negative consequences when the distinction between their roles was not clearly observed: when one usurped the function proper to the other, or one attempted to impose its *diktat* on the other. While the fifteenth century offers an example of an attempt by the theological faculties to impose their *diktat* on the magisterium, Jedin says, on the other hand, 'It can hardly be denied that in the recent past it was sometimes the case that theology was subjected to the *diktat* of the holders of magisterial authority.[29]

To conclude this comment on thesis 1: even from this sketchy survey, it should be evident that the ITC had good reason to say that the concrete ways in which the magisterium and theology have been related to one another and coordinated have been varied in the course of history.

The following three theses constitute Part I, under the heading:

*What the Magisterium and Theologians have in common
in performing their task*

*Thesis 2. The element that is common to the tasks of the
magisterium and of theologians, though to be realised in
ways that are analogous and proper to each, is 'to safeguard
the deposit of revelation, to seek ever deeper insight into
it, to explain, teach and defend it,'[30] for the service of the
people of God and for the whole world's salvation. This
service must first of all maintain the certainty of the faith;
this is done differently by the magisterium and by the
ministry of theologians, but it is neither right nor possible
to establish a hard and fast separation between them.*

In this thesis we again find a quotation from the address of
Paul VI to the International Congress on the Theology of
Vatican II. It would perhaps have been more effectively used
if it had included the phrase that shows that the pope was
describing the common *purpose* which both the magisterium
and theology aim to achieve (*idem propositum assequi
student*).

I think the key point of this thesis is to affirm that the work
of theologians is no less an ecclesial ministry than is that of
the bishops. They are both engaged in a ministry to the Word
of God (guarding, understanding, explaining, teaching,
defending it) — but this ministry to the Word is ultimately a
ministry for the salvation of people, since the Word was
revealed to us precisely 'for the sake of our salvation' (DV 11).
This justifies the idea that the theologian has a part in the
missionary task of the Church, even though he may personally
never preach the Gospel to anyone who has not yet accepted
it.

*Thesis 3. In this common service to the truth, the magis-
terium and theologians share a number of bonds in common.*

*1. They are both bound by the Word of God. For 'the
magisterium is not above the Word of God, but serves it,
teaching only what has been handed on, listening to it
devoutly, guarding it conscientiously, and explaining it
faithfully. From this one deposit of faith it draws everything which it presents for belief as divinely revealed.'*

(DV 10). Likewise, 'sacred theology relies on the written Word of God, along with sacred Tradition, as on a permanent foundation. By this Word it is most firmly strengthened and constantly rejuvenated, as it searches out, under the light of faith, the full truth stored up in the mystery of Christ.' (DV 24)

2. They are both bound by the 'sense of the faith' of the Church, both of past ages and of our own day. For the Word of God in a living manner pervades all ages in that 'common sense of the faith' of the whole people of God, by which 'the whole body of the faithful, anointed by the Holy One, cannot err in believing' (LG 12), in such a way that 'in maintaining, practising and confessing the faith that has been handed down, there results a unanimity of bishops and faithful.' (DV 10)

3. They are both bound by the documents of Tradition, in which the common faith of the people of God is set forth. Although the magisterium and theologians have different tasks with respect to these documents, neither can neglect such records of the faith which are stored in the history of salvation of God's people.

4. In performing their ministries, both are bound by the pastoral and missionary care they must have towards the world. While the magisterium of the Supreme Pontiff and the bishops is specifically called 'pastoral', still the scientific character of the theologians' work does not free them from pastoral and missionary responsibility, especially in view of how quickly even scientific matters are given publicity by modern means of communication. Moreover, theology, as a vital function to be exercised within and on behalf of the people of God, must have a pastoral and missionary purpose and effect.

'Common service to the truth'

When using this phrase, the members of the ITC may well have had in mind the concluding paragraph of Yves Congar's contribution to their symposium, where he said:

We must not think of the issue just in two terms: authority [of the magisterium] and theologians. We must think in three terms: above there is the truth, the transmitted apostolic faith, confessed, preached and celebrated. Beneath this, at its service, the 'magisterium' of the apostolic ministry, and the work or the teaching of theologians, as well as the faith of the faithful. It is a differentiated service, articulated organically, like all the life of the *ecclesia*.[31]

In his commentary on the statement of *Dei Verbum* that 'the magisterium is not above the Word of God, but serves it', Joseph Ratzinger makes the following pertinent observation:

> For the first time a text of the teaching office expressly points out the subordination of the teaching office to the Word, i.e. its function as a servant. One can say, it is true, that there could never have been any serious doubt that this was in fact the case. Nevertheless the actual procedure often tended somewhat to obscure this order of things, though it had always been acknowledged in principle.[32]

On the relationship of theology to the Word of God, the ITC again invokes the authority of *Dei Verbum*, and once more Ratzinger's commentary on this text is enlightening. Speaking of the idea that Sacred Scripture is the vital force by which theology must be constantly rejuvenated, he says:

> This thought had already been expressed in the encyclical *Humani generis*, where the further point had been made that experience proved that without a constant return to the sacred deposit of revelation speculation was bound to remain unfruitful. However, in the encyclical, this principle is rendered ineffective, by the peculiar limitation of the exegete's task to confirming what has been proposed by the magisterium. The principle can be fully effective only when theology has that immediate contact with Scripture which the text of *Dei Verbum* requires.[33]

The 'sense of the faith'

This term, as it is used in the second paragraph of thesis 3, seems to be intended in the objective sense: referring to what the faithful have believed and now believe. As I have already remarked earlier, I agree with Congar that when this objective sense is intended, it is better to speak of the *sensus fidelium*: the 'sense' or 'mind' of the faithful. The term 'sense of the faith' more properly refers to that supernatural 'instinct' for

187

the revealed truth, which is an aspect of the subjective gift of faith.

Both magisterium and theologians must pay close attention to what the faithful believe, and both have a role to play in determining whether any belief has the consistency and universality of consensus that would justify the conclusion that it could not be erroneous. I have already discussed the question of the infallibility of such a consensus in the last section of Chapter one.

The 'documents of tradition'

While the English word 'documents' suggests only written records of tradition (such as the writings of the Fathers, the decrees of councils, liturgical texts, etc.) the Latin term *documenta* can have a broader meaning. It could include other kinds of evidence of traditional faith, such as is preserved in the frescoes of the catacombs, the mosaics and stained-glass windows in churches, icons, sculpture, and other such physical records of what the Church has believed.

Pastoral and missionary responsibility

In publishing the fruits of his scholarly labours, even though his intention is to share his ideas with his colleagues, the theologian has to have a concern for the effect his ideas could have on a wider public, both within the Church and outside of it. He will sometimes have to weigh his responsibility as a scholar to share his work with his colleagues so as to profit from their reaction and criticism, against his pastoral responsibility toward the simpler faith of the Christian people. Obviously there can arise the problem of choosing between conflicting values, to neither of which can one give an absolute priority. This is treated more fully in thesis 8.

Thesis 4. Common — though at the same time different — is the manner, at once both collegial and personal, in which the magisterium and theologians perform their respective tasks. That 'charism of infallibility' which was promised both to the 'whole body of the faithful' (LG 12) and to the episcopal college in communion with the Successor of Peter, as well as to the Supreme Pontiff himself, head of this college (LG 25), must be made effective by the co-responsible cooperation and collegial association of the

188

members of the magisterium and of the individual theologians. This cooperation must be practised not only by the members of the magisterium and by theologians among themselves, but also between the magisterium and theologians, without any lessening of the personal responsibility of the individual theologian, which is indispensable, since without it the scientific study of the faith would make no progress.

'Co-responsible cooperation with personal responsibility'

The idea that the relationship between theologians and the magisterium is to be one of co-responsible cooperation and collegial association, and that the personal responsibility of the theologian is to be respected because it is indispensable for progress in the study of the faith, presents a 'model' of the relationship between the magisterium and theologians which surely reflects the spirit of Vatican II, but which the experience of the two decades since that council shows to be an ideal more easily described than realised. Effective collaboration between bishops and theologians on questions of doctrine calls for the establishment of structures and the acceptance by both sides of guide-lines that will help to ensure a cooperation that is genuinely co-responsible and collegial. Obviously this will best be done on the regional level. One suggestion that has been made is that each episcopal conference could establish a theological commission made up of the most respected theologians of its region, which could serve as the regular consultative body for the conference's committee on doctrine, and assist the conference, especially in the preparation of doctrinal statements.

A serious study has been made of practical ways to promote this kind of collaboration between bishops and theologians in North America by a joint committee of the Canon Law Society of America and the Catholic Theological Society of America. Its published report, edited by Leo J. O'Donovan, SJ, is entitled: *Cooperation between Theologians and the Ecclesiastical Magisterium.*[34]

Part II.
The Areas of Difference between the Magisterium and Theologians

Thesis 5. We must first speak of the difference between the functions which are proper to the magisterium and to theologians.

1. The function of the magisterium is authoritatively to maintain the catholic integrity and unity of the Church's faith and practice. From this there follow specific functions which, at first sight, seem rather negative in character, but which are actually a positive service on behalf of the Church's life. These include 'the function of authoritatively interpreting the Word of God, both in Scripture and in Tradition' (DV 10); the censuring of opinions which endanger the faith and morals of the Church, and the setting forth of truths which are especially relevant to the current situation. Although it does not seem appropriate for the magisterium to propose theological syntheses, still, in view of its concern for unity, it has to consider particular truths in the light of the whole, since the integration of particular truths into the whole is an important factor in truth itself.

2. The theologians' function can be described as one of mediating — in both directions — between the magisterium and the people of God. For 'theology has a two-fold relation, both with the Church's magisterium, and with the whole Christian community. In the first place it holds a sort of midway position between the faith of the Church and its magisterium.'[35] On the one hand, 'in each major socio-cultural region, theology, guided by the tradition of the universal Church, brings fresh scrutiny to bear upon the deeds and words revealed by God, recorded in the Scriptures and explained by the Fathers of the Church and by the magisterium.' (Ad gentes, 22) Moreover, 'recent research and discoveries in the sciences, in history and in philosophy raise new questions which also require fresh investigation by theologians.' (GS 62) In this way, theology 'is to provide the help which the magisterium needs in order to fulfill its mission as light and norm for the Church.'[36] On the other hand, by their work of interpretation, teaching, and translation into contemporary thought-forms, theologians integrate the doctrine and

190

admonitions of the magisterium into a broader synthesis,
and help the people of God to understand them better.
In this way, they provide 'effective help so that the truth
which the magisterium authoritatively proclaims, may be
spread abroad, explained, confirmed and defended.'[37]

The function of the magisterium

The key words in the sentence which describes the function
of the magisterium are: *auctoritative tueri catholicam inte-*
gritatem. While each of these words is well chosen to express
the specific role of the magisterium, this is particularly true
of the verb *tueri.* I have translated it as 'maintain', but one
could have used any of the words which the *Latin Dictionary*
of Lewis and Short gives as conveying the predominant sense
of *tueri* in classical Latin: 'to look to, care for, keep up, uphold, maintain, support, guard, preserve, defend, protect'.

One conclusion that follows from such a description of the
function of the magisterium, is that it can be expected to be
primarily conservative in its approach to questions that concern the Christian faith. This, of course, does not mean that
it is exclusively negative, or that its function is merely that of
a watch-dog guarding orthodoxy. In this respect, it is worth
noting that the new guidelines laid down by Pope Paul VI for
the CDF assign to this organ of papal magisterium a role of
promoting sound doctrine, in addition to the Holy Office's
inquisitorial function of examining questionable opinions and
censuring those judged dangerous to the faith.[38]

Among the 'positive functions' which the thesis ascribes to
the magisterium, the first is 'the function of authoritatively
interpreting the Word of God, both in Scripture and in
Tradition.' (DV 10) The Latin word which I have translated
as 'authoritatively' is *authentice*; the reader will recall that
this should not be translated into English as 'authentically'. It
must also be kept in mind that 'authoritatively' here means:
'with that kind of authority which is proper to bishops,
namely, the authority to speak in the name of Christ, in
virtue of episcopal ordination, and succession from the
apostles in their mandate to teach'. Indeed, the next thesis
of the ITC will speak of two different kinds of authority: one
proper to bishops, the other to theologians.

Not only do bishops, on the one hand, and theologians and

exegetes on the other, teach with different kinds of authority; they also have different tasks to perform in the overall function of interpreting the Word of God. It would be absurd to claim that in each diocese, the bishop is the person best qualified to give the correct exegesis of a text of Scripture or a statement made by one of the Fathers or councils of the early Church. The exegesis of texts of Scripture is the work of exegetes; the exegesis of the documents of tradition is the work of patristic scholars and historians of dogma. Few bishops are qualified for the kind of scholarly work that such exegesis entails.

Two further considerations come to mind. First: the magisterium has hardly ever defined exactly how any particular text of Scripture is to be interpreted. Secondly: it is generally understood in Catholic theology that when the magisterium invokes texts of Scripture in support of a doctrine it is defining, the weight of the solemn definition does not fall on the exegesis of those texts which is expressed or implied in the dogmatic statement. In other words, the exegesis of particular scriptural texts is not seen as the proper role of the magisterium.

What then does *Dei Verbum* mean when it ascribes the function of interpreting the Word of God, both in Scripture and in Tradition, to the magisterium? It seems to me it has to mean the function of discerning the consistent patterns, the general directions, which the Scriptures give in matters that concern Christian faith and practice, and of judging whether interpretations that are proposed are consonant with the Gospel message as it has been believed and lived in the Church. It is in this sense, I submit, that bishops are rightly called 'judges of faith and morals for the universal Church'. (LG 25)

The function of theologians

The description of the theologian's function as one of mediating between the magisterium and the people of God, is perhaps the most important idea that the theses of the ITC owe to the address of Paul VI to the International Congress on the Theology of Vatican II. This is the idea which Maurizio Flick judged most worthy of extended comment in his presentation of the ITC theses in an article for the *Civiltà*

Cattolica, which he entitled 'The Two Functions of Theology according to the Recent Document of the International Theological Commission'.[39]

These 'two functions of theology' involve a two-directional mediation: from the faith, culture and questionings of the people toward the magisterium; and from the pronouncements of the magisterium back to the people.

The first of these mediations has to do with the work of theologians which is preparatory to the statements of the magisterium, and on which the effectiveness of the official teaching to a considerable extent depends. Pope Paul VI spoke of this dependence when he said: 'Without the help of sacred theology the magisterium could no doubt protect and teach the faith: but it could hardly achieve that full and profound knowledge which it needs in order to perform its function in a fully satisfactory way.'[40]

The thesis draws upon Vatican II's Decree on the Church's Missionary Activity (*Ad gentes*) for the idea that theologians have a part to play in the inculturation of the Gospel in each 'major socio-cultural region'. Theologians are called upon to seek an understanding of the faith in the light of the philosophy and wisdom of non-European cultures, as it has already done in the light of the philosophy and wisdom of Greece and Rome.[41] In this way, they help the magisterium to know how to preach the Gospel more effectively to the people imbued with these cultures.

The thesis refers again to Vatican II, this time to *Gaudium et spes*, for the idea that it is the theologian's role to help the magisterium by seeking answers to the new questions that are constantly being posed to Christian faith by the rapid advances in every sphere of human knowledge which are so characteristic of the modern age.

The other mediation which theologians exercise is subsequent to the pronouncements of the magisterium, and involves interpreting them, translating them into contemporary thought-forms, rendering them more intelligible to people of varying cultures and levels of education. As M. Flick points out, this includes the challenge of presenting the teaching of the Church in a convincing way to a public, both within the Church and outside of it, many of whom are highly intelligent, well-educated and extremely critical.[42]

193

Thesis 6. The magisterium and theologians differ also in the kind of authority with which they carry out their respective tasks.

1. The magisterium derives its authority from sacramental ordination, which 'along with the office of sanctifying, confers also the offices of teaching and ruling.' (LG 21) This authority, which is called 'formal' is at once charismatic and juridical, and is the basis of the right and duty of the teaching office, insofar as this means sharing in the authority of Christ. Care should be taken that in the exercise of the authority attached to this ministry, the kind of authority which derives from the qualities of the person teaching, and from the matter itself which is taught, should also be effective.

2. Theologians derive their specifically theological authority from their qualifications as scholars. However, these cannot be separated from the distinctive character of their discipline, which, being 'the science of the faith', cannot be pursued without a living experience and practice of the faith. For this reason the authority which theology enjoys in the Church is not that of a profane science, but it is a truly ecclesial authority, which has its place in the order of authorities that derive from the Word of God and are confirmed by canonical mission.

The authority of the magisterium

While it is the teaching of Vatican II that episcopal ordination confers the office of teaching (*munus docendi*), it should be added that the bishop's authority to teach also depends on his membership in the episcopal college, which requires, besides sacramental consecration, also 'hierarchical communion with the head and members of the body'. (LG 22) Without this communion, he would lack a 'canonical mission' (LG 24).

On the other hand, it could also be noted that in the general councils of the Western Church, some men without episcopal orders have regularly been invited to share the magisterial authority of the episcopal college. For instance, at both Councils of the Vatican, the general superiors of clerical religious orders of men were among the 'Fathers' of the council, with the same voting rights as the bishops.

Authority is called 'formal' when it is derived from the

possession of an office to which such authority is attached. The thesis describes episcopal teaching authority as both 'charismatic' and 'juridical'. If I am not mistaken, the term 'charismatic' here refers to the sacramental basis of the bishops' teaching office. The term 'charism', derived from the Greek word *charis*, meaning 'grace', is properly applied to those distributed gifts of grace by which the Holy Spirit equips people for the various kinds of ministries or services which help to build up the Church.[43] Some such gifts, which we call 'vocations', are confirmed by sacramental ordination, which confers the charism, or grace-gift, for fulfilling the ministry for which one is ordained. Thus, in 2 Tim 1:6, Timothy is exhorted to rekindle the gift of God (*charisma*) that is within him through the laying-on of Paul's hands.

Inasmuch as the bishop's teaching authority is derived from the grace of his ordination, it can be called 'charismatic'. It is also called 'juridical', since it is also based on his canonical mission, and on his being in hierarchical communion with the Bishop of Rome and with the other members of the episcopal college.

The last sentence of the paragraph on the authority of the magisterium can be understood as an exhortation to the bishops not to rely exclusively on their formal or juridical authority to command assent to their teaching. O. Semmelroth's comment on this thesis suggests that what the ITC had in mind was the persuasiveness that the bishops' teaching could gain from either their own competence as theologians or their enlisting the help of capable theologians in the preparation of their doctrinal statements. Besides theological competence, however, one could also mention the need of skill in the arts of communication, with all that this could contribute by way of making a message intelligible and convincing to those to whom it is addressed.

The authority of theologians

As we have just seen, the teaching authority of bishops is described as 'charismatic' as well as juridical. This makes it all the more surprising that there is no hint, anywhere in these theses, of the idea of a charism for doing theology in the Church, or that the teaching authority of theologians could be called charismatic, as well as scientific.

The closest the ITC document comes to the idea of theology as a charismatic activity is the statement in thesis 7 that theology 'receives its dynamism from the life of the Spirit in the Church'. I shall return to this question in my comment on the next thesis.

Thesis 7. There is also a difference in the ways that the magisterium and theologians are related to the Church. It is obvious that both of them work in and for the Church. But there is a difference in the ways that each of them has an 'ecclesial' character.

1. Magisterium is an ecclesiastical office which is conferred by the sacrament of Holy Orders. Therefore, as an institutional element of the Church it can exist only in the Church, and its members can use their authority and sacred power only for the building up of their flocks in truth and holiness (LG 27). They are to do this not only for the particular churches of which they have charge, but as members of the episcopal college, 'each of them is bound by Christ's teaching and command to show that care for the universal Church which contributes to the benefit of the whole Church' (LG 23).

2. Theology, even when it is not practised in virtue of an explicit 'canonical mission', can be done only in a living communion with the faith of the Church. Consequently, any baptised person who both actively lives the life of the Church and enjoys scholarly competence, can undertake the theologian's task. This task receives its dynamism from the life of the Spirit in the Church, which is communicated through sacraments, the preaching of the Word of God and the communion of charity.

'Canonical mission' for teaching theology?

As I have already remarked, this thesis states clearly that one does not need an explicit canonical mission to *be* a theologian or to *do* theology in the Catholic Church. What remains unclear is whether these theses should be interpreted as favouring the view that one must have a mission to *teach* theology.

It is my impression, from the way that 'canonical mission' is spoken of in theses 1 and 6, that the members of the ITC considered it at least the normal thing that a person who taught theology would do so in virtue of a canonical mission. This impression is confirmed by the comments of P. Delhaye and O. Semmelroth on thesis 7, where both distinguish between teaching theology with a canonical mission, and doing personal research without it.[44] I think it is not irrelevant that the two members of the ITC who drafted the theses were German, because it is the peculiar situation of the Catholic faculties of theology in the German state universities that gave rise in the mid-nineteenth century to the notion of a canonical mission for university professors of theology.[45]

Prior to this time the term had been used to describe the conferral of hierarchical jurisdiction, e.g. when a bishop is named ordinary of a diocese or a priest is given charge of a parish. It was also used of the authorisation required to exercise the ministry of preaching. But there was no precedent in canon law for the requirement of such canonical mission for professors of theology. However, when the German bishops were faced, in the 1840s, with the problem of maintaining Catholic faculties of theology in universities that were now controlled by the state, they insisted that no one should be appointed to teach Catholic theology in the university without the approval of the local bishop, and no such professor should be retained if the bishop should withdraw his approval. Such an arrangement became legally binding on the German state universities by virtue of several concordats, most recently by the 1933 concordat between the German Reich and the Holy See.[46] Although these concordats did not use the technical term *missio canonica*, it became customary, at least in ecclesiastical circles, to use this term in referring to the episcopal approval required.[47]

With the promulgation of the Apostolic Constitution *Deus Scientiarum Dominus* in 1931, canonical mission became a requisite for teaching in ecclesiastical faculties authorised to grant degrees by the Holy See.[48] The new Apostolic Constitution *Sapientia Christiana*, regulating these faculties, also calls for canonical mission for those teaching disciplines concerned with faith and morals, adding as the reason for this, that 'they do not teach on their own authority, but by reason of the mission received from the Church.'[49]

While, up to this point, canonical mission had been required only of those teaching either in Catholic faculties of theology in state universities (where this was regulated by a concordat), or in ecclesiastical faculties granting pontifical degrees, the 1977 *schema* of the revised code of canon law extended the requirement of canonical mission to those teaching theology or related subjects in any institutes of higher learning whatsoever.[50]

Since we have now embarked on a question of canon law, I think it best to call upon an expert in that field. The following is the comment on the new law by the American canonist, John A. Alesandro.[51]

This canon engendered a great deal of discussion, many objecting to it as a needless 'condition of employment' which will be difficult to implement in all cultures throughout the world. The Fathers of the Code Commission amended the canon slightly so that is now reads:
'Those who teach the theological disciplines in any institutes of higher learning whatsoever should have (*habeant oportet*) the mandate (*mandatum*) of the competent ecclesiastical authority.'[52] The latest wording avoids the use of the technical term, 'canonical mission', which tended to equate the authorization to teach theology with the assignment of a person to an ecclesiastical office. Nevertheless, the implication of even the amended wording is clear. The right to teach theology in a formal academic setting rests not only on one's faith commitment and scholarly expertise but on hierarchical deputation as well. In this way, the theologian-teacher officially exercises the *munus docendi* on behalf of the church. This hierarchical concept suggests that one teaches theology as an agent commissioned by the church's juridically recognized leaders. . . .
From a theoretical point of view, the requirement of a *mandatum* represents an extremely significant shift in the canonical articulation of the relationship between hierarchy and theologian. At best it is a questionable experiment in directing Christian behavior which skirts perilously close to regimentation and opens the church to charges of institutionalized indoctrination. The 1917 canonical system of negative vigilance seems the wiser theoretical approach. What will result in concrete terms

from this shift to active deputation is a question to be answered by the history of the next decade, but it would not be surprising to see the longer canonical tradition prevail. If so, the requirement will soon evolve into a presumed permission, a development which may be equally fostered by bishops and theologians alike. The end result will be negative hierarchical vigilance in which the need for a *mandatum* will be invoked only in the rare occurrence in which a bishop finds himself in conflict with a theologian in matters seriously affecting faith and morals.

My own comment on the canonical requirement of a mandate from ecclesiastical authority for everyone teaching theology is that it reflects the 'model' of the relationship between the magisterium and theologians that characterised the thinking of Pope Pius XII, as exemplified in the following passage of his allocution *Si diligis* of 31 May 1945:

> Besides the legitimate successors of the Apostles, namely the Roman Pontiff for the universal Church and the bishops for the faithful entrusted to their care, there are no other teachers by divine right in the Church of Christ. However, the bishops, and in particular he who is the Supreme Teacher in the Church and the Vicar of Christ on earth, in fulfilling their task as teachers, can enlist other persons as helpers and advisors, to whom they confer authority to teach *[quibus facultatem docendi delegent]*. This may be given in a special way to the person, or may be connected with the office entrusted to him. Those who are thus called to teach, work as teachers in the Church not in their own name, nor by title of their theological scholarship, but by virtue of the mission which they have received from the legitimate magisterium. Their authority to teach remains always subject to that of the magisterium; it never becomes *sui iuris*, subject to no other power.[53]

I do not think that a Catholic theologian can question the truth of the last sentence of this quotation. But does the fact that the Catholic theologian is always subject to the authority of the magisterium justify the conclusion that he can teach only by virtue of a mandate or mission received from the magisterium? This would seem to suppose that there can be only one kind of teaching authority in the Church, namely, the hierarchical, and that anyone who has any authority to teach must be sharing in the pastoral authority of the hierarchy.

But the ITC has developed the idea, in theses 6 and 7, that the magisterium and theologians have different functions to perform in the service of the Word of God, and that they teach with different kinds of authority. To use the terminology of St Thomas, besides the *magisterium cathedrae pastoralis* there is also the *magisterium cathedrae magistralis*. The thesis proposed by Pope Pius XII in *Si diligis* seems to reduce all teaching authority in the Church to the teaching authority of the pastoral chair, so that whoever teaches theology must do so as sharing in the specifically pastoral teaching function and authority of the hierarchy. This is of a piece with the idea, also current in the time of Pius XII, that any apostolate of the laity must be seen as a sharing in the mission of the hierarchy, whereas Vatican II declares that 'through their baptism and confirmation all are commissioned to that apostolate by the Lord Himself'. (LG 33)

Vatican II also went on to say that besides being commissioned to the apostolate by their sacramental initiation, members of the Church 'of every rank' are gifted by the Holy Spirit with various charisms, by which they are made 'fit and ready to undertake various tasks or offices advantageous for the renewal and upbuilding of the Church' (LG 12). While Vatican II did not speak explicitly of a charism for doing theology in the Church, I believe that one can rightly apply what the council does say about charisms to the 'ecclesial ministry' of the theologian.

The charism for the ecclesial ministry of the theologian
The statement made in thesis 7 that 'any baptized person who both actively lives the life of the Church and enjoys scholarly competence can undertake the theologian's task' accords well with the teaching of Vatican II that the Holy Spirit distributes his charisms 'among the faithful of every rank'. While at one time practically all Catholic theologians were clerics, and hence necessarily celibate males, it is now obvious that laymen and women are also called to be theo-

logians. Vatican II expressed the Church's wish that many of the laity hear and heed such a call (GS 62).

The thesis goes on to say that the theologian's task 'receives its dynamism from the life of the Spirit in the Church, which is communicated through the sacraments, the preaching of the Word of God and the communion of charity.' All of this is surely true – but I do not understand why the ITC did not mention charisms among the ways that the life of the Spirit is communicated in the Church, and by which the ecclesial ministry of a theologian could also receive its dynamism.

A charism is a gift of grace; the presence of a genuine gift of grace is to be discerned by the signs that justify attributing phenomena to the work of the Holy Spirit. My thesis is that one can rightly judge that a person has received a charism for working as a theologian in the Church when there are evident signs that this person has received and is following *a vocation to do theology as an ecclesial ministry*. In my opinion such signs would be: that the person has all the gifts necessary to be a theologian, has conscientiously cultivated these gifts, and is devoting them generously and fruitfully to the service of the Word of God and his People.

Vatican II, in its Decree on the Apostolate of the Laity, makes a further statement about charisms which could have an important application to the question about the need of a mandate from the hierarchy to teach theology. The statement is as follows (AG 3):

> From the reception of these charisms or gifts, including those which are less dramatic, there arise for each believer the right and duty to use them in the Church and in the world for the good of mankind and for the upbuilding of the Church. In so doing, believers need to enjoy the freedom of the Holy Spirit who 'breathes where he wills' (Jn 3:8). At the same time, they must act in communion with their brothers in Christ, especially with their pastors. The latter must make a judgment about the true nature and proper use of these gifts, not in order to extinguish the Spirit, but to test all things and hold fast to what is good (cf. 1 Th 5:12,19,21).

I believe that this statement of Vatican II justifies the

conclusion that a genuinely ecclesial ministry, while it must be subordinate to the hierarchical ministry and submit to being judged and regulated by it, need not be understood as a *sharing* in the hierarchical ministry, or necessarily *derived from it*. An ecclesial ministry, and the right to exercise it in the Church, can be derived directly from a charismatic gift of the Spirit.

If then it is true that teaching theology is an ecclesial ministry for which a person can have a genuine vocation, and if such a vocation can rightly be seen to be a charism, it would follow from the above statement of the Council that the reception of such a charism confers a right and duty to use it in the Church. Now, since charisms are gifts which the Holy Spirit 'distributes to whom he wills', would it be inappropriate to speak of such a charismatically conferred right as a 'divine right'? Obviously, such a right would have to be exercised 'in communion with the pastors of the Church', with respect for their right to regulate its proper use.

But I do not see any reason why 'working in communion with' and 'under the authority of' the hierarchy, has to mean 'working as delegated by' or 'by mandate of' the hierarchy.

Joseph Ratzinger has noted a significant emendation of the earlier text of the Council's Constitution on Revelation, which suggests what the members of the Theological Commission might have thought on this question. The final text of *Dei Verbum* reads (n. 23):

Catholic exegetes and others who devote themselves to sacred theology should zealously combine their efforts. Under the watchful eye of the sacred magisterium, and using appropriate techniques, they should together set about examining and explaining the sacred texts in such a way that as many as possible of those who are ministers of the divine Word may be able to distribute fruitfully the nourishment of the Scriptures to the People of God.

Where this final text says that exegetes and theologians are to do their work 'under the watchful eye' (*sub vigilantia*) of the magisterium, the previous *schema* had said 'under the direction' (*sub ductu*) of the magisterium. This is Ratzinger's comment on this change of wording:

Vigilantia was used ... to replace the previous term

sub ductu, in order to express the fact that the function of the teaching office is not to lead the way. Progress is the concern of scholarship; basically, the teaching office has the negative function of marking off impassable terrain as such.[54]

I find striking similarity between Ratzinger's view of the proper role of the hierarchy vis-a-vis the work of exegetes and theologians, and Alesandro's suggestion that it was better expressed canonically by the 1917 Code as 'negative vigilance' than it is by the 1983 Code as 'positive deputation'.

I believe that there is an ecclesial ministry of teaching theology which is distinct from and not derived from the teaching authority of the hierarchy, even if it is necessarily subordinate to this and must accept its 'vigilance' over what it teaches and publishes. I do not see how the claim that 'besides the bishops there are no other teachers by divine right in the Church' can be reconciled with the mind of St Paul, according to whom 'God has appointed in the church first apostles, second prophets, third teachers' (1 Cor 12:28). I have criticised Hans Küng's use of this text, because he wanted it to mean that the *didaskaloi* of the New Testament church, and their successors (the theologians) in today's Church, are the only ones who can truly be said to have a divine right to teach in the Church. On the other hand, I do see in this text reason to question the view that besides the apostles and their successors there are no other teachers by divine right in the Church. As 'God appointed teachers' in the New Testament Church, I believe that the Holy Spirit is still 'appointing teachers' in today's Church, by giving people the charism of a vocation for the ecclesial ministry of doing and teaching theology.

Does this mean that there are 'two *magisteria*' in the Church? If we use the term *magisterium* as St Thomas did, of a teaching function with its proper teaching authority, then undoubtedly there are two *magisteria* in the Church. My objection to the expression 'two *magisteria*' is based on the fact that nowadays the term *magisterium* has become so closely identified with the hierachical teaching function and authority, that I think (with Rahner and others) that it would be too misleading to insist on speaking of theologians as having or constituting 'another magisterium'. But I cer-

203

tainly have no objection to speaking, as these theses of the ITC do, of theologians as having a teaching function and teaching authority in the Church that is different from that of the hierarchy, and that, in my view, need not be conceived as a sharing in, or derived from, that of the hierarchy. No doubt there is teaching in the Church that can properly be described as a sharing in the pastoral magisterium of the bishops: such as catechetical instruction, the teaching of religion in schools, perhaps even the basic courses in the seminary education of future priests ... But I do not see any justification for looking on the teaching that a theologian does in courses and seminars in university programmes for higher degrees in theology as a sharing in the pastoral magisterium of the bishops. I see no reason to abandon St Thomas's distinction between the *magisterium cathedrae pastoralis* and the *magisterium cathedrae magistralis*.

Thesis 8. The difference between the magisterium and theology is especially noteworthy as regards the freedom that is proper to each, and as regards the critical role they must exercise toward the faithful, the world, and one another.

1. The magisterium, by its nature and institution, is manifestly free in carrying out its mission. This freedom involves a great responsibility. For this reason it is often difficult, though always necessary, to use it in such a way that it not seem to theologians or to others of the faithful to be arbitrary or excessive. There are some theologians with an exaggerated esteem for academic freedom, who do not reflect enough on the fact that respect for the magisterium is one of the specific elements of the science of theology. Likewise, modern sentiments in favour of democracy sometimes give rise to a tendency to 'close ranks' against the magisterium, when it intervenes to prevent some harm to faith or morals. Although it will not be easy, the magisterium must always find a way of proceeding which on the one hand is free and forceful, but on the other hand is not arbitrary or such as would destroy peace and harmony in the Church.

2. To the freedom of the magisterium there corresponds the specific freedom of theologians, which flows from their genuine responsibility as scholars. This is not an unlimited freedom, for, besides being bound to the truth, it must also recognise that 'in the exercise of any freedom, one must observe the moral principle of personal and social responsibility' (DH 7). At the same time, the theologian's task of interpreting the statements of the past and present magisterium, of putting them into the context of the whole of revealed truth, and of seeking a better understanding of them with the aid of the science of hermeneutics, brings with it a function that is in some sense critical. This criticism, of course, must be of the positive, not the destructive kind.

Freedom and responsibility of theologians

Since pertinent passages of the documents of Vatican II are quoted so often in these theses, it is a bit surprising that no reference was made here to the statement of *Gaudium et spes* on the freedom to be accorded to all, whether clerics or lay people, who cultivate the sacred sciences.

It is hoped that many laymen will receive an appropriate formation in the sacred sciences, and that some will develop and deepen these studies by their own labors. In order that such persons may fulfill their proper functions, let it be recognized that all the faithful, clerical and lay, possess a lawful freedom of inquiry and of thought, and the freedom to express their minds humbly and courageously about those matters in which they enjoy competence. (GS 62).

If a theologian is going to pursue his vocation with genuine freedom, he has to be able to do research, to publish the fruits of his research, and to teach, with no limits set to his freedom other than the two mentioned in the thesis: namely, the truth, and his personal and social responsibility.

The problem is: how does one establish, in the concrete, the limits set by the truth, and the limits set by a sense of responsibility?

First: the limits set by the truth. Obviously, for the theologian, it is a question of the revealed truth, and for a Catholic, of revealed truth as this is handed on and understood in the Catholic Church. The *sensus Ecclesiae* is a norm of truth for the theologian who does his work 'in a living communion with the faith of the Church'. This *sensus Ecclesiae* is found most authoritatively in the doctrine that has been infallibly taught by the Church's magisterium, 'whether by solemn judgment or by its ordinary and universal magisterium' (D-S 3011).

Now, as Pope John XXIII pointed out in his opening address to the Fathers of Vatican II, the truth of the doctrine of the Church is one thing; the form in which it has been expressed is another.[55] So 'being bound to the truth' does not mean being bound to the formulas in which that truth has been expressed in the past, even in solemn dogmatic definitions. A new formulation, or new conceptualisation, is possible, provided it does justice to the truth of the dogma.

Of course the question will arise whether a new formulation really does justice to the truth of the dogma. A theologian may well believe that his interpretation is within the limits set by the truth of the dogma; others may dispute this. This is the kind of issue that calls for the critical function which theologians are to exercise with regard to one another. It may even call for the critical function which the magisterium exercises with regard to the work of theologians, when it judges an opinion incompatible with the truth of the faith. How such a critical function should be exercised is the subject of theses 10-12. The present thesis points out that it should be exercised in a way that avoids giving the impression of being arbitrary or excessive.

Perhaps the more troublesome question concerning the limits of truth within which a Catholic theologian has to work is raised by the assertion of Pope Pius XII that for a Catholic theologian, 'the sacred magisterium ought to be the proximate and universal norm of truth in matters of faith and morals' (*Humani generis*, D-S 3884). The schema of the Constitution on the Church prepared for Vatican II by the preparatory commission, adding a reference to this place in *Humani generis*, stated that theologians must always look upon the ecclesiastical magisterium as the 'proximate norm of truth'.[56] Although no such statement was retained in any document of the Second Vatican Council, Pope Paul VI, on several occasions, returned to Pius XII's description of the magisterium as the 'proximate and universal norm of truth' for the Catholic theologian.[57]

Now if by the magisterium here one meant the infallible teaching of the magisterium, I could understand describing this as 'the proximate norm of truth' with regard to those elements of Christian faith which have actually been infallibly taught. On the other hand, the statement as it stands would seem to mean that even the non-infallible or ordinary magisterium is to be accepted by Catholic theologians as a 'proximate and universal norm of truth in matters of faith and morals.' It is my guess that this is one of the statements that Yves Congar had in mind when he wrote that some of the claims made by the magisterium in modern times 'seem excessive and unreal'.[58] At any rate, this is what he says in reference to this claim, when speaking of the new approach taken by Vatican II.

> With regard to the magisterium, the Council re-established the traditional relationship of subordination of pastoral authority to what is given, to the object, in short the primacy of the *quod* over the *quo*. It did this both by insisting that the magisterium is bound to the Word of God and is at its service (LG 25,4; DV 10,2), and by not taking up the statement which the preparatory schema of 1962 had borrowed from *Humani generis*, namely, the idea that the magisterium is the 'proximate norm of truth'.[59]

It is obvious that the ITC did not take up this idea either, in the theses we are considering. It did say, in the first part of the present thesis, that 'respect for the magisterium is one of the specific elements of the science of theology.' But it also assigned to theologians a critical role with regard to the magisterium. I do not see what criteria would be available on which to base any criticism of magisterial statements, if one were to accept the magisterium itself as the proximate and universal norm of truth.

The critical role of theologians toward one another
Karl Rahner has deplored the reluctance of theologians to express criticism of one another.

> It is a false politeness and collegiality when theologians are too concerned to take pains to be 'indulgent' with one another. The indisputable decline in theological criticism is

to be deplored in this respect, and it is an extremely dangerous situation.[60]

Perhaps one reason for the indulgent attitude which Rahner deplores is the tendency, noted in the thesis, for theologians to 'close ranks' in the kind of solidarity more associated with organised labour than with critical scholarship. Rahner insists in another article that theologians should not fear to criticise one another's opinions, and even to defend the magisterium against a theologian when the case calls for this.[61]

The critical role of theologians with regard to the magisterium

The thesis sees this critical role entailed in the theologian's task of interpreting statements of the magisterium, putting them into a wider context, and applying to them the science of hermeneutics.

We can distinguish between the critical work theologians do with regard to defined dogmas, and the critical approach theologians may take toward the ordinary, non-infallible teaching of the magisterium.

Juan Alfaro describes the interpretation of dogmas which it is the theologian's task to undertake, as 'critical, methodical and systematic'. He observes that dogmas always arise out of a prior theology, whose concepts and language the dogmas make their own. Inevitably this theology will involve limitations, and the kind of historical conditioning which no human thinking can escape. It will involve presuppositions which may not have been recognised at the time, but which exercised a hidden influence on the way the dogma was formulated.[62]

The result, as Rahner expresses it, is that every dogmatic formula will represent a kind of 'amalgam' of a faith-content and a theological conceptualisation.[63] Thus it is possible, and can become necessary, for the theologian to exercise his critical role with regard to those elements in the 'amalgam' which do not really belong to the essential faith-content of the dogma, and which may now render the dogma less intelligible or even less credible to the modern mind. An example would be the association of the dogma of original sin with the assumption that the Genesis story of the creation and fall of man is to be taken as straightforward history.

Joseph Ratzinger has also spoken of the grounds on which

even radical criticism of papal doctrinal statements could be based.

> Criticism of papal pronouncements will be possible and even necessary, to the degree that they lack support in Scripture and the Creed, that is, in the faith of the whole Church. When neither the consensus of the whole Church is had, nor clear evidence from the sources is available, a definitive decision is not possible. Were one formally to take place, while conditions for such an act were lacking, the question would have to be raised concerning its legitimacy.[64]

The question of the limits of the freedom of Catholic theologians to exercise a critical function with regard to the ordinary, non-infallible teaching of the papal magisterium has been a matter of intense discussion since the publication of the encyclical *Humanae vitae* in 1968.[65] In the previous chapter I have spoken about the possibility of legitimate internal dissent from such teaching. What must be raised now is the further question about the limits of the freedom of Catholic theologians publicly to express their dissent from such teaching, if they are convinced that some statement of this magisterium is erroneous.

It will be recalled that according to the encyclical *Humani generis* of Pius XII, when a pope, in an encyclical, expresses his judgment on an issue that was previously controverted, this can no longer be seen as a question for free discussion by theologians (D-S 3885). The schema on the Church presented to Vatican II in 1962 by the preparatory commission followed Pius XII on this point,[66] but there is no such statement in any of the documents that were approved by the Council. There is, however, the statement of *Gaudium et spes* quoted above, to the effect that all the faithful, clerical or lay, are free to express their minds humbly and courageously about those matters in which they enjoy competence (GS 62).

While the documents of Vatican II make no mention of the possibility of legitimate dissent from ordinary papal teaching, the Council can be said to have expressed its own dissent from previous papal teaching on several important questions, such as religious liberty, and the identification of the Mystical Body of Christ with the Roman Catholic Church. Theologians who had been censured or silenced for their dissent on these issues during the pontificate of Pius XII came to be among the most highly respected *periti* of Vatican II. The Council could hardly have arrived at a number of its innovative decisions if it had not been for the preparatory work done by the theologians who had taken a critical stance towards what had been the official teaching of the Holy See.

One important aspect of the kind of teaching that is found in papal encyclicals, which justifies a critical approach by theologians, is the extent to which such teaching goes beyond the pastoral exposition and defence of the doctrine of the faith, and takes on the character of strictly theological discourse. As Yves Congar puts it:[67]

> In their encyclicals (the series begins with *Mirari vos* of Gregory XVI, 1832) modern Popes have *done theology*. And a specific kind of theology, the kind practiced in the Roman schools, whose personnel were recruited and kept under surveillance along a very definite line.

Archbishop Coffy has also noted the problem that arises from the fact that when the magisterium 'does theology' in its authoritative pronouncements, it inevitably makes theological options.

> The situation gains in complexity as one accepts theological pluralism — and how can one do otherwise when faced by facts? To accept pluralism is to accept that the faith can legitimately express itself in different theologies. . . . This explains the reaction of theologians when faced with certain interventions of the magisterium. They have the impression that the magisterium imposes on them its particular theology. What they ask is that it make explicit its theological options and abstain from presenting them as the only possible way of expressing the faith.[68]

It is my impression that the criticism of the ordinary magisterium that has been most consistently voiced by Catholic theologians in recent decades is along the lines suggested here by Congar and Coffy: namely, that on certain issues the official teaching of the Holy See (encyclicals, declarations of the CDF) seems to them to reflect, in too narrow a way, theological options which are not seen as representing the most widely respected theological opinion available in the Church today. If I am not mistaken, it was with the intention of providing a remedy for this situation that the Episcopal Synod of 1967 recommended the setting up of the International Theological Commission. The question is how effectively this body is being consulted in the preparation of the doctrinal statements that are issued by the Holy See. In any case, I do not see how one can deny to a theologian the right to express his criticism of what he perceives to be a strictly theological option, even when it is incorporated into a document of the ordinary magisterium.

At the same time, of course, such criticism must be of the positive, not the destructive kind, and in choosing the manner and medium of its expression, the theologian has to observe the moral principle of personal and social responsibility. What concretely does this involve?

With regard to the manner of expressing criticism or dissent, it seems obvious that it must not only be in accord with the canons of professional courtesy, but must also show the religious respect which is due to the bearers of pastoral authority in the Church.

It is not so easy to determine what the principle of personal and social responsibility requires with regard to the medium in which a theologian may express his criticism of official teaching. The question was fairly easy to decide when theologians could share their views with their professional colleagues through the medium of scholarly journals, with little likelihood that their ideas would reach the wider public. However, the 'information explosion' of modern times, and the tendency of popular journals to publicise any opinion that is critical of positions taken by those in authority, drastically increases the probability that what is carefully and moderately put forward in a scholarly article may subsequently be broadcast to the general public in a crude or tendentious way.

Pope John Paul II, in his address to the faculty and students of the Catholic University in Washington, D.C. (7 October 1979), said that theologians must take into account 'the right of the faithful not to be troubled by theories and

211

hypotheses that they are not expert in judging or that are easily simplified or manipulated by public opinion for ends that are alien to the truth'.[69] The question, then, is: does the possibility that the critical opinion which a theologian has published in a scholarly journal might be picked up and manipulated by the mass-media for ends alien to the truth, mean that theologians may never publish opinions which, if so manipulated, could 'trouble the faithful'?

The supposition of this question is that the kind of publicity which could trouble the faithful is an effect that is foreseen as possible, but is not intended. It would be another question if theologians deliberately sought to stir up public opinion against the teaching of the magisterium: this is mentioned in thesis 11 among tactics that would be harmful to a spirit of dialogue.

In the hypothesis that the kind of publicity that could trouble the faithful is an effect which the theologian does not intend, then the 'moral principle of personal and social responsibility' would require that he weigh the value which he intends to promote by publishing his criticism against the value which he foresees might be damaged by the unwanted publicity that might be given to his criticism. It seems to me that this would be a case of a conflict of values, neither of which can be simply given an absolute priority over the other. I do not see how one could maintain that the protection of the faithful from being troubled by the criticism of official teaching is a value that would always and necessarily have to be preferred to the value involved in the exercise by theologians of their critical function with regard to the magisterium. Nor do I see how they could exercise their critical function effectively if they could not share their views with their colleagues in serious theological publications. Such communication is the very life-blood of scholarly work. To stifle it would be to deprive the Church of a vital factor in its striving for the truth.

Thesis 9. The exercise of their functions by the magisterium and by theologians sometimes gives rise to a certain tension. This is not surprising, nor should one expect that such tension can ever be eliminated here on earth. On the contrary, wherever there is authentic life, there will also be some tension. Tension as such is not hostility

or real opposition; rather it is a lively stimulus and in-
centive for both sides to perform their respective tasks
in communion with the other, following the method of
dialogue.

One can only admire the realism, and at the same time the
optimism, of this approach to the problem of tension between
the magisterium and theologians. According to O. Semmelroth, this thesis provides a transition to the third part, which
will propose dialogue as a method, not to eliminate all tension
(which is recognised to be out of the question), but to make
it fruitful.

Part III
A Method for Improving the Relationship between
Theologians and the Magisterium

Thesis 10. Dialogue between theologians and the magis-
terium has its basis and is made feasible by the fact that
both sides share the faith of the Church and both are
engaged in ministry for the upbuilding of the Church —
a ministry that embraces all of their distinctive functions.
On the one hand, this unity in sharing the same truth is a
habitual communion which is prior to any actual dialogue.
On the other hand, this same unity can grow stronger
and more vital through the various kinds of interchange
which dialogue entails. Hence dialogue can be extremely
profitable for both sides: the magisterium can achieve
a deeper understanding of the truth of faith and morals
which it preaches and safeguards, while the theological
understanding of faith and morals can gain greater cer-
tainty from its corroboration by the magisterium.

Karl Lehmann, who worked with O. Semmelroth in
drawing up these theses, provided the brief commentary on
the third part, published along with the theses in *Gregorianum*.[70] In his comment on thesis 10 he stresses the fact that
to be fruitful, dialogue must not only arise out of a common
basis, but must also respect the diversity of the functions
proper to each of the partners. This thesis again describes
the function of the magisterium in terms of preaching and
safeguarding the faith, and that of theology in terms of under-

standing it. Through dialogue, each can receive something of the strength proper to the other.

> *Thesis 11. The dialogue between the magisterium and theologians is limited only by the truth of the faith to be preserved and explained. From this it follows, on the one hand, that a vast field of truth is available for such dialogue. On the other hand, this truth is not something we have forever to search for, as though it were doubtful or quite unknown. Rather, it is truth that has been truly revealed and has been entrusted to the Church to be faithfully preserved. And so this dialogue must be kept within the boundaries set by the truth of our faith.*
>
> *There are some kinds of behaviour which restrict the possibility of dialogue and make it less likely that it will achieve its purpose of serving the truth. A dialogue will surely founder when it becomes an 'instrument' for attaining some end in a 'political' way, that is, by applying pressures and ultimately prescinding from the question of truth. When one party 'unilaterally' takes over the whole field of the dialogue, he violates the rules of discussion. It is especially damaging to dialogue between the magisterium and theologians when the stage of discussion and debate is broken off prematurely, and measures of coercion, threat and sanction are employed all too soon. It is equally damaging when a discussion between theologians and the magisterium is carried on by resorting to the kind of publicity, whether in the Church or outside it, which is not adequately informed about the question at issue. This has the effect of introducing external pressures which are powerfully influential (e.g. the mass-media).*

Limits of the matter for dialogue

The thesis speaks only of revealed truth as matter for dialogue between the magisterium and theologians. But some of the questions that have occasioned the greatest tension between the magisterium and theologians in recent years have concerned the natural moral law. Hence it would have been better to describe the field of truth available for such dialogue as including all those 'matters of faith and morals' about which the magisterium speaks with authority.

Tactics damaging to dialogue

Of the tactics that are mentioned here, some would be employed by the magisterium, others by theologians; the thesis clearly intends to be evenhanded in assigning blame for the failure of dialogue.

The last two sentences of the thesis take a very negative view of the use of the mass-media by theologians with a view to influencing public opinion against a decision of the magisterium. As is well known, some of the dissent that followed the appearance of the encyclical *Humanae vitae* was of this kind. Referring in particular to a public declaration of dissent that originated in Washington, D.C., originally associated with twenty-one theologians, and subsequently signed by many others, Richard McCormick has offered the following assessment, from a moral theologian's stand-point, of what he calls 'public and organised dissent'.

> *Where dissent is both public and organized, it carries with it special risks, and hence demands special warrants.* Some of the *risks* in our day are: it appears to many to attack authority itself; it tends to polarise the persons exercising the various charisms within the teaching function; it tends to undermine the confidence of the faithful in the charism of the hierarchy; it tends to anticipate and prevent a truly personal reflection on the teaching by the faithful; it tends to associate theology with popular media rather than with serious, scholarly reflection. The *warrants* are two: (1) other forms of less sensational dissent are ineffective (2) in circumstances where an unopposed error would cause great harm.
>
> This harm would be traceable to two sources: first, the personal suffering of the faithful occasioned by the teaching if it touched their lives on a frequent basis; secondly, loss of credibility of the magisterium. . . .
>
> Therefore, given the availability of other styles of dissent and the fact that public organised dissent may easily disturb the proper interplay of the various charisms within the teaching function of the Church, the burden of proof would seem to be on those whose dissent is both public and organised. This is not to say that it is never justified. It is only to say that, in general, organised public dissent can easily threaten to derogate from certain

values profoundly associated with the common good. If this is so, the dissenter must show that the good to be achieved is at least proportionate to the foreseeable harm. If he does this successfully — in so far as this is possible in the circumstances — he has shown that the style of his dissent is both reasonable and Christian.[71]

Thesis 12. Before instituting any formal process about a question of doctrine, the competent authority should exhaust all the ordinary possibilities of reaching agreement through dialogue in order to clarify a questionable opinion (for example, by discussing the matter in person or by correspondence in which questions are asked and replies given). If no genuine agreement can be reached by such dialogical methods, the magisterium should employ a broad and flexible range of measures, beginning with various kinds of warnings, 'verbal sanctions'. etc. In the most serious kind of case, when all the methods of dialogue have been used to no avail, the magisterium, after consulting theologians of various schools, has no choice but to act in defence of the endangered truth and the faith of the believing people.

According to the time-honoured rules, the fact of 'heresy' can be definitively established only if the theologian accused of this has been clearly guilty of 'obstinacy', that is, if he has closed himself off from any discussion aimed at elucidating an opinion that seems contrary to the faith — and in effect, refuses to engage in dialogue. The fact of heresy can be determined only when all the rules concerning the interpretation of dogmatic statements and all theological qualifications have been applied to the case. In this way, even when a grave decision cannot be avoided, the genuine spirit of dialogical procedure can still be maintained.

This final thesis deals with the critical function which the magisterium exercises in regard to theologians when serious questions are raised about the orthodoxy of their teaching or their published writings. According to K. Lehmann, the thesis does not intend to discuss specific questions about the juridical procedure to be followed in such cases. What it proposes is that the method of dialogue be used at every stage: both prior to and during any formal process that is undertaken.

The principles of subsidiarity and decentralisation would seem to require that such dialogue begin at the diocesan level, and, if necessary, continue at the level of an episcopal conference, before a case is referred to Rome. If it is referred to Rome, the case will be handled by the Sacred Congregation for the Doctrine of the Faith, according to the rules of procedure approved by Pope Paul VI and promulgated on 15 January 1974.[72] It was not the intention of the ITC to express a judgment on these rules, or to suggest changes in them, but rather to suggest that the spirit and method of dialogue should characterise the procedure at every step.

It is well known that various aspects of the procedure of the CDF have been criticised in Catholic publications, especially in connection with the 'colloquium' to which Edward Schillebeeckx was summoned by the CDF in December 1979.[73] Given this criticism, one could suggest that the CDF, which surely approved this thesis of the ITC, review its procedure precisely with a view to making sure that there can be no legitimate complaint about a failure to respect a genuine spirit of dialogue at any point from the acceptance of a case by the CDF to a final deliberation and judgment by its board of cardinals.

One final word. A genuine spirit of dialogue calls for both sides to be willing to learn as well as to teach. In an allocution given just about six years prior to the opening of the Second Vatican Council, Pope Pius XII denounced the 'evident error' of thinking that theologians could be *'magistri Magisterii'*.[74] But was not the success of Vatican II due in large measure to the recognition by the magisterium — in the persons of the assembled bishops — of their need to learn as well as to teach? The four years of Vatican II are often spoken of, with nostalgia, as the golden age of collaboration between theologians and the magisterium. Anyone who lived in Rome during those years, as I did, saw abundant evidence that many bishops were willing to be taught by theologians, obviously careless of the accusation that they might be committing the error of accepting theologians as *'magistri magisterii'*.

If a teacher must keep on learning in order to teach well, he has to accept his need to be taught. This applies both to the *magisterium cathedrae pastoralis* and to the *magisterium cathedrae magistralis*. Fruitful dialogue is impossible when either claims a monopoly on the role of the teacher, and refuses to be taught by the other.

Notes

Chapter 1, pp. 4-23

1. Hans Küng, *Infallible? An Inquiry*, tr. E. Quinn, Garden City, 1971.
2. P. C. Empie, T. A. Murphy, J. A. Burgess, (eds.) *Teaching Authority and Infallibility in the Church* (Lutherans and Catholics in Dialogue, VI), Minneapolis 1978.
3. E.g. Lutherans in *Teaching Authority and Infallibility*, pp. 25, 65; Anglicans in Anglican-Roman Catholic International Commission, *The Final Report*, London 1982, pp. 62, 91. For the early Reformers, one can cite Luther: 'Credo Ecclesiam sanctam catholicam, ut impossibile sit illam errare etiam in minimo articulo' (*De servo arbitrio*, 1525, WA 18, 650). H. Ott declares: 'We Evangelical Christians can and must speak of the infallibility of the Church as such': *Die Lehre des I. Vatikanischen Konzils*, Basel 1963, p. 162.
4. Dogmatic Constitution on the Church, *Lumen gentium*, 9. (Hereafter LG).
5. *Summa Theologiae* 2a 2ae, q.1, a.9, ad 3.
6. LG 14.
7. *Acta Synodalia Concilii Vaticani Secundi*, III/1, p. 203.
8. H. Küng, *The Church — Maintained in Truth. A Theological Meditation*, tr. Ed. Quinn, New York 1980, p. 36.
9. 'Actus credentis non terminatur ad enuntiabile, sed ad rem,' St Thomas, *Summa*, 2a 2ae, q.1, a.2, ad 2.
10. Pius XII, encyclical letter *Humani generis*, AAS 42 (1950), p. 571.
11. LG 8. Earlier drafts of the Constitution on the Church had said: 'The Church of Christ *is* the Catholic Church.' The change from 'is' to 'subsists in' means that the Council no longer wished to assert such exclusive identification, but still to affirm that the Church of Christ continues to exist, with all its essential properties, in the Catholic Church.
12. *Summa Theologiae* 2, 2ae, q.45, a.2.
13. Usage of these terms is somewhat fluid, but I find Congar's treatment of them the most helpful. He says: 'On the one hand, there is the *sensus fidei*, which is a quality inherent in a *subject*, on whom the grace of faith, charity, the gifts of the Spirit confer a *faculty of perceiving the truth of the faith and of discerning anything opposed to it*. The *sensus fidelium*, on the other hand, is what can be grasped from outside, objectively, about *what the faithful, and especially*

219

layfolk, believe and profess.' 'Toward a Catholic Synthesis', in *Who Has the Say in the Church?, Concilium*, 148 (8/1981) p. 74.

14. For example, in *Decretum de SS. Eucharistia*, cap. I, D-S 1637; *Decretum de Sacramento Matrimonii*, D-S 1800.

Chapter 2, pp. 24-34

1. *Quodl.* III, 9, ad 3. For the history of the term *magisterium* see Y. Congar, 'A Semantic History of the Term 'Magisterium' ''', in *Readings in Moral Theology No. 3, The Magisterium and Morality*, eds. C. E. Curran and R. A. McCormick, New York, 1982, pp. 297-313, the original French article is in *RSPT* 60 (1976) 85-98.
2. *In IV Sent.* d.19, q.2, a.2, q^a 2 ad 4.
3. Const. Dogm. *Dei Filius*, Cap. III, D-S 3011.
4. Const. Dogm. *Pastor Aeternus* Cap. IV, D-S 3065.
5. Ibid., title of Cap. IV.
6. In Decree on the Pastoral Office of Bishops, *Christus Dominus*, n. 30, *magisterium* is used of the teaching role of parish priests as well.
7. Avery Dulles, 'The Two Magisteria: An Interim Reflection', *Proceedings, CTSA* 35 (1980) 155-69.
8. Among those who have expressed reservations about the attempt to reclaim the term *magisterium* for the role of theologians are Karl Rahner, in 'Lehramt und Theologie', *Schriften fur Theologie* 13, p. 74; Raymond Brown, 'The Dilemma of the Magisterium vs. the Theologians: Debunking Some Fictions', *Chicago Studies* 17 (1978) 291; Richard McCormick, 'Notes on Moral Theology', *Theol. Stud.* 40 (1979) 95.
9. Y. Congar, *Tradition and Traditions, An Historical and a Theological Essay*, London 1966, p. 201.
10. John H. Newman, *On Consulting the Faithful in Matters of Doctrine*, ed. J. Coulson, New York, 1961; originally published in *The Rambler*, July 1859.

Chapter 3, pp. 35-51

1. *Infallible?* p. 86.
2. Ibid., pp. 221-40.
3. *The Documents of Vatican II*, ed. W. M. Abbott, p. 98; the Latin text in *Acta Synodalia Concilii Vaticani II*, III/8, p. 10.
4. *Infallible?* p. 82. The page references in the following pages are to the same work.
5. 'The laity share in the priestly, prophetic and royal office of Christ and therefore have their own role to play in the mission of the whole People of God in the Church and in the world.' (n. 2).
6. Acts 6:1-6.
7. 1 Tim 3:1-2; Tit. 1:7.
8. If these letters are authentic, they were written during the reign of Trajan (i.e. before 117). R. Joly has recently attempted to prove that they must have been written a half-century after this: *Le dossier d'Ignace d'Antioche*, Bruxelles 1979. In the judgment of

G. Pelland, Joly, 'despite his erudition and ingenuity, has not reversed the traditional thesis concerning the authenticity and the approximate date of the letters of Ignatius.' 'Le Dossier des Lettres d'Ignace d'Antioche: A propos d'un livre récent', *Science et Esprit* 32 (1980) p. 296. Most reviewers of Joly's book share Pelland's view.

9. J. Fitzmyer, 'The Office of Teaching in the Christian Church according to the New Testament' in *Teaching Authority and Infallibility*, p. 196.
10. Ibid., p. 206.
11. Ibid., pp. 207, 206.
12. *The Martyrdom of St Polycarp*, n. 16: *The Apostolic Fathers*, ed. K. Lake, vol. II, p. 335.
13. Eusebius, *Hist. Eccl.* IV, 22; PG 20, 378-9.
14. Irenaeus, *Adversus Haereses* III, 3, 1; PG 7, 848.

Chapter 4, pp. 52-78

1. On this see Y. Congar, 'La "Reception" comme realité ecclésiologique', *RSPT* 56 (1972) 369-403; S. L. Greenslade, 'The Authorities Appealed to by the First Four Ecumenical Councils', in *Councils and the Ecumenical Movement* (Studies of the World Council, n. 5, Geneva, 1968), pp. 52-67; A. Grillmeier, 'Konzil und Rezeption', *Th. Ph.* 45 (1970) 321-52; W. Küppers, 'Reception, Prolegomenon to a Systematic Study', in *Councils and the Ecumenical Movement*, pp. 76-98; H. Sieben, *Die Konzilsidee der Alten Kirche*, Paderborn 1979.
2. Y. Congar, '1274-1974. Structures ecclésiales et conciles', *RSPT* 58 (1974) p. 379.
3. Letter to Cardinal Willebrands, 5 Oct. 1974, AAS 66 (1974) 620-25, see especially p. 620.
4. *Acta Synodalia Concilii Vaticani Secundi*, III/1, p. 251, K. Such truths are said to belong to the 'secondary object' of magisterium; I shall discuss this question in Chapter 6.
5. Abbott, p. 98. The Latin text is in *Acta Synodalia*, III/8, p. 10.
6. On the Church, On Divine Revelation.
7. On the Sacred Liturgy.
8. On the Church in the Modern World.
9. On the Instruments of Social Communication; On Ecumenism; On Eastern Christian Churches; On the Bishops' Pastoral Office in the Church; On Priestly Formation; On the Appropriate Renewal of Religious Life; On the Apostolate of the Laity; On the Church's Missionary Activity.
10. On Christian Education; On the Relationship of the Church to Non-Christian Religions; On Religious Freedom.
11. 'This Sacred Synod teaches . . .' e.g. LG 20, LG 21.
12. Examples of this are found in LG 39 and UR 3 and 4.
13. *Adversus haereses* III, 3, 1-2.
14. Athanasius, Bishop of Alexandria, appealed to Rome for support against the Arians; Cyril of Alexandria appealed to Pope Celestine

against the teaching of Nestorius, Bishop of Constantinople; Flavian, Bishop of Constantinople, appealed to Pope Leo I against the monophysite Eutyches.

15. According to the Roman doctrine, baptism correctly administered in a Christian sect was valid, and those so baptised, seeking to be reconciled with the Catholic Church, were not to be re-baptised. Cyprian and Firmilian held sectarian baptism to be invalid, and hence re-baptised those seeking reconciliation.

16. Firmilian's letter, containing the reference to what Pope Stephen had said, is to be found among the letters of Cyprian: *Ep.* 75, 17. *CSEL* III/2, 821.

17. *De Baptismo* 2, 4, 5. *CSEL* 51, 179.

18. 'Securus iudicat orbis terrarum', *Contra Ep. Parmen.* 3, 4, 24.

19. *Ep.* 54, 1, 1. *CSEL* 34, 159. Also *Ep.* 43, 19; *De Bapt.* 2, 3, 9; 4, 24, 31.

20. *Sermo* 131, 10; *PL* 38, 734.

21. *Contra Iulianum* 1, 4, 13. *PL* 44, 648.

22. *Contra Iulianum* 3, 1, 5. *PL* 44, 704.

23. *De Baptismo* 7, 53, 102. *CSEL* 51, 373.

24. W. De Vries, *Orient et Occident. Les Structures ecclésiales vues dans l'histoire des sept premiers conciles oecuméniques*, Paris 1974.

25. Ibid., p. 51.

26. Ibid., p. 140.

27. Yves Congar, *L'Ecclésiologie du Haut Moyen-Age*, Paris 1968, pp. 158-61.

28. Congar, *L'Ecclésiologie du Haut Moyen-Age*, p. 226ff.

29. English translation by T. C. O'Brien, in the Blackfriars edition of the *Summa Theologiae*, vol. 31, pp. 55-6.

30. *Decretum Magistri Gratiani*, I, 17, 5; ed. A. Friedberg, vol. I, p. 52.

31. The council to which St Thomas refers as the 'seventh' was the Third Council of Constantinople, now referred to as the Sixth Ecumenical Council.

32. Yves Congar, 'Saint Thomas Aquinas and the Infallibility of the Papal Magisterium', *The Thomist* 38 (1974) p. 92.

33. Ibid., pp. 89-90.

34. Such as St Albert the Great, whom Congar (art. cit., p. 92, note 25) quotes as follows: 'Si urgeret necessitas adhuc posset Papa convocato concilio peritorum, et invocato Spiritu Sancto, aliquid quod implicite continetur in symbolo Apostolorum explanare et ponere inter articulos explicitos' (III Sent. d. 21, a.8, ad 7). I translate: 'If there were some urgent necessity, the Pope, having called a council of experts, and having invoked the Holy Spirit, could clarify something that is implicitly contained in the Apostles Creed, and place it among the explicit articles.'

35. I refer especially to the Lutheran-Roman Catholic dialogue in the U.S.A., which has produced the following very useful volumes: *Peter in the New Testament*, eds. R. E. Brown, K. P. Donfried, J. Reumann, Augsburg/Paramus 1973; *Papal Primacy and the*

Universal Church, eds. P. C. Empie and T. A. Murphy, Augsburg 1974, and *Teaching Authority and Infallibility in the Church*, eds. P. C. Empie, T. A. Murphy, J. A. Burgess, Augsburg 1978.

36. See *Peter in the New Testament*, pp. 162-8. Also Raymond E. Brown, *Biblical Reflections on Crises Facing the Church*, New York/Paramus 1975, pp. 63-83.

37. Pope Honorius (625-38) was condemned as a heretic long after his death, by the Third Council of Constantinople. His blunder was in not having taken seriously enough the dispute whether there were two wills, or only one will, in Christ, and thus having seemed to countenance what was later condemned as the heresy of monothelism.

38. Joseph Ratzinger, *Das Neue Volk Gottes, Entwürfe zur Ekklesiologie*, Düsseldorf 1969, pp. 131-46. The 'patriarchal' role of the Bishop of Rome is his *regional* primacy over the *western* church: a primacy of *ecclesiastical* origin, involving an exercise of jurisdiction which the Bishops of Rome, during the first millennium, generally did not attempt to exercise over the eastern patriarchates. The strictly 'papal' role of the Bishops of Rome, or their 'petrine ministry', is believed by Catholics to be of *divine*, not merely ecclesiastical origin, and involves their responsibility, and hence their authority, regarding the faith and communion of the *universal* Church.

Chapter 5, pp. 79-118

1. Peter Chirico, in his book *Infallibility, the Crossroads of Doctrine* (Kansas City 1977), maintains that only 'universal meanings' are capable of being infallibly known or taught. An adequate presentation and discussion of his innovative theory of infallibility would deserve more ample treatment than I can give it here.

2. *Infallible?* p. 169.

3. Hermann J. Sieben, SJ, *Die Konzilsidee der Alten Kirche*, Paderborn 1979.

4. W. Hryniewicz, 'Die ekklesiale Rezeption in der Sicht der orthodoxen Theologie', *Theol. u. Glaube* 65 (1975) 250-265.

5. Yves Congar, '1274-1974. Structures ecclesiales et conciles dans les relations entre Orient et Occident', *RSPT* 58 (1974) pp. 360, 368.

6. G. Alberigo, 'Una cum Patribus', in *Ecclesia a Spiritu Sancto Edocta*, (Bibl. Eph. Theol. Lov. 27) Gembloux 1970, p. 302f.

7. Yves Congar, 'Saint Thomas Aquinas and the Infallibility of the Papal Magisterium', *Thomist* 38 (1974) p. 103.

8. Ibid.

9. The title in the original Latin is: 'Quaestio an romano pontifici in fide et moribus sit ab omnibus catholicis tamquam regulae inerrabili obediendum?' It was published by M. Maccarone in *Rivista di Storia della Chiesa in Italia* 3 (1949) 309-43.

10. Brian Tierney, *Origins of Papal Infallibility, 1150-1350. A study on the Concepts of Infallibility, Sovereignty and Tradition in the Middle Ages*, Leiden 1972, pp. 93-130.

11. B. M. Xiberta, 'De Doctrinis theologicis Magistri Guidonis Terreni', *Anal. Ord. Carm.* 5 (1923) p. 325. Xiberta also edited Terreni's *opusculum* on papal infallibility: *Guidonis Terreni Quaestio de Magisterio Infallibili Romani Pontificis*, Münster 1926.
12. Xiberta, *Guidonis Terreni Quaestio*, pp. 10, 16-17.
13. Ibid., p. 18.
14. Ibid., pp. 16-17.
15. Ibid., p. 8.
16. Tierney, *Origins of Papal Infallibility*, pp. 244-45.
17. Yves Congar, *L'Eglise de S. Augustin à l'époque moderne*, Paris 1970, p. 385.
18. Ibid., p. 401.
19. Yves Congar, 'L'Ecclésiologie, de la Révolution française au Concile du Vatican, sous le signe de l'affirmation de l'autorité', in *L'Ecclésiologie au XIXe Siècle* (Unam Sanctam 34), Paris 1960, pp. 77-114.
20. M. Cappellari, who published his work: *Il Trionfo della Santa Sede e della Chiesa* in 1799, at the nadir of papal prestige, was to be Pope Gregory XVI (1831-1846).
21. H. J. Pottmeyer, *Unfehlbarkeit und Souveränität: Die päpstliche Unfehlbarkeit im System der Ultramontanen Ekklesiologie des 19. Jahrhunderts*, Mainz 1975.
22. Congar, 'L'Ecclésiologie, de la Révolution française', p. 111.
23. August B. Hasler, *How the Pope Became Infallible, Pius IX and the Politics of Persuasion*, Garden City 1981.
24. J. H. Newman, *A letter . . . to the Duke of Norfolk*, London 1875, pp. 96-100.
25. Tierney, op. cit., p. 269.
26. G. Thils, *L'Infaillibilité Pontificale: Source, Conditions, Limites*, Gembloux 1969, pp. 194-211.
27. K. Rahner, 'On the Relationship between the Pope and the College of Bishops', in *Theol. Invest.* 10, London 1973, pp. 50-70.
28. See G. Dejaifve, 'Ex sese, non autem ex consensu Ecclesiae', *Salesianum* 25 (1962) 283-95; and H. Fries, 'Ex sese, non autem ex consensu Ecclesiae', in *Volk Gottes*, eds. R. Bäumer, H. Dolch, Freiburg 1967, pp. 480-500.
29. AAS 65 (1973) 399-400.
30. Avery Dulles, *A Church to Believe In*, New York 1982, p. 142.
31. Piet Fransen, 'The Authority of the Councils', in *Problems of Authority*, ed. J. M. Todd, Baltimore/London 1962, pp. 43-78.
32. Joseph Ratzinger, *Das Neue Volk Gottes*, Düsseldorf 1969, p. 144; H. Bacht, 'Von Lehramt der Kirche und in der Kirche', *Catholica* 25 (1971) pp. 166-7; H. Fries, 'Das missverständliche Wort', in *Zum Problem Unfehlbarkeit* ed. K. Rahner, Freiburg/Basel/Wien 1971) pp. 216-32; W. Kasper, 'Zur Diskussion um das Problem der Unfehlbarkeit', *St. Zeit* 188 (1972) p. 368; Y. Congar, 'Après Infaillible? de Hans Küng, Bilans et Discussions', *RSPT* 58 (1974) p. 245; G. H. Tavard, 'Infallibility: A Structural Analysis', in *Teaching Authority and Infallibility in the Church*, pp. 183-4; P. Chirico, 'Infallibility: Rapprochement between Küng and the Official

Church?' *TS* 42 (1981) pp. 531-4; A. Dulles, *A Church to Believe In*, New York 1982, p. 142.

33. Bishop B. C. Butler, 'Authority in the Church', *Tablet* 231 (1977) p. 479; also in 'The Limits of Infallibility', *Tablet* 225 (1971) p. 400.

34. R. McBrien, in *The Infallibility Debate*, ed. J. Kirvan, Paramus 1971, pp. 49-51; H. McSorley, 'Some Forgotten Truths about the Petrine Ministry', in *Proc. CTSA* 29 (1974) p. 196; G. Lindbeck, 'The Reformation and the Infallibility Debate', in *Teaching Authority and Infallibility in the Church*, p. 111.

35. 'A Letter Addressed to His Grace the Duke of Norfolk', pp. 96-100.

36. Yves Congar, 'La "reception" comme réalité eccésiologique', *RSPT* 56 (1972) 369-403, published in English as 'Reception as an Ecclesiological Reality', *Concilium* 7/8, Sept. 1972, 43-68; A. Grillmeier, 'Konzil und Rezeption', *Theol. u. Phil.* 45 (1970) 321-352; H. Bacht, 'Vom Lehramt der Kirche und in der Kirche', *Catholica* 25 (1971) 144-167 (see pp. 157-67).

37. It should be clear, from the preceding discussion, how I would interpret the statement made in the official *relatio* on LG 25 at Vatican II: '. . . definitions of a Council are also irreformable of themselves, and do not need the approbation of the people, as some in the East mistakenly hold, but rather they carry with them and express the consent of the whole community.' (*Acta Synodalia Conc. Vat. II*, III/1, 253) On the one hand, approbation is not needed to *confer* infallibility on a definition; on the other hand, one can hardly lay down the consent of the whole Christian community as a condition necessarily to be fulfilled before a dogma can be defined.

38. See 'Common Statement', and 'Reflections of Lutheran Participants', in *Papal Primacy and the Universal Church* (Lutherans and Catholics in Dialogue, V), eds. P. C. Empie and T. A. Murphy, Minneapolis 1974, pp. 9-33.

39. *Teaching Authority and Infallibility in the Church* (Lutherans and Catholics in Dialogue, VI). The following page references are to this work.

40. Anglican-Roman Catholic International Commission, *The Final Report*, London 1982.

41. Joseph Cardinal Ratzinger, *Theologische Prinzipienlehre: Bausteine zur Fundamentaltheologie*, München 1982, p. 209 (my translation).

42. *Letter to the Duke of Norfolk*, p. 110. The three texts are Mt 16: 16-19; Lk 22:32, and Jn 21:15-17.

Chapter 6, pp. 119-52

1. John C. Ford and Germain Grisez, 'Contraception and the Infallibility of the Ordinary Magisterium', TS 39 (1978) 258-312; M. Zalba, 'Infallibilità del Magistero Ordinario e Contracezione', *Renovatio* 14 (1979) 79-90.

2. *Infallible?* pp. 34-68.

225

3. Karl Rahner, 'Reply to Hans Küng', *Hom. Past. Rev.* 71 (Aug.-Sept. 1971) p. 19. J. A. Komonchak, *'Humanae Vitae* and its Reception: Ecclesiological Reflections', TS 39 (1978) 221-57.
4. Abp. James Hickey, 'The Bishop as Teacher', *Origins* 12/9 (29 July 1982), 142.
5. As reported in 'A Vatican Synthesis', *Origins* 12/43 (7 April 1983), 692.
6. On the source of this idea, see John P. Boyle, 'The Ordinary Magisterium: Towards a History of the Concept", *Heythrop Journal* 20 (1979) 380-98; 21 (1980) 14-29.
7. Mansi 51, 322.
8. J. Salverri, *De Ecclesia*, 3rd ed., BAC, Madrid, 1955, n. 543, p. 674.
9. *Commentary on the Documents of Vatican II*, Vol. 1, New York 1955, pp. 210-11.
10. 'Magisterium', *Sacramentum Mundi*, vol. III, p. 356.
11. *Lumen gentium* 25.
12. D-S 1501.
13. M. Bevenot, ' "Faith and Morals" in the Council of Trent and Vatican I', *Heythrop Journal* 3 (1962) 15-30.
14. D-S 1507.
15. Cardinal Meyer of Chicago raised this question in one of his interventions at Vatican II; see *Acta Synodalia Conc. Vat. II*, III/3, pp. 150-51, and the comment of J. Ratzinger in *Commentary on the Documents of Vatican II*, ed. H. Vorgrimler, vol. 3, p. 185.
16. L. Oeing-Hanhoff, 'Ist das kirchliche Lehramt für den Bereich des Sittlichen zuständig?' *Theol. Quartalschrift* 161 (1981) 56-66; E. Gutwenger, 'The Role of the Magisterium', *Concilium* I, 6 (1970) 51; R. S. Prendergast, 'Some Neglected Factors of the Birth Control Question', *Sciences Eccl.* 18 (1966) 218-19.
17. *Acta Synodalia Conc. Vat. II*, III/1, p. 251.
18. Ibid.
19. *Acta Synodalia Conc. Vat. II*, III/8, p. 89.
20. *Schema Primum De Ecclesia*, Canon IX, Mansi 51, 552.
21. Mansi 52, 1226-7. It should be noted that in this official explanation of the terms of the definition, Gasser described the secondary object of infallibility as truths which are not merely 'connected with revelation', but are *required* for the defence and explanation of the deposit of revelation: 'quatenus sine his depositum fidei custodiri et exponi non posset' (Mansi 52, 1226).
22. *Mysterium Ecclesiae*, AAS 65 (1973) p. 401.
23. J. Kleutgen, *Die Theologie der Vorzeit verteidigt*, Vol. I (2nd ed., Innsbruck 1878) p. 146. J. B. Franzelin, *De Divina Traditione et Scriptura*, Roma 1870, pp. 110, 547-51.
24. John J. Reed, 'Natural Law, Theology and the Church', TS 26 (1965) p. 55.
25. *Gaudium et Spes*, n. 50.
26. *Dignitatis Humanae*, n. 14.
27. Pius XII, Allocution 'Magnificate Dominum', 2 Nov. 1954, AAS 46 (1954) p. 671; Eng. tr. in *The Pope Speaks* 1 (1954) 380.

28. Mansi 52, 1224.
29. *Acta Synodalia Conc. Vat. II*, I/4, p. 48.
30. I quote this as it is given in Ford, Grisez, *art. cit.*, p. 302.
31. See note 1 above.
32. Ford, Grisez, art. cit. pp. 286-87.
33. Ibid., p. 287, footnote 65.
34. Ibid., p. 276.
35. Art. cit. p. 56.
36. Ford, Grisez, p. 295.
37. H. Küng, 'To Get to the Heart of the Matter', *Hom. Past.* 71 (June 1971) p. 21.
38. K. Rahner, 'Reply to Hans Küng', *Hom. Past.* 71 (Aug.-Sept. 1971) pp. 19-20. The reference to Pius XI is to the encyclical *Casti connubii*.
39. Ford, Grisez, p. 282.
40. Ibid., pp. 284-5.
41. Daniel C. Maguire, 'Morality and Magisterium', *Cross Currents* 18 (1968) p. 47.
42. Ibid.
43. Jakob David, 'Kirche und Naturrecht. Versuch einer neuen Grenzziehung', *Orientierung* 30 (1966) 129-33.
44. *Codex Iuris Canonici*, Can. 1323, §3. In the 1983 Code, this is Can. 749, §3.
45. Karl Rahner, 'Basic Observations on the Subject of the Changeable and Unchangeable Factors in the Church', *Theol. Invest.* 14 (1976) p. 15.
46. Among the moralists can be named F. Böckle, 'Unfehlbare Normen?' in H. Küng, *Fehlbar? Eine Bilanz*, Zurich 1973, pp. 280-304; Charles E. Curran, 'Pluralism in Catholic Moral Theology', in *Readings in Moral Theology, 3*, eds. C. Curran R. McCormick, New York 1982, pp. 364-87; J. David, 'Kirche und Naturrecht. Versuch einer neuen Grenzziehung', *Orientierung* 30 (1966) 129-33; Philippe Delhaye, 'Conscience and Church Authority', *Louvain Studies* 2 (1969) 355-75; Klaus Demmer, 'Kirchliches Lehramt und Naturrecht', *Theol. Glaube* 59 (1969) 191-213; Josef Fuchs, 'Sittliche Wahrheiten — Heilswahrheiten?' *St. Zeit* 200 (1982) 662-76; Bernard Häring, 'Magistero' in *Dizionario Enciclopedico di Teologia Morale*, 3rd ed., Roma 1974, pp. 583-94; Louis Janssens, 'Considerations on "Humanae Vitae" ', *Louvain Studies* 2 (1969) 231-53; Daniel Maguire, 'Morality and Magisterium', *Cross Currents* 18 (1968) 41-65; Richard McCormick, 'Notes on Moral Theology', *TS* 29 (1968) 709; *TS* 30 (1969) 660; Bruno Schüller, 'Zur theologischen Diskussion um die Lex Naturalis', *Theol. Phil.* 41 (1966) 481-503.
   Other Catholic theologians who share this opinion are: G. Baum, 'Doctrinal Renewal', *Jour. Ecum. Stud.* 2 (1965) 365-81; John P. Boyle, 'The Natural Law and the Magisterium', in *Proc. CTSA* 34 (1979) 189-210; P. Chirico, *Infallibility. The Crossroads of Doctrine*, pp. 184-92; J. A. Komonchak, *'Humanae Vitae* and its Reception.

Ecclesiological Reflections', *TS* 39 (1978) 221-57; J. P. Mackey, 'Teaching Authority in Faith and Morals', in *Morals, Law and Authority*, Dublin/Dayton, 1969, pp. 91-114; K. Rahner, 'Some Observations on the Subject of Changeable and Unchangeable Factors in the Church', *Theol. Invest.* 14 (1976) 3-23; G. Thils, 'Truth and Verification at Vatican I', *Concilium* 3/9 (1973) 27-34.

This opinion was also successfully defended in the doctoral dissertation: *Infallible Church Magisterium and the Natural Moral Law*, which William Levada submitted to the Faculty of Theology of the Gregorian University in 1970.

Chapter 7, pp. 153-173

1. *Documents of Vatican II*, Abbott, p. 715; *Acta Synodalia Conc. Vat. II*, I/1, 172.
2. Abbott, p. 98; *Acta Synodalia* III/8, p. 10.
3. *Lumen gentium*, 25.
4. L. Ciappi, 'Il magistero vivo di SS. Pio XII, norma prossima e universale di verità', *Sapienza* 7 (1954) 125-51; J. C. Fenton, 'Infallibility in the Encyclicals', *Amer. Eccl. Rev.* 128 (1953) 177-98; J. Salaverri, *De Ecclesia* (Sacrae Theologiae Summa, vol. I), 2nd ed., Madrid 1952, p. 692ff., n. 647ff.
5. Pius XII, encyc. letter *Humani generis*, AAS 42 (1950) 568; D-S 3885.
6. *Acta Synodalia Conc. Vat. II*, I/4, p. 50.
7. The pertinent section of this letter is given in English translation in K. Rahner, 'The Dispute concerning the Church's Teaching Office', in *Theol. Invest.* vol. 14, pp. 85-8; it is also given in a different English version, in K. Rahner, 'Magisterium', *Sacramentum Mundi* III, pp. 356-7.
8. Ibid.
9. B. C. Butler, 'Infallible; Authenticum: Assensus: Obsequium. Christian Teaching Authority and the Christian's Response', *Doctrine and Life* 31 (1981) 77-89.
10. Ibid., p. 84.
11. Ibid., p. 83.
12. *Acta Synodalia Conc. Vat. II*, III/8, p. 10.
13. John H. Newman, *An Essay in Aid of a Grammar of Assent*, ed. N. Lash, Notre Dame 1979, p. 148: 'Treating the subject then, not according to *a priori* fitness, but according to the facts of human nature, as they are found in the concrete action of life, I find numberless cases in which we do not assent at all, none in which assent is evidently conditional; — and many, as I shall now proceed to show, in which it is unconditional, and these in subject-matters which admit of nothing higher than probable reasoning. . . . Now let us review some of those assents, which men give on evidence short of intuition and demonstration, yet which are as unconditional as if they had that highest evidence.'
14. Ibid., p. 145.
15. Ibid.

16. *Acta Synodalia Conc. Vat. II*, III/8, p. 88, n. 159.
17. Ludwig Lercher, *Institutiones Theologiae Dogmaticae*, Vol. I, 5th ed., Barcelona 1951, p. 297.
18. *Dignitatis humanae*, 14.
19. *Acta Synodalia Conc. Vat. II*, IV/6, p. 769.
20. See note 7 above.

Chapter 8, pp. 174-218

1. The official Latin text, with a commentary by the two theologians who were most involved in drafting the theses for the commission, Otto Semmelroth, SJ and Karl Lehmann, is published in *Gregorianum* 57 (1976) 549-63. A French translation, with a very useful introduction by the General Secretary of the ITC, P. Delhaye, is given in *Documentation Catholique* 73 (1976) 658-65. (This translation was approved by the Secretariat of the ITC). An English translation was published by the Publication Office, USCC, 1977, and is reprinted in *Readings in Moral Theology No. 3, The Magisterium and Morality*, eds. C. E. Curran and R. A. McCormick, New York/Ramsey, 1982, pp. 151-70.
2. G. Caprile, *Il Sinodo dei Vescovi, Prima Assemblea Generale*, Roma 1968, p. 234.
3. Witness the observation made by Cardinal Garrone, reported by René Laurentin in *Le Premier Synode, histoire et bilan*, Paris 1968, p. 120, and the remark of 'the secretary of a congregation' reported by R. Rouquette in *Etudes* 327 (1967) 709.
4. G. Caprile, loc. cit.
5. AAS 61 (1969) 540f.
6. AAS 61 (1969) 431f.
7. AAS 74 (1982) 1201-1205.
8. I have been reliably informed that the ITC was not consulted in the preparation of any of these documents.
9. K. Rahner, 'The Congregation of the Faith and the Commission of Theologians', *Theol. Invest.* 14 (1976), p. 99.
10. The list of members is found in the *Annuario Pontificio*. The number is limited to thirty; they are appointed for a five-year term, and may be re-appointed.
11. He describes them as 'textes que l'on voit imparfaits': *Doc. Cath.* 73 (1976) p. 659.
12. German translation by Semmelroth in *Theologie und Philosophie* 52 (1977) 57-61; French version in *Doc. Cath.* 73 (1976) 662-5.
13. AAS 58 (1966) 889-896. Both citations from page 890.
14. Juan Alfaro, 'Theology and the Magisterium' in *Problems and Perspectives of Fundamental Theology*, eds. R. Latourelle and G. O'Collins, New York/Ramsay, 1982, p. 341.
15. Avery Dulles, 'The Church: Sacrament and Ground of Faith', in *Problems and Perspectives of Fundamental Theology*, p. 271f.
16. 'The Two Magisteria: An Interim Reflection', in *Proceedings, CTSA*, 35 (1980), p. 159; also *A Church to Believe In*, New York 1982, p. 122.

17. These were published as two articles in *RSPT* 60 (1976): 'Pour une histoire sémantique du terme "magisterium" ', pp. 85-98, and 'Bref historique des formes du "magistère" et ses rélations avec les docteurs', pp. 99-112. An English translation of both articles is given in *Readings in Moral Theology No. 3, The Magisterium and Morality*: 'A Semantic History of the Term "Magisterium" ', pp. 297-313, and 'A Brief History of the Forms of the Magisterium and its Relations with Scholars', pp. 314-31.
18. Hubert Jedin, 'Theologie und Lehramt', in *Lehramt und Theologie im 16. Jahrhundert*, ed. R. Baümer, Münster 1976, pp. 7-21; Max Seckler, 'Kirchliches Lehramt und theologische Wissenschaft', in *Die Theologie und das Lehramt*, (Quaest. Disp. 91), ed. W. Kern, Freiburg/Basel/Wien 1982, pp. 17-62.
19. *Chicago Studies* 17 (2/1978) 172-307; articles by E. LaVerdiere, 'New Testament Origins'; J. E. Lynch, 'Apostolic Fathers to Gregorian Reform'; Y. Congar, 'Gregorian Reform to Council of Trent'; M. D. Place, 'Trent to the First Vatican Council'; T. H. Sanks, 'Vatican I to the Present'; A. Dulles, 'The Magisterium in History: A Theological Reflection'.
20. M. Seckler, 'Kirchliches Lehramt' (see note 18 above), p. 22.
21. Ibid., p. 21.
22. 'Theologie und Lehramt' (see note 18 above), p. 14.
23. 'A Brief History' (see note 17 above), p. 320.
24. Op. cit., p. 16.
25. Pius IX, 'Inter gravissimas', 26 Oct. 1870, *Acta Pii IX*, pars. I, vol. 5, p. 260.
26. *Commentary on the Documents of Vatican II*, ed. H. Vorgrimler, vol. 3, New York 1969, p. 197.
27. 'A Brief History', p. 325. The reference to Seckler is to his article: 'Die Theologie als kirchliche Wissenschaft nach Pius XII und Paul VI', *Theol. Quartal.* 149 (1969) 209-34, especially pp. 220-25.
28. 'A Brief History', p. 327.
29. 'Theologie und Lehramt', p. 18.
30. Paul VI, Address to International Congress on the Theology of Vatican II, AAS 58 (1966), p. 891.
31. Congar, 'A Brief History', p. 328. I have slightly modified the English translation in the light of the original French, *RSPT* 60 (1976) p. 112.
32. *Commentary on the Documents of Vatican II*, vol. 3, p. 197.
33. Ibid., pp. 268-9. However, for this passage I prefer to give my own translation of the German, which is found in *Lexikon für Theologie und Kirche, Das Zweite Vatikanische Konzil*, vol. 2, Freiburg/Basel/Wien 1967, p. 577.
34. Edited by Leo J. O'Donovan, and published by the Canon Law Society of America, Washington, D.C., 1982.
35. Paul VI to the International Congress on the Theology of Vatican II, AAS 58 (1966) p. 892.
36. Ibid.
37. Paul VI, loc. cit. p. 891.

38. Pope Paul VI, 'Integrae servandae', AAS 57 (1965), p. 953. The new structure and operating procedure of the CDF are described by its Secretary, Abp Jérome Hamer, in his article: 'In the Service of the Magisterium: The Evolution of a Congregation', *The Jurist* 37 (1977) 340-57.
39. Maurizio Flick, 'Due funzioni della teologia secondo il recente documento della Commissione Teologica Internazionale', *Civ. Catt.* no. 3030 (1976) 472-83.
40. Paul VI, Address to Int. Cong. on Theol. of Vat. II, AAS 58 (1966) pp. 892-3.
41. The sentence of *Ad gentes* 22 which follows the one quoted in the thesis says: 'Thus it will be more clearly seen in what ways faith can seek for understanding in the light of the philosophy and wisdom of these peoples.'
42. 'Due funzioni', p. 474.
43. Cf. LG 12. See also F. A. Sullivan, *Charisms and Charismatic Renewal*, Ann Arbor/Dublin, 1982, pp. 9-15.
44. P. Delhaye, *Doc. Cath.* 73 (1976) p. 660; O. Semmelroth, *Th. Ph.* 52 (1977) p. 65, Eng. tr. in *Readings in Moral Theology no. 3*, p. 166.
45. Heinrich Flatten, 'Missio Canonica', in T. Filthaut and A. Jungmann, eds., *Verkündigung und Glaube*, Freiburg 1958, pp. 123-41.
46. AAS 25 (1933) p. 400.
47. The footnote added in the publication of the concordat with the State of Baden shows clearly that this was the term being used at the Vatican: AAS 25 (1933) p. 187, footnote 1.
48. AAS 23 (1931) p. 251.
49. *Normae Communes*, art. 27, § 1.
50. *Schema Canonum Libri III De Ecclesiae Munere Docendi*, can. 64.
51. John A. Alesandro, "The Rights and Responsibilities of Theologians: A Canonical Perspective", in *Cooperation between Theologians and the Ecclesiastical Magisterium* (see note 34 above), pp. 106 and 109.
52. This text is now canon 812 in the *Code of Canon Law* promulgated by Pope John Paul II on 25 January 1983, AAS 75/2 (1983) p. 147.
53. AAS 46 (1954) p. 314.
54. L TH K, Vat. II, vol. 2, p. 576 (my translation); a slightly different English version is found in *Commentary on the Documents of Vatican II*, vol. 3, p. 268.
55. Pope John XXIII, Opening address at the Second Vatican Council, 11 Oct. 1962, AAS 54 (1962) 792.
56. Schema Constitutionis De Ecclesia, cap. VII, n. 32; *Acta Synodalia* I/4, p. 52.
57. Paul VI, "Libentissimo sane", 1 Oct. 1966, AAS 58 (1966) 891; "Siamo particolarmente lieti", 11 July 1966, AAS 58 (1966) 653; "Praesentia vestra", 24 Sept. 1967, AAS 59 (1967) 962.
58. See note 28 above.

59. "Bref Historique" (see note 17 above), pp. 110-111 (my translation). Another English version in "A Brief History" (see note 17 above), p. 326.
60. K. Rahner, "Theology and the Church's Teaching Authority after the Council", *Theol. Invest.* vol. 9, p. 95.
61. K. Rahner, "Theologie und Lehramt", *Stimmen der Zeit* 198 (1980) p. 371.
62. J. Alfaro, "Theology and the Magisterium", in *Problems and Perspectives of Fundamental Theology*, p. 351.
63. K. Rahner, "Lehramt und Theologie", *Schriften* vol. 13, pp. 83-4.
64. Joseph Ratzinger, *Das Neue Volk Gottes*, Düsseldorf 1969, p. 144.
65. To mention just a few contributions: C.E. Curran and R.E. Hunt, *Dissent In and For the Church*, New York 1969; C.E. Curran, (ed.) *Contraception: Authority and Dissent*, New York 1969, especially the article in this by J. Komonchak, "Ordinary Papal Magisterium and Religious Assent", pp. 101-26; J.F. Kippley, "Continued Dissent: Is it Responsible?", *TS* 32 (1971) 48-65; K. Rahner, "On the Encyclical 'Humanae vitae'", *Theol. Invest.* 11, pp. 263-87; idem, "The Dispute concerning the Church's Teaching Office", *Theol. Invest.* 14, pp. 86-97; R.M. Gula, "The Right to Private and Public Dissent from Specific Pronouncements of the Ordinary Magisterium", *Eglise et Theologie* 9 (1978) 319-343; H. Küng and J. Moltmann (eds.), *The Right To Dissent, Concilium* no. 158 (8/1982).
66. *Acta Synodalia* I/4, p. 50.
67. "Bref Historique", p. 110.
68. Robert Coffy, "The Magisterium and Theology", in *Readings in Moral Theology No. 3, The Magisterium and Morality*, p. 212.
69. AAS 71 (1979) p. 1264.
70. *Gregorianum* 57 (1976) pp. 562-563.
71. Richard A. McCormick, "Notes on Moral Theology", *TS* 30 (1969) pp. 652-3.
72. AAS 63 (1974) 234-6. J. Hamer, Secretary of the CDF, has explained this procedure in the article cited in note 38 above.
73. Bas van Iersel, "Le colloque Schillebeeckx vu par un témoin", *Études* 353 (1980) 255-66; also some remarks of Y. Congar in his article "Les théologiens dans l'Église aujourd'hui", *Les Quatre Fleuves* 12 (1980) 22-7.
74. Allocution "Di gran cuore", 14 Sept. 1956, AAS 48 (1956) 709.

INDEX OF NAMES

INDEX OF TOPICS